NORWICH CITY

The Nineties

Edward Couzens-Lake

AMBERLEY

This book is dedicated to the Class of 1992/93 and all twenty-two players who made at least one league or cup appearance for the Canaries that season. Thank you all. It was one hell of a ride!

First published 2017

Amberley Publishing
The Hill, Stroud,
Gloucestershire, GL5 4EP

www.amberley-books.com

Copyright © Edward Couzens-Lake, 2017

The right of Edward Couzens-Lake to be identified as the Author
of this work has been asserted in accordance with the
Copyrights, Designs and Patents Act 1988.

ISBN 978 1 4456 6192 6 (print)
ISBN 978 1 4456 6193 3 (ebook)

British Library Cataloguing in Publication Data.
A catalogue record for this book is available from the British Library. *L796.834*

Typesetting and Origination by Amberley Publishing.
Printed in Great Britain.

Contents

Foreword by John Polston

I knew what I wanted to be on 1 January 1990. And that was to be a first-team regular at Tottenham Hotspur, the club I'd joined as a sixteen-year-old back in 1984.

They had a decent team back then, one that finished third in the old Division One at the end of the 1984/85 season. Peter Shreeves had some good players to call upon to with the likes of Ray Clemence, Chris Hughton, Graham Roberts, Glenn Hoddle and Ossie Ardiles all playing a prominent part in the team and at the club. There were also a few promising youngsters there with me at the time, and you may remember a few of them: Ian Culverhouse, Mark Bowen and Ian Crook were all at White Hart Lane when I signed for Spurs; none of us could ever have guessed we'd all eventually end up in Norfolk.

The biggest challenge any young player such as myself had at Tottenham back then was not only getting a chance of playing in the first team but staying put once you'd made it that far. Think of all the quality that the club had to call upon from the mid-1980s onwards; not only Clemence, Hughton, Hoddle and co. but also the big-money signings – Richard Gough, Clive Allen, Gary Lineker and Paul Gascoigne to name but four.

Their presence at the club and at the training ground was great for any young player. But it also made it a lot harder for players like me, who the club had brought in as schoolboys, to make any sort of impression unless, like Hoddle, you were already looking world class when you were still a teenager.

I ended up making just twenty-four league appearances for Tottenham in five years, so when the chance came to sign for Norwich in the summer of 1990 it was too good an offer to turn down. The Canaries had ended the 1989/90 season in tenth place, higher than both Manchester clubs, and in Dave Stringer had a good and well-respected manager. I'd actually played against Norwich when they came down to us that February and, although we won 4-0, they hit the post twice and looked good, not surprising really when you're up against players like Tim Sherwood, Dale Gordon and Robert Fleck. So I was looking forward to having them as my teammates.

I didn't have the best of starts at Carrow Road, mind. Paul Blades and I both made our debuts against Sunderland at Carrow Road and, although we won, I wasn't that happy with how I'd played. Dave Stringer wasn't that happy either when, three days later, we went down to Southampton and lost 1-0, courtesy of my own goal, a thumping header that gave Gunny no chance.

Dave Stringer then gave me a run of games in the reserves and, playing under Mike Walker, who was then reserve team boss, I began to settle into the area as a whole and get my game up to the level I wanted it to be at. I ended up making thirty-one league and cup appearances for Norwich that season and even contributed four goals at the right end, the first of which was the only one in a 1-0 win over Everton at Carrow Road, one that saw all four of us ex-Spurs lads playing in the same team. The four of us also played when Tottenham came to Carrow Road in April; we won 2-1 with goals from Lee Power and Ian Crook, which made for a very satisfying afternoon's work indeed – especially, I suspect, for Chippy!

Everyone rightly remembers the success we enjoyed after Mike Walker became manager, finishing third in the Premier League at the end of the 1992/93 season, although, looking back now, maybe we should and could have won it and done a Leicester City in the process. We were something like eight points clear at the top at one point and, had Mike been able to strengthen the squad at the time he needed to, then maybe, just maybe, that would have given us the push needed to go on and win it. Even so, finishing third was an incredible achievement and it remains the time in my career that most people want to speak about, especially the goal I scored against Aston Villa towards the end of the season – what a night that was. Good times and happy memories.

But I was also there when the club wasn't having such a good time during that decade. We finished sixteenth in the old Division One at the end of the 1995/96 season; Martin O'Neill had come and gone as manager, and for a while we even looked like we might slip down into Division Two. I played alongside Jon Newsome for much of that season and we were a decent partnership that was split up when he and Ashley Ward both left the club that March. A couple of weeks after they'd gone, we went up to Port Vale for a league match and lost 1-0 in front of just over 6,000 fans.

Running out at Carrow Road to play Bayern Munich and Inter Milan seems a long, long way in the past when you play in, and lose, games like that.

But that's football. If you're a professional player then you have to get used to the peaks and troughs in the game. You'll feel as if you're top of the world one moment and as if no one wants you the next. That means you have to enjoy the good times when they come and I certainly did at Norwich where there were, in my time at the club, a lot more good times than there were bad ones. It's a club I'll always have a lot of affection for and a time in my life that I recall with a lot of pleasure.

In closing, there is only one more thing to say: On The Ball, City!

John Polston
Norwich City Football Club 1990–98

John now lives near Reading, setting up and running Wokingham Boot Camps, where anyone can look to attain their fitness goals in a fun, friendly and supportive environment. For more information, go to www.wokinghambootcamps.co.uk

Introduction

If *Match of the Day* had been able to show highlights of all of the top-flight games played on Monday 1 January 1990, then it's a fair bet that the programme's producers would have wasted no time in slotting Norwich City's same-day meeting with Wimbledon right at the bottom of the programme's running order. But, to be fair, there were some matches played that day that might all have been considered much more attractive propositions to the viewing public than that game at Carrow Road could ever have been – Aston Villa's visit to Chelsea, for example, or the visit of Liverpool to Nottingham Forest. Then there was the meeting at Highbury between Arsenal and Crystal Palace or Coventry's game against Tottenham at Highfield Road.

All fixtures that would have easily merited the presence of John Motson or Barry Davies before the BBC would have considered giving anything other than cursory highlights with regard to the Canaries' encounter against Bobby Gould's notorious up-and-at-them side. Yet if it was regarded as a run-of-the-mill fixture then the same description could not be applied to Norwich City as a football club or their status in the game at that time, because the Canaries were a club on the up and up.

That 1989/90 season was still only the fifteenth campaign that Norwich City had enjoyed playing in the top flight of English football in their near 100-year history. Despite their relative naivety at that level, however, the club had enjoyed some hugely satisfying campaigns in among the elite of the game with best-ever league finishes of 10th (1976) and 5th (1987) preceding a nothing less than remarkable 1988/89 season, which not only saw the Canaries finish in 4th place in Division One, but also reach the FA Cup semi-final for the first time in thirty years. Talk throughout that season, astonishing as it will seem to us today, even suggested that the Canaries might be the potential winners of a League and FA Cup double.

That eventual final position of fourth, while ultimately disappointing, was still a remarkable achievement for Dave Stringer and his players. Yet it could have been so much more than that. Norwich's comfortable 2-0 win over West Ham at Upton Park on 27 March 1989 saw the club consolidate its position of second place in the Division One table. At that crucial point in the season, the Canaries were just three points behind leaders Arsenal but had a game in hand. More to the point, third-placed Liverpool were five points adrift of the Canaries with Norwich due to play both them and the Gunners before the end of the season. This meant that, with Liverpool due to visit Carrow Road in Norwich's next league game, a win for the Canaries would have seen them go an eyebrow-raising eight points clear of the Reds. For the Merseysiders, formidable as they were, that might have been too large a gap to make up. Consequently, the race for the title over the remaining weeks of the season would have been played out between Norwich and Arsenal. And make no mistake about it, the title of Football League Division One was well within the club's capabilities. An equivalent of what Nottingham Forest had achieved in 1978 and Leicester City achieved in 2016 was, at that late stage of the season, more than a distinct possibility.

With a run of crucial games coming up and mindful of the need to boost an attack that relied rather too heavily on Robert Fleck, Canaries boss Dave Stringer had previously chosen to miss his side's 1-0 win over Derby County on 11 February in order to cast a watchful eye on a teenage striker who was beginning to make a name for himself at Southampton. The player in question was Alan Shearer, then just eighteen but already, as far as the Canaries scouting team would have been concerned, one who was worth signing, his pace and raw aggression seen as a perfect complement to Fleck in the Norwich attack.

The Canaries must have been very close at that time to making an official bid for Shearer. There is no way that Stringer would have taken time out to watch a player on the same day as his own team were playing unless he had been fully briefed on Shearer's talents beforehand. This was no speculative trip, no last-minute decision to take in a game in the hope of seeing someone, anyone, stand out of the crowd. That sort of thing was the responsibility of the club's scouts, anonymous individuals whose weeks were spent travelling up and down the counties' motorways in order to see as many reserve-team games as they could in the faint hope of unearthing a diamond, just as Norwich had done with players like Ian Culverhouse and Dave Watson. Shearer was different; he was already close to being the finished article and if Norwich were to have any chance at all of prising him away from the south coast, then they needed to act quickly and with conviction. That meant sending the first team manager along to take a look for himself – a very public show of intent.

Shearer, playing as part of an attacking trio alongside Danny and Rodney Wallace, had a quiet game on the day with Kevin Moore, an uncompromising defender cast in the same mould as Stringer, scoring

Southampton's goal in a 1-1 draw. Shearer's relative anonymity in the match is unlikely to have made Stringer think his journey had been a wasted one but, for one reason or another, any interest that the Canaries had in the player ended shortly afterwards, meaning Norwich fans were ultimately denied the tantalising prospect of an attacking duo of Shearer and Robert Fleck. Yet all was not quite lost. After determining that, for whatever reasons, Shearer was not an option, the Canaries moved on and a little over a month later announced the signing of striker Dean Coney from Queens Park Rangers instead.

Coney had made his debut in the aforementioned 2-0 win over West Ham, coming off the bench to replace Fleck and making a good first impression. Maybe at twenty-five and with over 250 senior league appearances behind him for the Hoops and Fulham as well as caps for England at U21 level he was seen as less of a gamble, a safer bet for Norwich than the still-developing Shearer? Coney was, at the very least, a player who would hit the ground scoring, rather than a future prospect who might, given time, establish his place in the team over the next year to eighteen months or, like so many before him, fade into obscurity after a promising start to his career. Thus, given the choice of their club either signing Coney, a familiar name who was in his prime, or the promising but raw and still relatively inexperienced Shearer, most Norwich fans at the time, this one included, would have opted, without hesitation, for Coney. As Sir Alex Ferguson famously said, 'Football. Bloody hell.'

Bloody hell indeed. Norwich's win over West Ham should have been the springboard for the club to get the results needed in order to win the League Championship. Looking back now, a run of six wins and two draws from the Canaries last nine league games following the West Ham match would have been enough, especially as both Liverpool and Arsenal were among their opponents during that run. But it was not to be. Liverpool came to Carrow Road on 1 April and won 1-0, courtesy of a goal from Ronnie Whelan. Four days later the Canaries' lost 2-0 at Nottingham Forest, meaning that their glorious tilt at the most unlikely league title success since that of Derby County in 1972 was as good as over.

Disappointments aside, however, it had been a glorious season for the club, the best in their history by some considerable margin, a fact that, arguably, remains the case to this day. They'd started the season with an unprecedented six successive away wins in the league, reached the semi-finals of the FA Cup and topped the table from September through to the new year. It was, if you were into your clichés, real 'boy's own stuff' and promised much for the future prospects of the club. This was, of course, providing that the Canaries could keep hold of some of their better players in the summer of 1989, their successes of the previous season now resulting in the inevitable and very much unwanted attentions of big clubs with even bigger chequebooks.

The new season and the new decade that came with it was set to be a very interesting one indeed.

Edward Couzens-Lake
July 2017

CHAPTER ONE

Striking Issues

Prior to the signing of Tanner, Stringer had given a league debut to Ipswich-born Adrian Pennock who'd come through the Canary ranks, having originally signed on associated schoolboy forms. It would be his one and only appearance for the club.

Henrik Mortensen, scorer of a spectacular goal on his debut. (*Photo courtesy of Norwich City Football Club*)

People are not always at their best on New Year's Day. A week or so of time spent with family coupled with nothing less than extraordinary efforts at eating and drinking with, to cap it all off, a last gasp and very late night out at the end of it all in order to see in a new year with all the forced bonhomie and false hope that it invariably brings can leave even the most vigorous constitutions a little strained and emotional.

Which means that there were probably quite a few Norwich fans who, upon waking up on the morning of Monday 1 January 1990, remembered that the Canaries match later that same day was against Wimbledon and so chose to give it a miss. Sure, you'd crawl out of bed and endure the thumping headache inherited from the night before for the visit of Arsenal, Chelsea, Manchester United, Tottenham and just about any of the other nineteen teams that were competing alongside you in Division One that season. But Wimbledon? Never mind having a raging hangover from the night before, going to see them play was like watching one. And one hangover on New Year's Day was more than enough for most people to cope with.

For all of the reputation for brutality that accompanied them wherever they went, the Dons were not quite the side that had, according to popular footballing folklore, psyched Liverpool out in the Wembley tunnel prior to their victory over them in the 1988 FA Cup final. But only just. With players like Eric Young, Carlton Fairweather and John Fashanu among their blue-clad ranks, there would always be a degree of physicality in their approach, while in midfielder Denis Wise they possessed, technically, a very good footballer, but one who would complement that with an innate tendency to snarl, bicker and bait his opponents throughout the game. It was a footballing culture that wasn't altogether accepted or even approved of in the English game at that time, but it worked for them, becoming an added weapon to their not inconsiderable matchday armoury that included some other very fine footballers indeed, not least former Nottingham Forest goalkeeper Hans Segers and John Scales, a classy centre-back who would later go onto play for Liverpool and Tottenham as well as England.

So Wimbledon were no mugs and, despite their reputation, their game was about more than mugging their opponents, as some of their results that season had shown. A great example of this had been their 5-2 win over Chelsea at Stamford Bridge on 2 December, a game that had seen Terry Gibson and Wise score a goal apiece in addition to one from vastly underrated club stalwart Alan Cork. In Gibson, the Dons had everything that a Wimbledon striker was not meant to be. Fairweather, Fashanu and Cork were all physically strong strikers who'd hold an opponent up as easily as they could hold the ball up, uncompromising figures who went in where it hurts and came out smiling. Tough guys in other words. Gibson stood at just 5 foot 4 inches tall but he was a fast and tricky goal poacher, an opportunist who expected the ball to be played to his feet. And he was quality, no question. He'd made his debut for Tottenham when he was just seventeen and had also played for Manchester United, signed as a direct replacement for the Barcelona-bound Mark Hughes.

Gibson took his place in the Dons attack alongside Fashanu for that New Year's Day clash against Norwich at Carrow Road and spent much of the game an isolated figure as Norwich dominated proceedings from kick-off, drawing three wonderful saves out of Hans Segers in the process. Had it been a boxing match, as the old adage goes, then Bobby Gould might have thrown in the towel. Yet, as the end of the game drew close and Norwich's attacks became all the more wanton with it, Gould, a better coach than many would give him credit for, saw an opportunity to throw a little caution to the wind himself and sent Keith Curle, nominally a defender, into his club's attacking lines. His snap decision paid immediate dividends as, with the Norwich defence suddenly uncertain as to who should be marking who as Curle strode forward, Gibson made the most of the resultant confusion, snatching an injury-time winner for the visitors.

That disappointing 1-0 defeat was Norwich's third by that score in a week. The Canaries had previously lost to Manchester City at Maine Road on Boxing Day before succumbing to Crystal Palace four days later in the 'traditional' festive encounter between the sides at Selhurst Park. Prior to those matches, the club had won its previous three fixtures 'on the bounce', the 1-0 win over Derby County at Carrow Road lifting Norwich to fourth place in the Division One table, the position they had ended the previous season in.

Good times. But three consecutive defeats without even scoring a goal had not been on the agenda. Little wonder that Stringer had shown such an interest in Shearer the previous March and little surprise that he had, in the end, spent £350,000 on Coney in an attempt to give Robert Fleck some much needed support (and competition) in the Canaries' attack. It was an attack that was now misfiring with just four goals scored in nine league games, that run stretching back to a 2-0 win over Aston Villa on 11 November – even one of those goals had been an own goal from Villa's Derek Mountfield.

The Canaries' ongoing inability to score goals is reflected in the relevant statistics from the end of the 1988/89 season. They'd finished it in that laudable fourth place but the number of goals the Canaries had scored in their thirty-eight league games had been just forty-eight, an average of just 1.27 goals scored per game). That total was just four less than relegated

Middlesbrough, while, in their nineteen league games at home, the club had managed to score only twenty-three goals, the joint fourth lowest in the whole division.

So it was a concern that, rightly, Dave Stringer had been trying to address for some considerable time. One major problem was that the signing of Dean Coney had not worked out as everyone might have reasonably expected. He'd ended the 1988/89 campaign with just one goal from his eight league appearances and that was one that he barely knew about, coming as the result of a Nigel Spink clearance in the game against Aston Villa that had hit him and gone back past Spink and into the Villa goal as a result. Oddly enough, that was Coney's penultimate game for the Canaries that campaign as he was dropped for the club's final three matches and replaced by Robert Rosario, a player much admired and respected by his teammates, not least Robert Fleck. The popular Glaswegian's thoughts on Coney are unknown but he valued Rosario as someone who took the knocks and created plenty of chances for others in the process. It showed. Rosario ended the 1988/89 season with just four goals from twenty-seven league appearances; yet, for all that, was now regarded as a better option than Coney, the £350,000 man, for the club's last three games in a season where, for much of it, they had been genuine contenders for the league title.

Luckily for Norwich, the game against Arsenal on 4 November 1989 had seen the return of Malcolm Allen to their starting line-up. Welsh international Allen, signed from Watford for just £175,000 in August 1988, was twice the striker that Coney was for the club – and at half the price. He'd ended the 1988/89 season with twelve goals from thirty games, hardly prolific but it still made him a better option than Coney and, perhaps, Rosario. Yet he never really seemed to find favour with Stringer as one of his first choice strikers and of the thirty-five league appearances he eventually made for Norwich, eleven of those came as a substitute. Thus, after a run of three games partnering Fleck in the Norwich attack in February/March 1990, his transfer request was accepted by the club and he joined Millwall.

The decision to sell Allen at a time when goals were in such short supply at Carrow Road seemed an odd one then and, looking back, remains that to this day. Norwich ended the 1989/90 season even more goal shy than they had been the previous campaign with just forty-four goals scored (an average of 1.15 per game) in their thirty-eight league fixtures, with over a third of them coming before the end of September. Of that total, twenty-four had been scored at Carrow Road with only Wimbledon (twenty-two) and the three relegated teams (Sheffield Wednesday, Charlton and Millwall) scoring fewer at home. The lack of goal power was now a very serious and ongoing problem that had affected the club for three consecutive seasons, so it was little wonder that Stringer had spent much of his time looking for players that might be able to help improve on these numbers.

In such goal-shy times, therefore, the club was lucky to have had the services of Robert Fleck to call upon. He'd joined the club from Rangers for a then club record fee of £580,000 in December 1987 and, for the rest of that 1987/88 season as well as the following four campaigns, was the club's attacking talisman. He was an immensely likeable and charismatic member of the Canaries' playing squad, both among his teammates and the club's support with whom he held a remarkable rapport with from day one.

Fleck ended the 1989/90 season as the Canaries' top scorer with twelve goals from thirty-four League and Cup matches. As a player and personality he was as popular with the Norwich fans as the unfortunate Dean Coney was the polar opposite, with sections of the Canary support taking every opportunity to barrack him whenever he appeared on the pitch or even took possession of the ball. Supporters, then and now, may champion their right to express their opinions on the form and value to the club of a player with the argument that they 'pay their wages' (a claim that, at least today, is spurious at best) but, as is nearly always the case, the effect of such obvious supporter discontent goes far beyond the target. Coney, not unnaturally, could not have helped but feel his confidence ebbing away whenever he heard the criticisms aimed at him. But so would his teammates, aghast and disillusioned themselves that one of their teammates was getting so much stick from those they had assumed were their own. It wouldn't have gone unnoticed by opposing managers and coaches either, who would have put pressure on Coney from the off, closing him down and encouraging him to make mistakes thus, in their doing so, raising the collective ire of his critics even more.

Coney eventually became so disillusioned and unhappy with the way his career at Norwich was going that he handed in a transfer request, allegedly stating at the time that, '...the fans have it in for me'. You could hardly blame him for wanting out but, before he had the chance to do so, he suffered a snapped cruciate ligament in a reserve team game meaning that his career was now in limbo until he recovered his fitness and proved it enough to persuade another club to sign him. The opportunity to do so in England never came about, however, and he eventually joined Hong Kong-based Ernest Borel before returning to England to play at non-league level for Farnborough Town (when he was still in his twenties) before joining Carshalton Athletic.

Quite why Coney endured such a miserable and short-lived time at Norwich is a mystery. He was, of this there is no doubt, a quality player, one who welcomed his move to Carrow Road when he signed, saying that he was joining a 'footballing side'. Some of his ex-teammates have no doubts as to his ability, with former Fulham teammate Gordon Davies (scorer of 114 league goals in 247 games for Fulham) describing him as someone who was more about making and creating chances for other players rather than doing so for himself. The problem was, as far as the Norwich fans were concerned, that the club already had one of those types of player in Rosario.

Robert Fleck was a big fan of Rosario, however, describing him as an underrated player and one who'd put his head in where it hurts, describing him as, '...a great player and a great character to have in the dressing room'. BBC Radio Norfolk presenter and journalist Rob Butler was also a big fan of Rosario and looks back on both the player and that time at the club with a lot of fondness.

18th August 2012. Not a date etched into the memories of Norwich City fans. The Canaries were, as usual beaten at Fulham's Craven Cottage, 5-0 this time but for me it was a special day. I met one of my heroes.

Big Bob ... Rosie ...'that donkey'; just three names we all remember Robert Michael Rosario by. He really did split the Norwich City fans, but for me he was special. I idolised him as a child, and on that sunny day in West London when I finally got to interview the big man for BBC Radio Norfolk he was charming and genuinely touched by my excited handshake as we exchanged pleasantries.

Rosario was brought to Carrow Road in 1983 by Ken Brown after impressing in non-league. My first top flight game wasn't until 1987 and by then I was already a huge fan of his after watching him numerous times in the reserves. There were three reasons why I loved him (remember I was just a kid) 1 – he had the same first name as me. 2 – My sister REALLY fancied him – he had a bit of the Andrew Ridgeley about him, and, 3 – He used to play with his socks rolled down – and for some reason, an 8 year old me really respected this in a player! I'd also seen him playing tennis at the Norwich Sport Village once and waited patiently to say hello to him after he'd finished his five sets, he was so friendly afterwards and gave me a high five.

I'll be honest, I loved every single Norwich player back then. It was an amazing squad. Dale Gordon was my absolute favourite with Flecky a close second, but Big Bob was the one I pretended to be down at Thorpe Rec. Yellow socks rolled down, trying to header my mates crosses in, and usually missing much like the man I was trying to be.

It was these misses that made Rosario a 'boo-boy' for the Canary faithful. This upset me on numerous occasions. We were one of the best teams in the country at the time, maybe if Rosie had have come along 20 years later he would have been much more useful in the top of The Championship/ bottom of Premier League purgatory that we now find ourselves in. He was tall but not slow, he was good in the air and a very good 'hold up' man. It was in the days managers used to love the big and little men up front. I always thought Robert Fleck used to enjoy partnering Big Bob. The two Roberts up front. I was the third Robert in spirit!

Then on 9th September 1989 I saw the greatest goal I'd ever seen at Carrow Road – and Robert Rosario scored it. It was also the greatest game I'd ever witnessed up until then. Southampton were the visitors, Paul Rideout gave them an early lead (that was after our hero had nearly scored an own goal), then it happened. Rosario banged in THE goal of the season (Saint and Greavsie picked it). An absolute peach of a half volley, go and watch it on YouTube now, it's there with a lovely Kevin Piper voiceover. I was nearly on the pitch, the Family Enclosure in the South Stand had never seen such scenes! Finally the whole of the ground was in unison celebrating the skill of my hero. The game finished 4-4, we had been 4-2 down. Rosario scored another that day and had the game of his life.

Rosie ended up leaving us in 1991 and signing for Coventry. I wasn't as upset as when Gordon and Fleck finally packed their bags but it was still a sad day for me. I felt a real connection to Rosario, I used to stick up for him while others around me booed his every touch. He wasn't everyone's cup of tea but I've always had a soft spot for big old-fashioned centre forwards and that's what Rosie was. He was never going to be a Grant Holt or a Chris Sutton but there was just something about him that I loved. When I told him this on that sunny August day in 2012 he was genuinely touched, proof perhaps that we should give the players we love to a boo and moan about a break sometimes?

By the way, would you agree that Brian Clough is the greatest ever club manager in England? He rated Big Bob and made him his last ever signing. What a world we live in eh?

Robert Rosario. One of my all-time favourite Norwich players, I'll never forget him.

As Rob said, Rosario certainly did divide opinion among the Norwich support, something which you couldn't claim also applied to Coney for whom the terrace derision was pretty much total. But, and crucially, Rosario had that backing and support of his teammates who considered him to be what is known in the game as a 'players player', that is, one who will get through an enormous amount of work, often to little or no recognition in response, for the good of the team, the type of pro that, as Eric Cantona once said of his France teammate Didier Deschamps, was the team's 'water carrier'. Rosario's stand-out moment as a Norwich player was unquestionably that stunning strike against Southampton in that thrilling 4-4 draw, a fiercely hit volley from 30 yards that looks as if it was still accelerating as it passed Tim Flowers in the Saints goal.

Reliving that goal today may well leave the viewer in a thoughtful and retrospective frame of mind, wondering quite what could have been for Rosario for both himself and the Canaries had he been given more of an opportunity to hone and demonstrate his skills in his time at the club. Watch that goal again. It's one that demonstrates, almost perfectly, power, skill, exceptional balance and a flawless technique, a quartet of playing attributes that most players might possess two or three of in total, but rarely, if ever, all four.

You don't score a goal like that by luck. Nor are they a fluke. It might have seemed a one-off moment of yellow and green glory for Rosario. But, albeit in glorious hindsight, it shouldn't have been his Canary epitaph.

Back to the 1989/90 season though and, with the turn of the year being marked by that defeat to Wimbledon, Dave Stringer was, for the time being, continuing to show his faith in Rosario. He'd already had some opportunities in the game before he'd joined Norwich from non-league Hillingdon Borough, having already had trials with Tottenham, Brentford and Watford, all of whom saw in his tall and physically imposing figure the sort of dominating, albeit old-fashioned number nine, that English football, at that time, still doted upon. This was a playing policy, an obsession even, that had seen England take Mark Hateley to the 1986 World Cup finals. Hateley was a rather more proficient goalscorer than Rosario but then he had benefitted from playing in sides where he was surrounded by top-quality teammates. He also benefitted from playing in a Glasgow Rangers side who were so superior to the very great majority of teams that they played that he couldn't help but benefit from the myriad chances that would have been laid on for him by players of the calibre of Trevor Steven and Oleksiy Mykhaylychenko.

Here's a question: Would Hateley have scored with such easy abundance had he been a Norwich player during that 1989/90 season? It seems unlikely, just as it seems likely that, had Rosario somehow switched places with him and been playing for Rangers in the early 1990s, he could, and would, have come close to emulating Hateley's achievements. Certainly, for Hateley at least, the game was up when, later in his career, he played for the likes of Queens Park Rangers and Hull City in England. Surrounded as he was at those clubs by fellow professionals who, for the most part, could be described as 'workmanlike' at best, he struggled to make any sort of impact at all, scoring five goals in thirty-three appearances for QPR and just three in twenty-seven for Hull City. What he had done with consummate ease in Scotland with Rangers didn't seem to come so naturally upon his return to English football. Robert Fleck, on the other hand, had little to no difficulty adapting to English football after he'd joined Norwich for £580,000 in 1987. By the end of the decade he'd become one of the most popular players in the club's history, not only among the fans but his teammates as well, thanks, in no small part, to his larger-than-life personality. Make no mistake about it, the Fleck you saw on the pitch – effervescent, larger than life, an energetic and infectious presence who played with a smile on his face and passion in his heart – was the same Fleck that the Norwich players had grown used to in the inner sanctums of the club's training ground and Carrow Road dressing rooms.

A major player at the club then, of that there is little doubt. But also one that more than lived up to that reputation on the pitch. He ended that 1989/90 season as the club's top scorer for the second consecutive season with twelve league and cup goals, five ahead of left-back Mark Bowen, who had contributed seven from a then full programme of thirty-eight league games played. Fleck's total had come from just twenty-five starts in the league after injury had ruled him out from November through to late December. His presence was missed. It was a Fleck-less nine game period during which City had only scored nine goals, five of which had come in two games, Arsenal (3-4) and Aston Villa (2-0). It was therefore becoming more and more evident that, for all of Rosario's qualities as a centre forward as well as his undoubted popularity at the club, scoring an abundance of goals, odd as it may seem, was not one of the things he was going to do and that without Fleck in the side, Norwich were always going to struggle to do just that.

With Fleck missing, Coney completely out of sorts, Malcolm Allen seemingly out of favour and Rosario proving that he was more of a creator of chances than a taker of them, Norwich manager Dave Stringer badly needed to freshen up his attack with a new face – an Alan Shearer maybe? One option Stringer might have taken was that of Lee Power, an eighteen-year-old striker who had been making a name for himself in the club's reserves with a string of good performances that had also included his fair share of goals. Stringer, however, resisted the temptation to throw Power into a team that would have demanded an instant return rather than have the luxury of easing him in slowly and, although Power made an appearance off the substitutes' bench for his debut against Aston Villa (replacing, ironically, Fleck) on 28 April, it would be his only appearance of the season. There was, however, the option of giving one of his summer signings a first start and so it was that, with Fleck still out injured, twenty-one-year-old Henrik Mortensen was called up to the first team to make his debut, playing alongside Rosario, in the home game against Sheffield Wednesday on 2 December 1989.

Mortensen, who'd signed for the club two months earlier, certainly had an impressive footballing CV. He'd started his career with Aarhus in his native Denmark before moving onto Anderlecht in Belgium where he not only won a Belgian First Division 'A' winners' medal but also played in both the European and European Cup Winners' Cup competitions. Quite an accomplishment for such a young player and quite a coup for Norwich to be able to sign a player with such an impressive CV and burgeoning reputation for a relatively small fee – Danny Wallace had, after all, cost Manchester United £1.2 million when he'd joined them from Southampton at around the same time.

Needless to say, the arrival of Mortensen created a tremendous amount of interest in and among the Norwich support and a far larger attendance than normal turned up to see him make his club debut in the reserves where he obliged expectations by scoring via an overhead kick. It was, for Norwich, fairly unprecedented stuff. You just didn't do that sort of thing at the club, even in a reserve match, especially if you were a young debutant who'd just moved to England to live and work. Excitement at his arrival and potential now reached fever pitch and those who were now clamouring for him to get an opportunity in the first team saw their wishes fulfilled when Stringer named him in the starting line-up for the first-round Zenith Data Systems Cup game against Brighton at Carrow Road on 29 November. Mortensen didn't disappoint his growing army of fans there either, scoring again as the Canaries racked up an easy 5-0 win in front of a disappointing attendance of just 5,704, most of whom had come just to see the new boy play. Two games played, two goals scored. Had Dave Stringer finally unearthed the player who was going to solve the Canaries' goalscoring problems?

It may well have been the case that the Canaries' goalscoring crisis had forced Stringer's arm as regards Mortensen and that, in reality, he may well have not wanted to have pick him for the first team as quickly as had been the case. The young Dane had been signed with the future in mind and, with Norwich already well stocked on some admittedly misfiring strikers when he'd joined the club, it would have been reasonable to expect that Mortensen's first real opportunity would have come the following (1990/91) season after, as it was now expected Coney, Allen and possibly even Rosario would have left the club for pastures new. Yet, with Fleck still missing and with the club's resident strikers at the start of the season having scored just four goals between them up until the end of November, Stringer might have thought he had little choice. Mortensen was therefore given his full league debut and the No. 8 shirt (replacing Allen) for the game against Sheffield Wednesday at Carrow Road on 12 December 1989.

For all the fuss being made about strikers, it was ironic that the one who made a swift and deadly impression upon the game almost straight from the start was Wednesday's No. 9 David Hirst. He would have been, had Norwich been able to afford him, the perfect playing partner for Fleck in the Norwich attack. Hirst was, at the time, as near to a complete striker as you could get; as good with the ball at his feet as he was in the air and with no mean turn of pace as an added asset he would, in time, make three appearances for England, scoring in a 2-0 win in a friendly against New Zealand. Hirst had his admirers in the game, none more so than Manchester United manager Alex Ferguson, who tried to buy him from the Owls on no less than six occasions, making a bid of £3 million for him in 1992. Wednesday rejected that bid (it's perhaps safe to say that, if Hirst had been a Norwich player at that time, chairman Robert Chase might have found such a bid irresistible), just as they did a further five until, fed up with the Owls insubordination, Ferguson switched to his second choice striking target, the player in question being Eric Cantona, then at Leeds United.

Hirst made up half of a formidable striking partnership at Hillsborough with Dalian Atkinson and it was the latter who set him up for the games' opening goal, Hirst seizing the opportunity with typical ease after only fourteen minutes. For Norwich, who had Tim Sherwood filling in at right-back, this was obviously an early setback but not one that led them, as some Canary sides have been prone to do in similar circumstances, to fall apart. Indeed, conceding that early goal merely spurred Norwich on to greater efforts and the equaliser, when it came, was via a spot kick that was converted by Andy 'For me Clive, that was a penalty' Townsend just eight minutes later, awarded after – who else – man of the moment Mortensen had been taken out by future Norwich manager Nigel Worthington. Mortensen continued to impress throughout the game, one that the Canaries won courtesy of a Phil King own goal shortly before half time. It hadn't been the best of afternoons for Wednesday's full-backs but it was turning out to be a very good one for Norwich, who climbed three places up the Division One table to fifth as a result of the win. Three points and up to fifth in the table and a new star rising in the east. Striking crisis, what striking crisis?

Two more league wins swiftly followed with former Midland giants Nottingham Forest and Derby County (both 1-0) seen off in the process with, after a close range effort from Rosario seen off the Rams, Norwich jumping up another place to fourth in the Division One table. That win was all the more impressive for the Canaries given that it was Derby's first defeat in seven, a run that had included six successive wins with a defence that was one of the toughest to unpick in the league. All reasons for Stringer to smile. Yet his biggest smile of all might have been reserved for Mortensen, whose quick thinking and pass had led to Rosario's goal. The two of them were proving to be quite a partnership in the making and, with the still-injured Fleck doubtless keen to regain his place in the side as soon as he returned to full fitness, the Canaries' striking problems seemed to have been, at least for the time being, well and truly annulled.

Which is why that 1-0 defeat to Wimbledon at Carrow Road on New Year's Day 1990 was such an unexpected and morale-quashing disappointment. Norwich City will, according to many of the club's fans, always have a tendency to flatter to deceive and that run of games going into 1990 was turning into yet another example of that. But it didn't end there. In their next league game, a fortnight after that set back against the Dons, a trip to Loftus Road to play QPR presented the Canaries with an ideal opportunity to get their league campaign back on track; yet, rather than take the opportunity to do that against Don Howe's inconsistent Hoops, Norwich turned in another poor display that saw substitute Colin Clark gifted the Hoops winner after an error by Andy Linighan. From the highs that had followed that win over Derby County, Norwich now headed back to Norfolk from West London on a run of just one win in six games.

That lone victory had been in an FA Cup third-round replay against Exeter City, deemed necessary after Norwich had escaped being the victims of a giant-killing down at St James Park via an eighty-sixth-minute equaliser from Robert Fleck after another Glaswegian, Bobby Williamson, had put the Grecians ahead a minute earlier. With Fleck and Rosario now restored to the Canaries front line, Norwich had won the replay 2-0 in a bad-tempered game that might, had it not been for some strong arm refereeing from official Peter Foakes, got out of hand. A scrappy and bruising encounter then but at least it was a win, one that meant that Norwich could at least have made the trip down to Loftus Road with some optimism, optimism that was subsequently blown out of the water by Linighan's uncharacteristic error. The Canaries had now slipped down to nineth place but would, at least, have a chance to make amends in their next league game, one that saw the visit of Manchester United to Carrow Road.

It is interesting to note that the attendance for that game, played on 21 January 1990, was 17,370, less than those who had turned up for that FA Cup third-round replay against Exeter a week and a bit earlier. Were Exeter a bigger draw than the Red Devils? Of course not. But then this was a Manchester United team that was, seemingly endlessly, going through a period of transition under their increasingly beleaguered manager Alex Ferguson, something that the attendance reflected; indeed, it was one that was bettered on eight different occasions at Carrow Road in league games that season.

Manchester United down there among the also-rans? Surely not. But yes, they most certainly were. Much has been made and written of Ferguson's early travails at Old Trafford and, pending the Red Devils trip to Carrow Road, they merit a brief revisit here, certainly as far as that 1989/90 season was concerned. They'd begun it with two expensive additions to their playing squad, namely Neil Webb, signed from Nottingham Forest, plus the former Norwich skipper Mike Phelan. He'd served the Canaries with great distinction and no little class since joining from Burnley in 1985 but now, four years after joining Norwich, he felt his career needed an upgrade. Logically, if that is what he wanted, at least from a career point of view, Manchester United were not his best option. They'd finished the 1988/89 season in eleventh place, eleven points behind Norwich who had also, for good measure, done the double over them in the league. Phelan, Webb and a third signing, West Ham's Paul Ince, would form the core of Ferguson's new midfield for the next campaign, one which had started extremely well with a 4-1 win over defending champions Arsenal on the opening day but had slowly faded away, a grim low point being reached in a 5-1 defeat at the hands of their biggest and most hated rivals Manchester City, a game and performance that precipitated a banner in the Stretford End that stated, 'Three years of excuses and it's still crap ... ta-ra Fergie'.

Norwich now found themselves in the position of hastening Ferguson's fate and, if a Canary win did, as expected, prove to be the end of the line for the former Aberdeen boss, it would mean Manchester United would be looking for their fourth manager in under a decade. The problem with that, of course, was that Dave Stringer had been doing so well since he had replaced Ken Brown as the man in charge at Carrow Road that there was no guarantee that the Red Devils wouldn't have had Stringer on a potential list of replacements for Ferguson, for they were, even then, a big draw for both players and potential managers – even one as 100 per cent yellow and green in hue as Stringer. Would, had the chance arisen, Stringer have been interested in swapping Norwich for Manchester? It is an intriguing thought.

United and Ferguson went into the Norwich game on a run of nine games without a win. As a consequence of this, they were not expected to improve on that poor sequence anytime soon, with Norwich expected to arrest their own relatively disappointing poor run of form with a victory that would lift them back in the lower reaches of the top ten. Defeat for United on the other hand might have left them in one of the Division One relegation places. All compelling stuff, so much so, in fact, that the producers of ITV's *The Match* programme chose it for their live game of the weekend, eager, no doubt, to see some sort of end game being played out for Ferguson under the obsessive glare of their cameras.

The programme, presented by Elton Welsby, featured a pre-Sky Sports Andy Gray as the studio guest, Gray making the observation before the game that, '...United are playing a team under as much pressure as they are'. That may well have been the case. But there is no way that even a fifth consecutive league defeat for the Canaries would have marked the beginning of the end for Dave Stringer. Ferguson, on the other hand, was under massive pressure to deliver and to do so in style and there is little doubt that his intent was to take the game to Norwich and to win all three points on the day. Caution was never his watchword and this was reflected in his matchday squad, which included four very offensively minded players in Mark Robins, Brian McClair, Mark Hughes and Danny Wallace. Stringer, on the other hand, opted to keep faith with the same starting XI that had lost the Canaries last three games, hoping trust and persistence would be rewarded.

Norwich's 2-0 win, the goals coming from Robert Fleck in the seventieth and eighty-fifth minutes, was well deserved and ranks as, perhaps, the Canaries' best performance of that 1989/90 season. With Rosario taking both the knocks as well as providing the knockdowns alongside Fleck in that Norwich attack, one that was backed by a midfield quartet (Dale Gordon, Andy Townsend, Ian Crook and David Phillips) that was, and remains, as good as any Norwich manager has been able to select, the Canaries were dominant for large tracts of the game and very good value for their win, one that saw the cries for Ferguson's head reach unheard of heights. But enough of Ferguson and Manchester United because this was as significant a result for Stringer's side as it had been his opposite number that afternoon. It was a performance and result that gave Norwich an opportunity to push on and look to match their fourth place finish at the end of the previous campaign or, at the very least, look to make it into the top six. Sadly, this was not to be the case. The Canaries featured in a live TV game again the following weekend, the BBC opting to show their fourth round FA Cup game at home to Liverpool. Unfortunately for the watching millions, it was a poor game played in the sort of icy conditions that are more likely to induce a weather-related injury rather than a thrilling game of football. Both clubs were ultra-cautious in their efforts as a result of this, with Norwich coming closest to scoring when Robert Rosario's header beat both Glenn Hysen and Bruce Grobbelaar only to skip agonisingly over the bar. The Canaries travelled to Anfield for the replay three days later only to lose 3-1, the defeat coming before a trip to Tottenham the following weekend, which saw Gary Lineker score a hat-trick in the home sides 4-1 victory.

The defeat at White Hart Lane seemed to knock all of the confidence and swagger out of the Canaries, the *joie de vivre* of the previous season's football now becoming a fond yet distant memory. A run of six more league games with just one win to show for it (1-0 at Charlton on 3 March) saw Norwich in danger of slipping out of the top ten if they failed to get a good result at Everton three weeks after that rare win. It didn't happen. Norwich went ahead through David Phillips shortly before half time but three Everton goals in the second half sealed their fate, that 3-1 defeat seeing the visitors slip down into eleventh place in Division One, the club's lowest league placing for nearly two years. To add insult to injury, two of Everton's goals had come from Tony Cottee headers, not something the Norwich back four on the day would have looked back on with any great pleasure given that, at just 5 foot 7 inches, Cottee was probably the shortest player on the pitch.

But perhaps that increasing defensive frailty that was becoming more and more evident as the season wore on could be blamed on a series of injuries to key players that left Stringer struggling to fit square pegs into round holes. A long-term injury to Ian Butterworth in January meant, at one point, Stringer had no option other than to play Rosario at centre-back in the aforementioned game at Charlton, one which saw the striker paired with loan signing Nick Tanner. He'd been borrowed from Liverpool and signed, no doubt, with fervent hope that he would turn into another Dave Watson. That mix of on loan debutant and in and out striker at the heart of the Canaries defence for that game sounds a recipe for disaster but Norwich prevailed thanks to a goal from Robert Fleck.

Prior to signing of Tanner, Stringer had given a league debut to Ipswich-born Adrian Pennock in a game against Southampton at The Dell, one that Norwich lost 4-1 with Matt Le Tissier contributing a hat-trick. Pennock had graduated to the first team through the Canary ranks, having originally signed on associated schoolboy forms, but his time and opportunity as a Norwich player was a brief one, the heavy defeat at Southampton signalling both the beginning and end of his career at the club. Such was, by now, the dearth of defensive options available to Stringer that he even gave Tim Sherwood the opportunity to play alongside Andy Linighan in the Canaries rearguard and, although he was more well known as a midfielder, his strength and all-round ability meant that, even if centre half was neither his best or preferred position, he did well enough to keep his place alongside him, making nine appearances in total before reverting back to his midfield enforcer role the following season.

Norwich had therefore started the 1989/90 season with question marks over their attacking options only to end it with similar questions being asked about their back four. It was an issue that Stringer would clearly have to address over the pending World Cup summer.

The Canaries' 1989/90 campaign ended with two entertaining score draws, at Aston Villa (3-3) and at home to Arsenal on the final day where, after twice going ahead, Norwich had to settle for a 2-2 draw, the goals coming courtesy of Mark Bowen and Ruel Fox, that hard-earned point seeing Norwich end the season in tenth place. It had been a campaign that, if hardly disappointing (could the Canaries ever have successfully followed up a fourth place finish in addition to reaching an FA Cup semi-final?), had, nonetheless, been a frustrating one. This had been particularly evident in the club's disappointing run of league form after Christmas, which had seen just five wins in twenty league games, part of a season that had, to adopt an old footballing cliché, been one of two halves with a promising start, which had seen, at one point, Norwich move up to third place in the Division One table. The club had, however, ultimately fallen away from the sort of heights that they had been getting used to experiencing as a combination of injuries and that ongoing problem of still not having found a striker who could guarantee twenty goals a season took its inevitable toll.

Then there was the ongoing issue about the club's inability to hold onto its best players. Mike Phelan had departed the club the previous summer for Manchester United, while, a year prior to that, Kevin Drinkell, a player that the club maybe missed more than any other, had left for Glasgow Rangers. With Andy Linighan, Andy Townsend and Robert Fleck now all drawing more than admiring glances from other clubs, it was apparent that the biggest problem Dave Stringer would have over the summer would be retaining their services when the inevitable bids came in as he, they and everyone else in and around the club, supporters included, knew they would.

It was going to be a long hot summer at Carrow Road. But at least there was a World Cup to look forward to.

CHAPTER TWO

One Step Forward, Two Steps Back

The uncomfortable situation that Norwich fans had to live with, one that is long familiar to all with a yellow and green hue, is that no one outside of Norfolk really fancied them as anything else other than rural upstarts who might occasionally raise a curious eyebrow or two.

Mark Robins, scorer of two goals in the Canaries' first ever Premier League match. (Photo courtesy of Norwich City Football Club)

Once the excitement of England's 1990 World Cup campaign in Italy, one that had seen the Three Lions exit the competition at the hands of West Germany at the semi-final stage, had died down, interest slowly, almost reluctantly, turned to the domestic league season to come, one that would be Norwich's fifth consecutive campaign playing at the top level of the game in England out of a total of fourteen spent as an unlikely, if popular, member of English football's elite.

There had been some impressive finishes during that time. Tenth (1975/76); fifth (1986/87) and fourth (1988/89) emphasised the steady progress that the Canaries had made under Ron Saunders, John Bond, Ken Brown and Dave Stringer, especially that illustrious latter trio, but, for all of that, the Canaries invariably found themselves tipped for relegation at the start of each Division One season and, as the 1990/91 campaign drew ever closer, sure enough, Norwich were again one of the clubs tipped to struggle.

Admittedly, it didn't help matters that, as in previous summers, 'big club' interest in some of Norwich's best players had again seen some significant departures from Carrow Road. In this case, the major departures in the summer of 1990 were the two Andy's; Townsend, who joined Chelsea for £1.2 million, and Linighan, who also opted to head south, in this case to join Arsenal for £1.25 million. Those figures made good reading for the accountants, a total of nearly £2.5 million received for two players who between them had cost the club around £650,000, a hearty profit that would unquestionably have brought a very big smile to Robert Chase's face. It wasn't such good news for everyone else connected with the club though, whether that was the management and coaching staff, playing squad or fans. Both players had been massive assets to the club over the last couple of seasons, assets on the pitch rather than on a balance sheet. Linighan, who'd joined the club as a replacement for Steve Bruce, had proven himself to be an exceptionally good player, one who, like Bruce, was effective in both penalty areas and drawing praise from Dave Stringer, who'd said of Linighan, '...he is good in the air, comfortable on the ball with both feet and, for a big lad, is quite quick'. It was rare but justified praise from a man who didn't easily dish out the plaudits. Linighan made 102 league and cup appearances during his time at Norwich, scoring eight goals in the process, although, as we will see later, the most important goal he ever got for Norwich was scored while he was wearing an Arsenal shirt.

Andy Townsend, on the other hand, always felt as if he was someone who merely saw Norwich as football's version of Clapham Junction railway station, somewhere to briefly stop at before taking the next step in his football career. He'd signed for the Canaries from Southampton in 1988, his departure from The Dell taking many Saints fans as well as, in all probability, many of his teammates by surprise as he had, up to then, been regarded as a pivotal member of a gifted squad that included players like Jimmy Case, Matt Le Tissier and Danny Wallace. Townsend had particularly impressed during Saints second league match of the 1987/88 season, setting up a goal for Kevin Moore from a corner as well as hitting the bar from a free kick in his side's 1-0 win over, you've guessed it, Norwich City. He clearly made a big impression on the then Norwich manager Ken Brown with his performance on the day, one that would have been passed on and noted by Stringer who, a year later, probably couldn't believe his luck in luring Townsend away from Southampton for just £300,000, a ludicrously low amount for a player who went onto excel at Carrow Road as well as at Chelsea and Aston Villa.

Big players who would be missed. They would clearly have to be replaced but how much of the money that Norwich had received for their leading pair would be made available for Stringer to strengthen his squad? The answer to that question was under half of the total amount received for them. Yet Stringer invested it well, bringing in three new defenders in John Polston from Tottenham, Paul Blades from Derby County and Colin Woodthorpe from Chester. Blades and Polston made their Canary debuts in the opening league fixture of the 1990/91 season, which saw a narrow win over Sunderland at Carrow Road. Goals from Dale Gordon and Tim Sherwood had given Norwich what looked like a comfortable lead at half time only for Peter Davenport and Marco Gabbiadini to level things up, the latter's fierce shot in the sixty-third minute an early contender for Carrow Road's goal of the season award. The Canaries were shaken but, fortunately, not quite fully stirred and eventually sealed the win when Ruel Fox scored in the seventy-third minute.

Three points, three goals scored and more than decent debuts from the two new men. The new season was up and running. The continuing emergence of Ruel Fox as one of the Canaries key players was one of the highlights of the 1990/91 season for both the club management and supporters. He had made his senior debut for Norwich back in the 1986/87 campaign in a Full Members Cup game against Coventry City before making his full league debut in a league game against Oxford United a few days later. Fox went onto make a further two league appearances for Norwich that season before making thirty-four league starts in the 1987/88 campaign. He then dropped out of contention again over the next two seasons, making just seven league starts in the 1988/89 and 1989/90 seasons as Dale Gordon and David Phillips firmly established themselves as the first-choice wide players under Dave Stringer at that time. Under such circumstances, Fox wouldn't have been blamed if he had chosen to continue his football career elsewhere. By the start of the 1990/91 season, he was twenty-two and at the time in his professional life where he needed to be playing regularly so he and the club would have seen that campaign as being crucial for him. Fox made the very most of the opportunity he was given by Stringer during that season, making twenty-eight league appearances in all and contributing four goals, one of which had been in the season opener against Sunderland as well as his grabbing the equaliser in a 1-1 draw at home to Liverpool on 10 October 1990, a well earnt point for the Canaries that brought Liverpool's run of eight successive league wins since the start of the season to an end. That unexpected point against the league leaders was a rare highpoint for the Canaries in what was, despite that encouraging win over Sunderland, a disappointing start to the season. The hope and optimism that an opening day win always generates was swiftly followed by four consecutive league defeats, these coming against Southampton (1-0), Leeds (3-0), Crystal Palace (0-3), and Manchester City (2-1). Four games, four defeats and nine goals conceded, not the best of starts for new boys John Polston and Paul Blades.

Polston may not have been that archetypal big and uncompromising centre-back, but Blades was. He'd first announced himself to the football watching nation as the winner of ITV's *Penalty Prize* competition in 1978 when he was just thirteen, going onto win caps for the England youth team before signing for Derby County on apprentice forms in 1981, turning professional a year later. Like Polston, however, Blades found his path to the Derby first team hindered by both the presence and personality of big name and personality players like Peter Shilton, Mark Wright and Dean Saunders, three individuals who must have been quite a daunting prospect for any young player looking to impress and break into first-team contention. However, having joined Norwich at the same time as Polston, Blades now found that with Polston, after an uncertain start, now beginning to carve out a very capable central defensive partnership with Ian Butterworth, his opportunities in the Canaries first team were becoming somewhat limited. Three good players then, all looking for one of two places in Dave Stringer's first team. Not a particularly good situation for any of them to be in, particularly Blades, but a very nice problem for Dave Stringer to have.

Stringer had, if you remember, been so short of defensive cover the previous season he'd had to resort to signing Nick Tanner on loan from Liverpool for six games, give the unfortunate Adrian Pennock his league debut before, just as quickly, abandoning him as an option before giving midfielder Tim Sherwood a run of games at centre half. That was a situation that, to his credit, Sherwood coped with admirably, even if it meant that the club temporarily missed out on his tenacious presence in midfield.

That draw against Liverpool was a rare high spot in a poor league run since the opening day win against Sunderland that had seen Norwich lose six of their next seven matches, an extremely disappointing sequence that had included a 3-0 defeat at newly promoted Leeds as well as an embarrassing 3-1 reverse at Carrow Road against Luton for whom Lars Elstrup scored a fourteen-minute hat-trick. A 2-0 reverse at Arsenal followed a week after that, a result that saw the Canaries sink down into seventeenth place in the Division One table. What was now particularly worrying for the Canaries, in a season that was already looking as if it might be one of struggle, was the fact that, again, they were simply not scoring enough goals with just seven scored in those opening eight league fixtures, three of which had been against Sunderland. The defensive shortages that had come to the fore towards the end of the previous season may well have been addressed with the arrivals of Polston and Blades, yet the old problem of not having a reliable goalscorer was still evident, with Robert Fleck expected to shoulder much of the responsibility himself again.

The defeat against Luton was bad enough but there was worse to come at the beginning of December with what turned out to be the Canaries' worst performance under the management of Dave Stringer. It was a humiliating 0-4 defeat to Wimbledon at Carrow Road on 1 December, a result and performance that stunned the 12,324 in attendance, a small but hardcore support who had, as always, steeled themselves in anticipation for the Canaries annual roughing up at the hands of the Dons. A physical battle would have been what they expected but the very last thing on their minds would have been a total capitulation. Yet that is exactly what they got for their entrance money. Because make no mistake about it, the Canaries were woeful. Out thought and out fought, the opening half hour saw Wimbledon dominate to such an extent that there must have been, at one point, very real fears that they would achieve double figures. John Fashanu started the rout, running clear of an exposed defence after less than thirty seconds to fire past Gunn before Warren Barton and John Scales, both defenders, made it 3-0, with Fashanu scoring his second and his sides fourth on twenty-eight minutes. You couldn't even say that goal made it game over as a match, at least how we all might recognise one, wasn't taking place. Wimbledon were in complete control of the game to such an extent that a massive sit down protest took place in the Barclay stand on the final whistle. There hadn't been supporter discontent at this level at Norwich since seat cushions had been lobbed onto the pitch in protest at the end of Ron Saunders last game in charge nearly thirty years previously. Things invariably had to be grave to incur the wrath of any Norwich City fan and this game and performance most certainly did that.

Dave Stringer had to react after such a game but what could he reasonably do? Norwich's squad wasn't overflowing with ready-made replacements for those who had played against Wimbledon; indeed, if it had, then he might have felt justified in making eleven changes for the Canaries next match, another home game, this time against Southampton. But Stringer didn't have that luxury and made just two changes to the team that had been bullied into abject submission by Bobby Gould's side, with Paul Blades making way for a recalled John Polston while Robert Rosario returned to the starting line-up in favour of Lee Power.

It would be too simplistic to suppose that these two changes made all the difference to a Norwich side that clearly prospered in playing against a team that, like themselves, preferred to pass and caress the ball rather than physically assault it. This was particularly evident when, after the Saints had gone ahead in the sixth minute via a typically spectacular Matt Le Tissier strike, the Canaries stayed loyal to their game plan with calm heads and steady minds prevailing as they sought to get themselves back on level terms.

That reward was not too long in coming, David Phillips scoring the equaliser with just under ten minutes of the half left with a typical long range effort, meaning that Dave Stringer would not have needed to say much to his players at half time other than to encourage them to do what they did best (i.e. pass and move). This would have been in stark contrast to how he might have been feeling the previous week when, already 4-0 down to Wimbledon, he would have felt he didn't have enough time to say what needed to be said. All that Norwich needed to do now was to start the second half as they had ended the first, putting pressure on the Southampton defence through their elegant passing game and to wait for the mistakes to come, as they surely would. And come they did, a fifty-fourth-minute howitzer of a back pass from Neil Ruddock giving Tim Flowers no chance as it flew past him. Then, mindful of how the icy conditions might have affected the speed and flight of Ruddock's back pass, Glenn Cockerill wafted an altogether far too gentle effort back to Flowers two minutes later, as underhit as Ruddock's had been overhit, something which gave the ever-aware Mark Bowen time enough to take advantage, stealing in to steer the ball past the unfortunate Flowers for Norwich's third and final goal.

The Canaries performance in that 3-1 win contained everything that had been missing in the Wimbledon debacle. Where there had been panic, there was calm; where play had been hurried, it was considered; and, most importantly of all, where there had been self-doubt, there was confidence and self-belief. If the Wimbledon game was unquestionably their worst performance of the season, then this one was up there as one of the best, positive proof that this was a very good side in the making, one that could, given the right additions to the playing squad, justifiably find itself challenging for a finishing place in the top six. Hyperbole? Hardly, as Norwich had already proven themselves good enough to do just that on two separate occasions in the previous four years.

Someone who failed to make any sort of impact on the game that afternoon was the Southampton number nine, a certain Alan Shearer. Yes, the very same Alan Shearer who had been the focus of both Norwich's and Stringer's attention a little less than two years earlier. A lot had happened since Norwich had seemingly been on the verge of signing the then twenty year old, not least, for Canaries fans, the much vaunted signings of Dean Coney and Henrik Mortensen as the apparent alternatives to the Saints' young striker. Shearer was having a fairly decent 1990/91 season individually; indeed, he would end that campaign with fourteen goals from forty-eight league and cup appearances, hardly stellar figures but still more than any Norwich player would manage by the end of the campaign. Southampton were, however, having a disappointing league season themselves, something which must have been very frustrating to Shearer. The defeat at Norwich had seen them drop to seventeenth place in the Division One table, five points behind Norwich who were looking, in contrast to the Hampshire side, a team on the up and up. Shearer's time would come, and how, at Blackburn Rovers, who he joined for £3.6 million a little under eighteen months later, forming a deadly and much-talked-about striking partnership with Chris Sutton, who, at the time of that Southampton match, had not even made his senior debut for the Canaries.

Norwich followed up that win against the Saints with two more, a 2-1 success at Sunderland followed by a 1-0 win over Everton at Carrow Road. The Canaries were, by now, missing Robert Fleck, who had been ruled out for a few weeks having had surgery on his knee, with Lee Power partnering Robert Rosario in those two games. It was, however, a defender who had come to the rescue with the only goal of the game against the Toffees, John Polston's header on thirty-eight minutes the first of the six goals he would score in 104 league appearances for the Canaries, while equal praise was due to goalkeeper Bryan Gunn, who had made three crucial saves in the dying minutes of the game from each of Graeme Sharp, Mike Newell and Pat Nevin. A hard earnt but thoroughly deserved win therefore for the Canaries, who were now back up to ninth place in the table.

By the beginning of March 1991, Norwich were still holding their own in the top half of the Division One table, an uncompromising and occasionally overtly physical 0-0 draw at Derby on 23 February doing just enough to keep them there. With the Canaries now eight points clear of the relegation zone and continuing to play well, albeit in frustratingly hot patches (the 3-1 win over Southampton and a 3-1 canter at Crystal Palace) punctuated by unexpected dreadful ones (a 2-6 home defeat to Nottingham Forest on 2 January), there seemed little to no danger of the Canaries being drawn into a life or death struggle at the end of the table. Which, in itself, could have been regarded as success. After all, nearly every top-flight season for the Canaries throughout the 1980s and 1990s commenced with them being tipped for relegation, as predictable then as it is today. Yet, following the success of that, admittedly, unprecedented 1988/89 campaign, rising levels of expectancy around the club had dared suggest that Norwich could, and should, now look to move on and establish themselves as a permanent fixture in or around the top ten rather than just looking to make up the numbers.

If the levels of expectation and all the pressure that goes with it had been on the up and up around Carrow Road, then maybe some of the heavy defeats the club had also ensured that season were serving as an invaluable reality check? Nottingham Forest's emphatic victory had seen Norwich swept aside by a new, young, exciting and occasionally precocious Forest side that Brian Clough was putting together, one that featured the likes of Stuart Pearce, Des Walker, Roy Keane, Scott Parker and Nigel Clough, outstanding talents who made up the core of Clough's side and who, at the average age of just twenty-four, looked set to have glittering futures ahead of them in the game, whether that was with him at Forest or at bigger clubs. Yet couldn't Forest fans argue that they were already playing for a big club? Clough had already led them to a League Championship, two European Cups (now the Champions League), one European Super Cup and four League Cups. That had been in the days of Peter Shilton, Viv Anderson, Kenny Burns, John Robertson and Trevor Francis. Forest now had a new cast of footballing talents and, under Clough's watch, if any club looked set to break the stranglehold that Liverpool had on the English game in the 1990s and emerge as serious contenders for league titles and cups alongside the men of Anfield and Arsenal, then surely it was going to be the team from the City Ground, rather than the one at Carrow Road.

The uncomfortable situation that Norwich fans had to live with, one that is long familiar to all with a yellow and green hue, is that no one outside of Norfolk really fancied them as anything else other than rural upstarts who might occasionally raise a curious eyebrow or two. Those heavy defeats against Luton and Wimbledon had only served to reinforce that image, one that suggested that, rather like West Ham, the Canaries were a team who could, on their day, 'turn it on', but, regardless of that, were still one that tended to crumble in fixtures where the opposition either didn't let you play, as had certainly been the case against Wimbledon, or were better than you at playing your type of football, as Forest had seemingly proved with that emphatic victory. Besides, teams with aspirations of reaching the top didn't concede six goals in a game of any kind, let alone one played at their own ground, an infallible logic that was hard to mount a counter argument against.

As it turned out, there were no goals to be seen and very little action of any kind when the Canaries arrived at Plough Lane for the return league fixture with Wimbledon. No goals, little action to talk about, and, in front of a crowd of just 4,041, hardly any spectators either, the lucky ones being those who chose, for one reason or another, to do something else on that particular Saturday afternoon. Yet, in surviving the inevitable onslaught played at a ground where, if you were bored, you could watch the London buses pass by on the adjacent roads, Norwich gave themselves a little bit of credibility with that well earnt point. A fortnight later, the Canaries made the trip to Luton, a collective goal of more footballing atonement on the minds of players and fans alike after that September surrender to the Hatters at Carrow Road.

The fact that Norwich achieved exactly that by winning 1-0 speaks volumes of the positive attitude that Dave Stringer's men would have taken into that game, fortified, no doubt, by the recently won point in South London. Luton dominated the match from the kick-off and had numerous opportunities to win convincingly only for their best efforts to be thwarted by Bryan Gunn, the Norwich keeper performing heroics with several excellent saves. With Gunn in such good form, it looked as if one Norwich goal would be enough to win the game and, sure enough, the Canaries made the most of one of their rare breaks on goal with Tim Sherwood converting David Phillips' pass in the twenty-first minute to win an unlikely but very welcome three points for the Canaries. Another 0-0 draw, this time at home to Arsenal, followed a week later, a result and point that meant that the Canaries had now gone 407 minutes without conceding a league goal, an admirable achievement that spoke a lot about how Bryan Gunn was organising and managing his defence, one that had been leaking goals in a most alarming manner earlier in the season but was now looking as secure as the dungeons at Norwich Castle.

A 2-1 win at home to Tottenham on 10 April saw the Canaries move back up into tenth place in the First Division, handily placed, as it turned out, for the run in. Norwich were on forty-two points with only goal difference separating them from Queens Park Rangers in ninth place – Norwich with a game in hand. Tottenham (forty-five points) were in eighth place, whist Wimbledon (forty-eight) and Manchester City (fifty-two) were in seventh and sixth places, respectively, but, crucially, Norwich also had games in hand over them. It wasn't, therefore, beyond the realms of possibility that Norwich could, with a good run of results following that success over Tottenham, push for a place near to the top six and, in doing so, at least retain their place in the top ten, a finishing position which would have been an encouraging base from which to prepare for the 1991/92 season.

A not totally unrealistic goal. Finishing in the top six might have been one that was just out of the Canaries' reach by now but if they at least strived to achieve that then, surely, a finishing place in the top ten would be almost assured, one that would be a very good foundation for the following season. It was certainly something to aim for and, for Norwich, gave those remaining six matches added frisson, a reason to play well and compete at a time when some other clubs, marooned in mid-table (and with no added prize money to play for by moving from fourteenth to eleventh place) would have been going through the motions. Not something that Dave Stringer would contemplate. 'Going through the motions' wasn't something he ever did as a player and it most certainly wouldn't be something he would consider as a manager, something that his players would have been aware of within five minutes of first meeting him. He would have expected nothing more than a committed and focused end to the season from his players and woe betide anyone who slipped below the high standards that he constantly set.

If this narrative was the basis for a Hollywood film, it would now detail, together with some stirring music by Hans Zimmer and a montage of Canary goals, celebration and overall jubilation as the Canaries ruthlessly swept aside each of their opponents at the end of that season on their way to an unexpected but stirring top-six finish.

But this is not Hollywood. We're talking Norwich City, where the unexpected comes as standard. Thus, following their win against Tottenham, Norwich welcomed Chelsea to Carrow Road a week later. The Blues, with former Canary Andy Townsend in the ranks, had nothing to play for, big-time Charlie's from West London with their eyes on the beach. Would Kerry Dixon and Dennis Wise be up for it? The popular consensus was that they wouldn't and that they would suffer the same fate as Tottenham had done a week earlier. Yet the Tottenham side that Norwich had beaten that day had been very much an understrength one with a named matchday squad of sixteen that included names like Tuttle, Hendon and Garland.

Their minds would have been on a pending FA Cup semi-final with Arsenal, a case of Wembley being in the club's collective thoughts rather than the beaches and clubs of Ibiza. This meant that they were never going to be the same Tottenham that had beaten Norwich 2-1 earlier in the season, a Tottenham that included Gary Lineker, scorer of both their goals that day.

If, therefore, anyone thought that Chelsea would be turned over in the same cavalier fashion, they'd have been wrong. Wrong, in fact, to the tune of 3-1 as the Blues (playing, for some reason, in red and white) enjoyed a profitable days work in Norfolk, goals from Dennis Wise and Gordon Durie (two) sealing their win, with Norwich's lone reply coming courtesy of John Polston. It was a disappointing result that came with an even more disappointing performance, one that had shades of the capitulations against Wimbledon and Luton against it.

Two more heavy defeats followed at Liverpool (3-0) and Nottingham Forest (5-0). Three games played, three defeats, one goal scored and eleven conceded. Not so much the form of a team hoping to end the season with a push towards the top six as one that wanted to see how close it could get to the relegation places. Dave Stringer had, by now, given up on picking his strongest possible eleven in these closing fixtures, choosing instead to give a few of the club's up and coming players their full league debuts. Daryl Sutch made his first full appearance at Liverpool, with Robert Ullathorne making his Canary bow in that defeat at Nottingham Forest, not a game he will want to be reminded about too often. Then, for the home fixture against Queens Park Rangers on 4 May, Stringer summoned an eighteen-year-old striker from the club's youth team, a player who had originally been rejected by the Canaries when he was twelve but had since done enough to be invited back on YTS terms, proving, in time, to be as effective a player at centre half as he was at centre forward. Chris Sutton duly made his Norwich City debut in that game, coming on as a substitute to replace Robert Fleck in the Canaries 1-0 win and doing enough in his cameo appearance to be selected for the next game, albeit again from the bench, which saw Norwich revert to their bad old ways in losing 2-1 to Aston Villa. Three days later, Norwich headed north to play Sheffield United in their last league game of the season, going ahead through a John Polston goal after just eight minutes but eventually succumbing 2-1 thanks to two quick fire efforts from Tony Agana. His presence and performance throughout the game made it very clear, not that it needed to be emphasised again, that here was the sort of player that the Canaries had needed all season – a fast, strong and brave striker who had shown throughout his career that he knew where the goal was. Scoring goals was, again, something which the Canaries had struggled to do all that season, the total of forty-one goals scored in thirty-eight league games ending up as the fourth worse in the league, with two of the three teams that ended the season more goal shy than Norwich (Sunderland and Derby) ending up being relegated.

So, from entering the final stretch of a season with the hopes of pushing for a place in or around the top six at its conclusion, the Canaries ended the 1990/91 campaign in fifteenth place, five places lower and with eight points fewer than they'd accrued at the end of 1989/90 season; that and fewer goals scored (three) but a lot more conceded (twenty-two). You didn't need to be Jimmy Hill to work out that, since that remarkable 1988/89 season, the Canaries were now in freefall.

The club also found itself with work to do on the pitch. At some points during what had turned out to be a very disappointing season, some Norwich fans, frustrated at what they saw as a talented and extremely capable squad of players not performing to expectations, start to take those frustrations out on, rightly or wrongly, those who they deemed to be underperforming. The unfortunate Dean Coney had previously been a target for spectator ire (Coney had gone so far as to publicly comment 'the fans have got it in for me') now, with Coney long gone, the new target for terrace criticism turned out to be midfielder Tim Sherwood. Sherwood, hardly a shrinking violet, was not going to ignore what he would have seen as unjust criticism and ended up responding with a few gestures aimed back at the fans after he's scored in a 2-2 draw against Coventry, a game that saw former Canary Robert Rosario, another player who had endured a lot of stick from the Norwich support, get some sort of revenge by setting up Micky Gynn for one of Coventry's goals. Mark Bowen also made his feelings clear, commenting on the 'lack of atmosphere' at the club's home games, a claim that was backed by supporters favourite of Fleck.

Then, to add insult to injury, the club announced that season ticket prices for the 1991/92 season were set to be increased, a decision that, as you would expect, did not go down at all well among the fans of the club, particularly as the season had been, overall, a disappointing one, especially after that exceptionally poor run in that saw the Canaries lose seven of their last ten league games. It was, however, a considered response by the club in the wake of the fact that the 1991/92 season would end up being the last under the present Football League structure, the campaign after that, 1992/93, being the one where English football's new 'Super League' would kick-off with, over a year before it was set to commence, the financial importance of being one of that league's founder members already becoming very obvious.

English football was preparing itself for a change of cataclysmic proportions, the aftershocks of which are still, a quarter of a century later, having a dramatic (and not always good) effect on the game to this day. It was clear, at least to Robert Chase and his board of directors at Norwich City, that the Canaries would need to strengthen their squad prior to the new season commencing and that, in order to do this, any and all forms of extra income would have to be secured. And if that meant asking the fans to pay more in order to give the Canaries the best possible chance of being part of the 'whole new ball game' that tantalisingly sat just over the horizon, then that is what would have to be done. A board decision then but one which would publicly have to be fulfilled by the manager. It would now be up to Dave Stringer to identify the players that he wanted and for the club to give them reason enough to want to join. Whether or not the players in question would turn out to be up to the extremely high expectations and demands that would be made of them from day one (the sort of pressure that had turned Dean Coney from a high-profile England U21 international and top-flight regular to professional obscurity in Hong Kong within three eventful years) remained to be seen.

One thing that was missing from the Canaries preseason in the summer of 1991 was the club's 'traditional' high-profile trip abroad. In previous years the club had made the most of the summer break by flying off the squad plus most of the management and coaching team, as well as the board of directors, to an exotic location of two – for example, China (1980 and 1990), the USA (1981 and 1987), Kenya (1983), Norway and Sweden (1985) and Gibraltar (1988). There would be no such 'jolly' (masquerading as preseason training) in the summer of 1991 as the club, ever mindful that the coming season would be one of the most strategically important in their history, focused on a round of low-profile warm-up matches and intensive preparation for what lay ahead. This also, of course, gave Dave Stringer time to evaluate the squad that he had ended the previous season with, as well as work on bringing in new additions. There was also, as was regularly the case at this time of the year, the very real threat of one or two of the Canaries leading players being tempted away by other clubs with, at this particular time, fans left wondering if Mr Chase and his board would actively listen to, or even encourage, big-money bids for the likes of Robert Fleck, Dale Gordon or Tim Sherwood, three high-profile players who were known to have admirers at other clubs, Fleck in particular.

It came as a pleasant surprise, therefore, when the summer came and went with no significant departures from the club's playing staff, the only move out sanctioned being that of twenty-year-old reserve-team striker Robert Taylor, who, after being released, joined Birmingham on a free transfer. In hindsight and with the club having struggled to score goals over the preceding couple of seasons, it seems a strange decision to have let Taylor leave without at least giving him a chance to show if he was first-team material. This was, after all, an opportunity that had been given to quite a few of the club's young players in previous seasons, Jason Minett, Lee Power, David Smith, Daryl Sutch, Chris Sutton and Robert Ullathorne among those who had been 'promoted' to the first-team squad by Dave Stringer. Sadly for Taylor, and for whatever reasons, no such chance had come his way, despite his scoring eleven goals for the reserves in the 1989/90 season before spending the Summer of 1990 on loan with Norwegian side FK Mjølner.

Just the one out but two new faces in with, very significantly, the club's transfer record being broken in the process. The player in question was Darren Beckford, who'd made quite a name for himself at Port Vale since he'd joined them from Manchester City in 1987. Unlike the unfortunate Robert Taylor, Beckford had at least been given a chance in the first team at Maine Road, given his City debut by Billy McNeill in a game against Middlesbrough on 20 October 1984 and going onto make a further ten league appearances for them, but with no goals to show for it. He subsequently had a spell on loan at Bury (twelve league games, five goals scored) before joining Port Vale in 1987 for just £15,000. He ended up scoring seventy-two goals in 178 league appearances for them, garnishing the interest of several clubs in the process. The Canaries, given their shortage of both goals and strikers, were, not surprisingly, one of the clubs that had taken note of his goalscoring ability and all-round game. Beckford was fast, strong and as good in the air as he was with the ball at his feet – and he could finish. As an all-round goalscoring package, he and the Canaries seemed a perfect fit and, once he had signed for that then club record fee of £925,000, Dave Stringer, a man not normally given to making potentially outlandish statements, described Beckford as, '...the answer to the Norwich supporters prayers'. No pressure there then. Perhaps, at that point, the Norwich fans might have been rather more wary of Beckford's now former manager, John Rudge's later description of him, which was, 'Darren Beckford was a brilliant striker for the Vale, but a nightmare to manage'. Given Dave Stringer's expectancy that all of his players maintained a strict sense of discipline and professional behaviour at all times, it looked as if Beckford, a lively and unpredictable character, might have ended up as lively off the pitch, where, according to former teammate Robbie Earle, he'd sometimes stop working in the middle of a training session and ask why he was doing that particular exercise, as he undoubtedly was on it. Clearly, the relationship between him and Stringer was going to be an interesting one.

Earle had also, if reports at the time were correct, been a summer target for Stringer, with the Norwich manager hopeful of making a double signing and bringing in both players at the same time. Earle would certainly have been a valuable acquisition to the Norwich squad had that been the case. He was a hard-working attacking midfield player who got more than his fair share of goals, racking up a total of seventy-seven in 294 league appearances for Vale. It was the sort of strike rate that a goal-shy team like Norwich would have found exceedingly valuable in the 1991/92 season and the prospect of Earle linking up with Ian Crook and Robert Fleck must have been an exceedingly tantalising one for Stringer. It was, however, a prospect that only ever remained just that and Earle eventually signed for Wimbledon with Sam Hammam, then the Dons chairman, later claiming that he had locked Earle in a room and only agreed to release him on condition that he signed for the club! Wimbledon ended up paying around £775,000 for Earle, plus an agreement to pay Port Vale 30 per cent of any subsequent sell on fee, terms that might have been just a little too steep for Robert Chase given that the club had already committed just under £1 million for Beckford.

The Canaries still needed to bolster their defence and midfield, however, and with the signing of Rob Newman from Bristol City, they procured a player who could fulfil either role with consummate ease. Newman, by trade an attacking right midfielder, was given the somewhat unkind description of 'utility player' when he signed for the Canaries, for as well as playing on the right-hand side of midfield, he could also slot into any one of the other three positions across a four-man midfield, as well as, if required, into the back four, especially at centre half. He'd been at Bristol City for nearly a decade and had made over 400 league and cup appearances for the Robins in that time, the sort of consistency and reliability in a player that any club would cherish. The Canaries paid £600,000 for Newman, meaning that he and Beckford had, between them, set the club back a little over £1.5 million. It was a hither-to-unprecedented outlay for the club to commit to and a sign of their determination to be part of football's 'whole new ball game' the following August when the new 'Premier League' kicked off for the first time. It was portrayed as a footballing land of milk and honey that the Canaries desperately wanted, and needed, to be part of from the beginning, as it would be offering the sort of worldwide commercial prospects that came with sustained membership that would soon make the Canaries £1.5-million summer outlay look like small change.

Norwich opened their 1991/92 league campaign with a home game against Sheffield United, who had also been their opponents on the last day of the previous season. Hardly the sort of opening fixture to get the pulse racing then; yet, despite that, it still drew a crowd of 16,380 to Carrow Road eager, no doubt, to see the Canaries two new signings in action for the first time.

Newman, wearing the No. 9 shirt, and Beckford, wearing No. 10, duly made their Canary debuts as part of a conventional 4-4-2 formation; Beckford alongside Fleck in the Norwich attack with a midfield quartet comprising of David Phillips, Rob Newman, Ian Crook and Dale Gordon behind them, the aforementioned striking duo an example of the classic partnership of the small, mobile striker playing alongside the big target man, with both set to profit from Dale Gordon providing pace from the wide positions and Ian Crook abundant passing guile from the Norwich midfield.

There didn't seem an obvious weak link in the team. With Bryan Gunn back in goal after missing the last four league fixtures of the previous season (Gunny was more than adequately covered by the extremely capable and popular Mark Walton) and Ian Culverhouse, Mark Bowen, Ian Butterworth and Paul Blades making up the back four, it looked as if Dave Stringer had been fortunate enough to start the season by being able to name a starting XI that wasn't far off being the strongest available to him, although those who missed out, especially John Polston, Jerry Goss and Ruel Fox, would have been entitled to suggest they should have been in contention to start as well. Reassuring evidence, therefore, of the strength in depth that Norwich now had across their squad. There was, it seems, reasonable grounds for optimism at Carrow Road.

Optimism lasted all of four minutes, which is how long it took for Brian Deane, a specialist at scoring early goals on the opening day of the season, to put the Blades ahead. His typically opportunist strike came from nowhere and acted as the cue for the Blades, then managed by Dave Bassett, to adopt an immediate 'what we have, we hold' mentality, focusing on keeping their shape and frustrating the Canaries at every opportunity. Bassett's side then looked to have won the game when, against the run of play, Colin Hill scored their second goal after seventy-three minutes, a fitting if unpopular reward for him and his team's ability to maintain its discipline and shape throughout the match.

With Beckford withdrawn to make way for Ruel Fox, Norwich looked to up the ante in that last quarter of an hour with Stringers gamble of taking off his record signing paying off as Fleck, rumoured to have asked for a move in the summer, scored two goals, his second coming in the eighty-ninth minute. It sealed a fortuitous point for the home side who now had four days to work out where and how things had gone wrong before a potentially tricky away game against Queens Park Rangers the following Wednesday. But if Stringer was tempted to change things around for that game, he resisted the urge, naming the same starting XI for that game, despite Fox impressing all who witnessed his cameo appearance on the Saturday. Thankfully, the faith he placed in his players paid off and saw Norwich get a deserved 2-0 win with Man of the Match Dale Gordon scoring one of the goals while Rob Newman, who had swiftly and effectively settled into the Canaries' midfield, got the other, converting a cross from the ever-impressive David Phillips. For Darren Beckford, Norwich's other new signing, it was, as it had been at the weekend, another quiet game, the imposing striker finding life against top-flight defenders, in this case David Bardsley and Danny Maddix, a playing step up from what he had been used to with Port Vale in Division Two. This might not have been too much of a problem had Beckford been signed by one of the leagues bigger clubs where he would be afforded time to settle down into both the culture of the club and its playing philosophy. At Norwich, however, things were, by necessity, different. Beckford had cost the Canaries close to £1 million and was a marquee signing, one designed to show that the club meant business and would do whatever it took retain its top-flight status. Unfortunately for Beckford, that large outlay and all the accordant publicity that came with it had an accompanying caveat; he'd need to live up to both the big fee and the faith that had been placed in him by the Canaries' hierarchy by scoring goals, and quickly, something that Ricky van Wolfswinkel also found to his cost when he became the Canaries' record signing twenty-two years later.

By the end of August 1991, Norwich had played five league games, winning one, drawing three and losing one, a 1-0 defeat to Tottenham at Carrow Road on 31 August. Gary Lineker, the scorer of the lone goal that afternoon, had, upon signing for the North Londoners from Barcelona in 1989, gone seven league games before notching his first for his new club, one that had come, coincidentally, in a 2-2 draw against Norwich at Carrow Road. So Lineker would have been only too familiar with the pressure and expectation that came with being a big money signing. But then he'd already proven himself as a world-class striker with Everton, Barcelona and England. Tottenham had known he'd come good, even if it took five, ten or fifteen games for him to get going. As it was, despite his 'late start' that campaign, he still ended as the First Division's leading scorer by the close of the season with twenty-four goals to his name.

No one expected Darren Beckford to do the same with Norwich. Yet, by the end of the Tottenham game, a few questions were already being asked of him. Five games played, no goals to his name, and, perhaps more significantly, by the end of the first week of September, one that had seen Norwich draw 1-1 with Everton before losing 3-0 to Manchester United at Old Trafford, Beckford had been substituted in five of Norwich's first seven league games. On each of those occasions he'd been replaced by Ruel Fox, who must, by this stage, have been wondering what he needed to do in order to get a start. But Fox didn't have to wait for much longer. For the visit of West Ham on 14 September, Dave Stringer opted to drop Beckford in order to give Fox his first start of the season, the Ipswich-born midfielder repaying his managers faith by opening the scoring after just thirteen minutes. Despite Mike Small equalising for the Hammers two minutes later, a thirty-ninth-minute goal from Dale Gordon sealed a 2-1 win for the Canaries, lifting them up two places in the Division One table to fourteenth. For Darren Beckford it must have been a frustrating afternoon. He'd gone from being the stand-out player and big-name draw at Port Vale to a striker who was struggling to score at his new club and had been dropped as a result, only to see his replacement do in under a quarter of an hour what he still hadn't been able to do in seven matches.

The Canaries had scored nine goals in their opening eight games. One of those goalscorers, Robert Fleck, had now gone seven games without a goal, a statistic that would have been as much a concern to the Canaries fans as Beckford's apparent inability to score at all. It was a puzzle. Much had been expected of the striking partnership between the two of them, especially as Fleck had spoken well of the one he had formed with Robert Rosario before the latter had grown weary of the stick he'd been getting from parts of the Carrow Road crowd and sent himself to Coventry. Clearly, Fleck preferred to play alongside a traditional target man but, for whatever reasons, the much anticipated one between himself and Beckford wasn't working out for either of them.

In among all of this yellow and green footballing angst, you might, were you a Canary fan, have been forgiven for forgetting all about the man who'd originally been signed with the hope that he would be able to provide a sure-fire remedy for the club's shortcomings in front of goal.

Henrik Mortensen, remember him? Unlike the unfortunate Beckford, he'd made an immediate impact after signing from Danish club Aarhus. He'd scored on his reserve team debut before following that up with another goal in his first-team debut, following that up by winning a penalty in his league debut against Sheffield Wednesday a few days later. It was all a bit *Boy's Own* stuff even if, with his pop star looks and carefully coiffured hair, Mortensen looked as if he would be more at home on a fashion catwalk rather than a football field. Mindful of his youth and inexperience of English football, Dave Stringer had been protective of Mortensen for the remainder of that 1989/90 season, one that the young Dane completed with fifteen league appearances (of which twelve were starts) to his name but no goals.

The following season (1990/91) saw Mortensen make just three league appearances, all of which came from the bench, plus one in the FA Cup when, in a 3-1 win over Sweden, he replaced David Smith, promptly scoring his first, and only, senior goal for the club in the eighty-sixth minute. He went onto become a regular scorer for the club's reserve side, totalling twenty-five goals from fifty-four games, stats that, had he done it at first-team level, would probably have seen him end up as another multimillion-pound departure for the club. Sadly, following his sustaining a pelvic injury in a reserve game at Ipswich, Mortensen eventually had to quit the game, his undoubted promise put to an end by a professional footballer's greatest enemy, a cruel and very low-key end to a career that had, at its peak, seen him play in European club competition for Anderlecht.

His departure was just one of a growing number of disappointments for the Canaries on the striker front. Dean Coney, Robert Rosario and Malcolm Allen had briefly come and gone again, a growing list to which Mortensen's name could now be added. With doubts also lingering over the long-term prospects of Lee Power at the club, as well as the very real fact that Darren Beckford genuinely looked as if he was struggling to adapt to the demands of top-flight football, one thing was clear: those ongoing concerns about a lack of regular goalscorer or two within Dave Stringer's squad were now in danger of turning from a temporary inconvenience to a full on crisis. Matters were not helped when, shortly after he was part of the Norwich side that laboured to a 0-0 draw at home to Nottingham Forest on 2 November, Dale Gordon, at the time the club's leading goalscorer that season, signed for Glasgow Rangers for £1.2 million, a sale that, predictably, provoked unbridled fury from the club's support with chairman Chase once again being accused of putting profit before results. Gordon's departure also grew some stinging rebukes from the local press with one *Norwich Evening News* reporter, David Cuffley, asking the question, 'Is There Life After Dale?' while, when asked to comment about the matter, Canaries boss Dave Stringer admitted, 'Anyone who thinks I like losing my best players must need his head examined.'

Stringer, clearly, was feeling as frustrated about Gordon's sale as the club's fans were and it seems almost certain that his frustration at repeatedly having his best players sold from under him was beginning to make him wonder if he really wanted all the stresses and strains that went with managing the club that he adored. Ever dignified, he chose to carry on with what he had got but the seeds of doubt that ultimately led to him resigning his position as manager before the end of that season were very likely propagated by Gordon's sudden and unexpected departure.

By the time Gordon headed north there had been at least one glimmer of light on the horizon – a first Norwich City goal for Darren Beckford.

It had come in his tenth appearance for the Canaries, a 3-1 defeat to their traditional spoilers, Wimbledon. A tiny crowd of just 3,531 had dotted itself around the Dons ramshackle Plough Lane ground to see their side lift themselves up to seventh place in Division One with that win, the last under manager Ray Harford, who was set to join Blackburn. Everywhere you looked, it seemed, players and managers were moving onto bigger and better things. Stringer had already seen Andy Townsend and Tim Sherwood do just that while Dale Gordon would soon be following. Now the allure of more money and a very real chance of winning some silverware had tempted Harford away from Wimbledon, a club that, like Norwich, was continuing to punch above its weight despite losing their star performers on a regular basis. The balance of power in English football, one that had long seen a fair scattering of both playing and coaching talent distributed throughout the leagues, was now drifting inexorably towards the bigger clubs, with Harford willing to give up his position as manager of a top-flight club in order to become a number two at a club in a league below them but one that was very upwardly mobile from a financial point of view with Jack Walker happy to sink as much of his personal fortune into Blackburn as possible to ensure not only their promotion that season but to give them more than a fighting chance of winning the league. Norwich would, later that season, see Tim Sherwood willingly drop down a division to join Walker's side, now Harford would soon be coaching the ex-Canary. What chance did clubs like Norwich and Wimbledon have of competing with the new money coming into the game? Very little it seemed-and this was, remember, still nearly a year before the Premier League started.

Beckford struck again for the Canaries in their 2-1 defeat at Liverpool on 30 November, following that up with his third goal of the season a week later as Norwich drew 3-3 at home to Crystal Palace. Had he finally 'arrived'? Was the player who had so successfully bossed and bullied defences during his time at Port Vale now ready to do the same with Norwich City? If the jury was out on that particular question, there is no doubt that everyone connected with the club wanted to see him achieve great things with the Canaries, especially as, once Dale Gordon had left the club, Robert Fleck was repeatedly tipped as being the club's next big name to be on his way, with Tottenham being particularly keen on adding the Scottish international striker to their already formidable array of goalscoring options that included Gary Lineker, Gordon Durie and Paul Walsh. Chelsea were also interested and had, in the summer of 1991, invited Fleck down to London for informal talks about a possible move, something that he later admitted he was more than willing to consider. Despite both parties willingness, however, the move never got past that initial discussion stage with Norwich chairman Robert Chase advising Fleck that the club would not sanction his departure that summer.

Given that Chase's business model at Carrow Road was based on signing players for relatively modest fees, raising both their games and profiles before selling them on again for a vast profit, this decision was a very surprising one. Yet, when balanced against the importance of the Canaries commencing the 1992/93 season as members of the FA Premier League, it now makes a lot of sense. Chase would have been very aware of the extra money and the far wider business and overall commercial interest there would have been in the English game once the first Premier League season got under way. Norwich's participation in the Premier League was therefore a massive priority with everything at Carrow Road and the training ground at Trowse being focused on achieving just that. This meant that selling your best player/most valuable asset was, for once, not something that would be entertained. It didn't mean, however, that the club would not consider bids for the same players once Premier League membership was assured and Fleck duly got Chase's promise that the chairman would not stand in the way of his move to Chelsea the following summer, in return for which the popular striker would not rock the boat and continue, as he always had, to give everything to the cause as a Norwich City player.

By the halfway point of the 1991/92 season, marked on Boxing Day with a 2-1 defeat at Manchester City, Fleck had scored five league goals from twenty league games, a modest total that might, had he been anyone else, made him the subject of the same sort of terrace criticism that had been afforded to some of his less than fortunate (and equally under-firing) predecessors in the Canary attack. This was not, however, the case. Fleck remained a hugely popular figure at the club, well liked by his teammates and adored by the club's support. He was guaranteed to give 100 per cent in every match he played, to run, sweat and occasionally bleed for the Norfolk cause. Football supporters the world over can forgive players many a finer detail regarding their game if they are seen to be giving their total and absolute all in every game, and Robert Fleck most certainly did this. He'd also had, in the club's 3-2 win over Coventry City on 23 November, a new strike partner. The game itself had been very much a nip and tuck affair with Kevin Gallagher putting Coventry ahead only for Mark Bowen to equalise shortly after half time. Gallagher then put the visitors 2-1 up and that pretty much looked to be that before Fleck's equaliser with five minutes left, before substitute Chris Sutton scored the Norwich winner in the last minute, his first goal for the club in his first game of the season. Food for thought for Dave Stringer perhaps, especially as Darren Beckford had, again, been substituted earlier on.

Sutton had looked set for a career in sport, one way or the other, almost since birth. His father, Norwich-born Michael, had joined the Canaries as part of the club's ground staff in 1960, going onto progress through the ranks at the club, ending up making fifty-four league and cup appearances, during which time he scored three goals. After spells with Chester and Carlisle United, he returned to Norfolk, spending time in non-league football with Gorleston Town and Yarmouth Town before taking on a part-time coaching role at Carrow Road. Position wise, Sutton senior was described as a 'utility' player, something which can be seen in one of two ways: either not good enough to establish himself in a specific position or role, or, the one I prefer, a player with sufficient skills to be able to play in more than one position or role on the pitch, a quality that makes him as valuable as, even more so, than one who is adequate in one position but would struggle in any other.

This was an issue that Chris Sutton would have to contend with in early part of his career. He was initially seen as a centre-back, playing in nine consecutive games in that position for Mike Walker at the start of the 1992/93 season as like-for-like cover for either John Polston or Ian Butterworth. However, as those early games for the club had proved during the previous season, Sutton's height and physical presence, allied to a great first touch, were more suited for the game of a traditional centre forward than a centre half, proof of this coming in the Canaries FA Cup run that campaign where, playing as a striker, he scored three goals in six games; an impressive brace against Notts County at Carrow Road followed by an instinctive header to win an epic quarter-final replay against Southampton. Could it be that the answer to the club's ongoing striking deficiencies were about to be answered by an eighteen year old who was not long out of the club's youth team?

On New Year's Day 1992, the Canaries welcomed Aston Villa to Carrow Road, mindful that their opponents, fifth in the Division One table at kick-off, would provide a good test as far as their ongoing top-flight credentials were concerned. Norwich were sat in fourteenth place at kick-off but were only six points clear off the relegation places. That wasn't exactly a cause for concern at this early stage but, if the club was gone into the last quarter of the season with the focus more on building for the following season than worrying about ending this one being relegated, then Aston Villa would provide an ideal opportunity to commence a good sequence of results, with winnable games against Oldham, Sheffield United, Southampton and Luton, all clubs that were struggling at the wrong end of the table, to follow.

With Chris Sutton now reverting to what was then thought of as his best position, playing alongside Paul Blades in the Canaries back four, Norwich were full value for money in an entertaining game that they won 2-1. They took the lead in unusual circumstances, Robert Fleck converting a fifty-sixth-minute penalty at the second attempt after Les Sealey had saved the first, referee John Martin ordering it to be retaken as Dariusz Kubicki was deemed to have encroached into the area before the ball was struck. Cyrille Regis equalised after seventy-four minutes, that goal the prelude to some sustained Villa pressure and some nervous states of mind but, fortunately for the home support, that state of affairs didn't last for long with Robert Ullathorne scoring the winner from a David Phillips cross just four minutes later. Norwich's win lifted them two places up the table to twelfth and with those four consecutive games to come against teams Dave Stringers' side might reasonably have been expected to beat, it was hoped, maybe even expected that, by the time the Canaries travelled to Highbury to play Arsenal on 11 February their top flight status might already have been more or less confirmed for another season.

Football would be a much more enjoyable game if every match our team played was decided on paper, rather than grass.

On paper, the fixtures against Oldham, Sheffield United, Southampton and Luton were all winnable games for the Canaries. But even if expecting that it would result in a twelve-point haul was a little presumptuous, then one of nine or ten points most certainly wasn't. You could understand why, as none of the aforementioned quartet were having the best of seasons. Take, for example, Southampton. The Saints had dropped down to twenty-second and bottom of the table on the day that Norwich were beating Aston Villa, while Oldham seemed to be in freefall, a situation exacerbated by their having conceded ten goals in heavy defeats to Chelsea and Manchester United. Then there was the blunted Blades, Sheffield United, who'd been in and around the bottom three since the beginning of the season while Luton, who would end up being relegated anyway, had won just three of their opening twenty league fixtures that campaign. So maybe a full haul of points wasn't such an unrealistic proposition.

Yet, as things turned out, it was. Very much so. The game against Oldham at Carrow Road started promisingly enough, Darren Beckford's eighth goal of the season looking like it would give the Canaries a deserved half-time lead. Yet, against the run of play and right on half time, a long throw in into the Norwich penalty area caused pandemonium among the Norwich defence, giving Andy Holden all the time and space he needed to head home the equaliser. Then, just after the hour mark, Holden crossed the ball over to Graeme Sharp, which the experienced Scottish striker was able to head into the path of Paul Bernard, who, unmarked and seemingly invisible, was only too happy to finish the job in hand and put Oldham 2-1 up, a lead which they held onto for the rest of the match with some ease, much to the disquiet of the alarmingly low attendance of 10,986 at Carrow Road.

A week later, the Canaries made the long haul up to Bramall Lane to play Sheffield United, three wins in eleven days and pretty much a permanent occupant at the bottom of the table until early November. Norwich needed to dig in and show some resilience in order to match the Blades physical game and they just about coped with their hosts traditionally rumbustious approach until Bryan Gunn was forced to go off with a back injury early in the first half. No substitute goalies in those days meant an outfield player was forced to put on the green shirt and gloves, always an entertaining prospect at any football match – unless it's your team that has to do so. Darren Beckford did the honours for the Canaries and so very nearly became the hero of the afternoon as a series of saves kept the Blades at bay. But he couldn't hold out forever and was finally beaten when midfielder Ian Bryson scored after a shot from Kevin Gage had beaten Beckford but hit the bar.

Two games played, two defeats and the need for a replacement goalkeeper for the remainder of the season when it was confirmed, post-match, that Gunn's injury would mean he wouldn't be appearing in Canary colours again until August at the very earliest. Luckily for Norwich, they had the very capable Mark Walton to call upon as a replacement for Gunn and he duly took his place in the Canaries line-up for the home game against Southampton a fortnight later, a game that saw additional defensive reshuffling needed by Dave Stringer, who, not for the first time that season, was forced to play David Phillips as a makeshift right-back. Phillips, a very underrated player while he was at Carrow Road, coped admirably with the enforced role change but, with a goalkeeper making his first appearance of the season thrown into the mix as well, it was a potentially shaky Norwich back four who went out to face the Saints; yet, shaky or not, they prevailed, winning 2-1 thanks to goals from Robert Ullathorne and Robert Fleck. Any signs, however, of that much-needed victory resulting in an upturn of form were swiftly swept away the following week when Norwich faced Luton, a dreadful Norwich performance in the first half giving Luton manager Jim Ryan, whose team had lost their last three fixtures, the opportunity to point out to them at half time that Norwich were there for the taking. He would have been right. The Canaries managed to follow up their appalling first half display by being even worse in the second half, with David Preece and Mick Harford the scorers in their 2-0 win.

Norwich had gone into that run of four games in early January confident of getting nine, maybe ten points out of them but equally aware that had they performed at anything like the high standards they were capable of (and had already shown) that season they could, quite capably, have won all four of them, meaning that, by the time the Canaries travelled to Arsenal on 11 February, they'd have been on thirty-nine, forty, or possibly forty-two points and would, with it, have almost certainly guaranteed their participation in the following seasons Premier League. As it was, had Norwich won all of those games, they would, prior to the Arsenal game, have been sixth in the table and three points above their hosts on that day. Yet, after the grim run of results and form they had just been on in those four games, they were now in sixteenth place and just six points above the relegation places – with, as well as Arsenal, games against Liverpool, Manchester United, Sheffield Wednesday (up into fourth and loving it), Arsenal (again) and eventual Champions Leeds United to come.

A very real case of 'squeaky bum time' at Carrow Road when it needn't, and most certainly shouldn't, have got to anything like that stage.

Typically, after such a poor run of form, one that had, like it or not, seen Norwich become of the clubs being talked about as genuine relegation possibilities at the end of the season, the Canaries travelled down to Highbury to play reigning champions Arsenal and ended up sharing the points after an excellent all-round performance earned them a 1-1 draw. Dave Stringers' immediate response to the defeat at Luton was to recall Chris Sutton and play him in what was now clearly his best and favoured position, in attack. With Darren Beckford missing out, it would be the first time that Sutton and Robert Fleck would combine as the Canaries attacking spearhead and it was an option that, at least after this one match, looked as if it might have some promise with the two very different types of players appearing to dovetail well together. Ruel Fox also started the match for the first time that year and, with Fleck and Sutton proceeding to give the much-vaunted Gunners back four of Lee Dixon, Steve Bould, Tony Adams and Nigel Winterburn a torrid evening, Fox was left to pretty much run the show, which he did in some style, hitting the crossbar ten minutes into the game, executing the perfect finish to put Norwich ahead just short of the hour mark and generally dominating throughout, a display good enough to guarantee him a starting place in the Norwich team for the rest of that season.

That well-earned point meant that Norwich would have gone into their next game, a home clash against Liverpool with the sort of renewed confidence that might not have been thought possible after the collapse at Luton. Could they maintain the very high standards that had now been reset at Highbury? For many Canary fans, another draw would have been a good result, positive proof that progress, of sorts, was being made after the hugely disappointing run of results over the previous few weeks. But that was, and remains the case, the lot of the Canary fan to this day. Exhilarating and frustrating in equal measures is the Norwich City way, with no greater evidence of that than in that 1991/92 season, one that saw miserable and utterly soul-destroying home defeats to Oldham Athletic and Notts County played out before a near disbelieving Carrow Road, yet still one that saw witness to wins at Chelsea as well as impressive home victories over Aston Villa, West Ham and a Coventry side that in Robert Rosario and Kevin Drinkell had included two ex-Canaries in their ranks.

Liverpool, on the other hand, were a different proposition altogether. They arrived at Carrow Road on 22 February in third place and on a run of just two league defeats in their previous games, a finger in the eye for those who were continuing to suggest that they were a 'spent force' under Graeme Souness and still a side, for all of Souness's much-criticised rebuilding of his squad, that contained high-quality players like Mark Wright, Dean Saunders, Ray Houghton, Ian Rush, Jamie Redknapp and Steve MacManaman.

A 'spent force'? Probably not. Except that on a memorable afternoon for the 20,411 spectators present (an increase of 9,751 on that for the game against Southampton three weeks earlier) Norwich made Liverpool look exactly that, the Canaries dominance reflected in their magnificent 3-0 win. Yet, if the win and margin of victory was impressive, the one thing that stands out, even today, above them is the manner of the performance that went with it. Norwich bullied, bossed and dominated Liverpool from start to finish, something that was thought of as unthinkable for any side to do in many a previous year; yet, for a team that had, in recent seasons, lost to Liverpool 4-1 (twice), 4-0, 5-3, 6-2 and 6-0, the combination of such a convincing win with a side order of swagger to go was little short of a footballing sensation, one which saw the pressure and constant criticism that Souness had been subject to since he succeeded Ronnie Moran as manager a little under a year earlier get substantially more vociferous. Music to the ears of the joyful Norwich support who had been accustomed to having their noses rubbed in the dirt by the Merseysiders.

Norwich's will to win and greater desire was reflected in all three of their goals. The opener had come about via a typically surging run forward by Jeremy Goss, who'd found Chris Sutton overlapping him on the Norwich right, Sutton continuing his run before hitting a pass across the Liverpool penalty area that Colin Woodthorpe had bundled over the line at the second attempt, Woodthorpe one of three Norwich players in the Liverpool penalty area who were awaiting that final ball.

Norwich's second was the result of a poorly hit back pass by Mark Wright, which was seized upon by the ever-predatory Fleck who made no mistake. Fleck then added his second and Norwich's third, winning the ball just inside his own half from Glenn Hysen (playing in his last game for the Reds) before surging forward, unchallenged, to goal and placing a shot just beyond Grobbelaar, which crept over the line despite Mark Wright's somewhat half-hearted attempt to stop it. And maybe he could have done. But, by then, Wright and his Spice Boy teammates had long given up the fight and just wanted to get home.

For once, the journey back from Norwich would have been one that they wouldn't have enjoyed. Not that anyone in Norfolk would have been particularly bothered.

Two more good league performances followed: a 4-3 win over Crystal Palace at Selhurst Park, one that saw Norwich score three goals in thirteen dazzling minutes and a dour but well-disciplined o-o draw at Coventry City. Eight points from four games, satisfactory progress and a mini run that had, by the time the Canaries welcomed Notts County to Carrow Road for an FA Cup fifth round match on 15 February, saw them back up to tenth in the table with, finally, talk of relegation beginning to fade into the background. That welcome little run in the FA Cup, however, was about to prove to be something of a distraction, one that very nearly cost Norwich their top-flight status after all. Robert Fleck has since mentioned he believes, along with other senior Canary players at the time, that the club's focus on their run to the competitions semi-finals in 1989 cost the Canaries a very genuine chance of winning the League title that season. Speaking in *Fantasy Football*, Fleck said,

We could have pushed Arsenal and Liverpool all the way to the title that season. The worse thing that happened was getting to the semi-final of the FA Cup ... Dave (Stringer) was starting to rest players and think about the Cup more, rather than going all out for the League. We spoke about it, it was decided this is what we were going to do, and to some players it was, 'yes, the FA Cup semi-final, how often do you get that close to Wembley? But we could, we should, have gone for it in every game.

Now, three years later, the Canaries were, once again, heading into the last four of the competition, Chris Sutton's headed winner in a quarter-final replay against Southampton seeing Norwich through to a last four meeting against Sunderland, then in Division Two. If the Canaries had been close to the twin towers in 1989, then they must now have felt as if they were looking up Wembley way. That quarter-final win had come after two defeats in the league, against Chelsea (0-1) and Nottingham Forest (2-0), but with euphoria of the win over the Saints still very much in and around the club and city, Norwich followed up that last-gasp win with, just three days later, a 4-3 victory over Everton at Carrow Road, Darren Beckford scoring a hat-trick in front of, again, a hugely disappointing crowd of just 11,900. That win elevated Norwich back up to thirteenth place in the Division One table with forty-four points, twelve clear of Luton and the two clubs between them in the relegation places. This meant that, even if the Canaries were by no means mathematically safe from relegation, it would take a spectacular drop in league form between then and the end of May to put them in any real danger of going down.

Which is exactly what happened. Maybe the prospect of another FA Cup semi-final was weighing heavily on the Canary players' minds, maybe, as Fleck suggested, it became a priority and, with that, the proper due diligence and attention that should have been paid to their remaining league fixtures wasn't all it should have been. It's a moot point now, of course. Yet, the fact remains that out of the remaining eight league fixtures that followed the win over Everton, Norwich gained just one point from a possible twenty-four, the 1-1 draw at home to Wimbledon on the penultimate day of the season enough to ensure that the Canaries would retain their place in among the elite of English football and become, as had been the target from day one, a founder member of the new FA Premier League. Norwich's goal in that game, scored by Robert Fleck, had been their first in seven league games, eight if you include the aforementioned semi-final against Sunderland, which Norwich lost 1-0. It was another depressing statistic in among a very frustrating and disappointing end to the 1991/92 season for the club, one which had sometimes flashed with promise and even had occasional brilliance thrown in, but which had, for the most part, been most unsatisfactory, especially given all the club had achieved over the previous few seasons.

As far as Dave Stringer had been concerned, that point won against Wimbledon was enough to see him sign off and out from the job he had carried out with so much care, passion and total commitment since he had succeeded Ken Brown in 1987. His resignation, the day before Norwich's final match of the season, a 1-0 defeat at newly crowned Champions Leeds, was unexpected but, on reflection, maybe not that surprising. He'd become increasingly frustrated with having to see his best players lost, time and time again, to the allure and, unquestionably, transfer fees waved in the faces of the club's board by their top-flight rivals. Among those that Stringer reluctantly saw depart under his management were Steve Bruce, Mike

Phelan, Kevin Drinkell, Andy Linighan, Andy Townsend and Dale Gordon; in addition to all of that, he had long known that the summer of 1992 would see Robert Fleck leave the club as well. He'd had enough, later admitting to Rick Waghorn in his excellent book *12 Canary Greats*:

> I was filleted to be honest. It had taken its toll on me … I'd probably had enough myself by that time in terms of being manager. I didn't want to move anywhere else. Norwich was my club – always has been. So I said to the chairman: 'I'm going to resign'. I don't think he wanted it to happen, but there you go. I did come close before – over Andy Linighan. When he left – because I thought he was a big part of the team...I said to the chairman: 'Well, I'm resigning!'. But he talked me out of it...if you get a decent player, his own ambitions are going to say to him: 'I want to go on, go out and play for bigger clubs, get the bigger prizes and everything else'. And I thought this is never, ever going to change. The supporters are getting frustrated with it and I thought I'm going to be on the rack here all the time...I'll always be the one in the middle. So did I want all that?

Clearly, Dave Stringer did not. And you can hardly blame him. Had the unthinkable happened at the end of the 1991/92 season and Norwich had been relegated, he almost certainly would have paid the price for it with his job, sacked without a second thought from the club that he loved and loyally served for almost all of his working life, a decision that, if carried out, would have been an even more disgraceful one than that which saw Ken Brown dismissed by the club in the autumn of 1987. Brown had, like Stringer, guided the club to unprecedented levels of success including a League Cup win and a fifth place finish in Division One, both achievements that would, had it not been for Heysel, seen Norwich qualify for European football the following season. Fortunately for Dave Stringer, the same ignominious fate did not await him and he left the club with his head held high and his reputation, which he retains to this day, of being 'Mr Norwich City' still very much intact. There is no doubt that, given he was still only forty-seven when he resigned his post at Carrow Road, coupled with all he had achieved during his time at the club (that had included managing the Canary youngsters to success in the 1983 FA Youth Cup) that he could have had his pick of jobs to go to had he decided to continue his management and coaching career elsewhere. Yet, as he himself admitted, Norwich were 'his' club and the thought of going anywhere else didn't even receive the remotest consideration.

A Norwich City legend in every sense of the word.

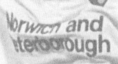

CHAPTER THREE

Premier League

The Norwich players returned to Norfolk at the end of July as fit as they had ever been in their professional lives, but, as importantly, the squad had bonded and found a real unity and togetherness during that time, something which would have been as equally an important goal to Walker and Deehan as working on those fitness levels had been.

Ian Crook, Midfield maestro.
(Photo courtesy of Norwich City Football Club)

Once the fall out surrounding Dave Stringer's shock resignation as Norwich City manager had settled, talk, inevitably, began with regard to who his successor might be.

Both Stringer and his predecessor, Ken Brown, had been internal appointments as Norwich replicated the tried and trusted method by Liverpool (i.e where the identity of the club's next manager was always known, even before he had taken the job). Hence Bob Paisley stepping up after Bill Shankly's retirement in 1974 before Paisley himself was succeeded by Joe Fagan, who, in turn, was followed by Kenny Dalglish. Such a policy not only meant a certain amount of managerial stability within a club, it also meant that any new incumbent was also deeply familiar with how the Reds worked as a club and what sort of players he would have to call on when the time came for him to pick his first Liverpool side. It was a policy that yielded rich dividends for Liverpool and one that had also worked well at Norwich with both Brown and Stringer enjoying more success at the helm than John Bond, recruited at no little expense from Bournemouth in 1973, had enjoyed at the club, although, in fairness to Bond, his greatest gift to Norwich City was how he had dragged the club, kicking and screaming, out of football's dark ages almost as soon as he was appointed.

If Norwich were to continue the same business model following Stringer's departure, then the obvious choice and overwhelming favourite would have been David Williams, who'd worked alongside Stringer as his assistant. Williams certainly had the experience as well as the credibility for the top job. He was player-manager of Bristol Rovers from 1983 until 1985, accepting the position as Bobby Gould's replacement at Eastville when he was only twenty-eight, still one of the youngest ever appointments to such a role in senior English football. In addition to that, he'd also had a spell as caretaker manager of Wales in 1988, prior to the appointment of Terry Yorath. With Williams an exceedingly popular player and coach at the club, his accession looked a formality and much of the early days of the 1992/93 preseason in Norfolk were spent waiting for Is to be dotted, Ts to be crossed, and for Williams appointment as Norwich City manager to be confirmed

Except, of course, that it never happened. The likelihood is that David Williams would have been delighted to have been offered the job. But, for reasons that remain unknown, he was not offered it. He consequently left the club and was appointed as assistant manager to Tony Pulis (a more contrary pairing in football management you can hardly imagine) at Bournemouth that July with Pulis, himself only thirty-four at the time, stating that, 'David knows what the job is about following his Rovers, Norwich and Wales career at playing and coaching level. He's a thinker and level headed and a shrewd tactician and it was Norwich's loss at not giving him their managers job'.

Williams may well, of course, have made the decision that with no swift invitation made to him to take over following his one game in charge as caretaker manager (the 1-0 loss to Leeds United on the last day of the season) that his time at the club was up, especially as new rumours began to surface about Robert Chase and the Norwich board considering a break in tradition by looking for a suitable external candidate for the job, something that might have meant Williams would have been out anyway. There were certainly no shortage of possible targets with names like Brian Little, then at Leicester City, and John Beck, who'd achieved a minor miracle in getting Cambridge United to within two wins of a place in what was now the Premier League, (although his footballing methodology might not have gone down too well at Carrow Road) both getting more than a passing mention, while, among the usual plethora of well-known playing names looking to move into management, Bryan Robson, then beginning to wind down his career at Manchester United, was postulated as a strong contender.

The man who Robert Chase eventually offered the post to was ex-Liverpool and England defender Phil Neal. Neal's first managerial role had been at Bolton Wanderers, who he went onto guide to a place in the Third Division play-offs in 1990 and 1991, missing out on promotion on both occasions. Bolton then finished thirteenth in the Third Division at the end of the 1991/92 season, which was enough to see Neal sacked by the club, his glittering career as a player seemingly not something he was, as yet, able to replicate as a manager. Regardless of those disappointments, though, his standing in the game was still attractive enough to Chase for the Norwich chairman to offer him the chance to resurrect it with the Canaries, an opportunity that Neal must have found extremely tempting. He'd been sacked by a club that had finished mid-table in Division Three one day before being invited to take over one that was about to take part in the very first season of Premier League football the next. It was quite an offer and one that certainly came out of the blue. Yet, for all that, and with a three-year contact his to sign, Neal's reluctance to uproot his family from their Merseyside home and relocate to Norfolk became a major obstacle and, in the end, either Neal walked away or Chase withdrew the contract offer. In glorious hindsight, it does look as if Neal made the wrong choice, for he didn't return to football in a managerial role after Norwich's offer to him fell through until he accepted an offer to take over as manager of Coventry City in October 1993. He promptly lost his first game in charge of the Sky Blues 5-1 and lasted for less than eighteen months at Highfield Road before being sacked.

With Williams gone and Neal being something of a false start, Robert Chase now had a problem. He'd wanted a new manager appointed as swiftly as possible, meaning that the new man would have had the entire preseason to cast an eye over his squad before making the appropriate decisions on who he might see as pivotal players and those who he might see as not having a future at the club under his management. This was common sense, a decision made easier for him by Stringer's early departure, the now ex-Norwich manager as aware as anyone that his successor (and it's likely that Stringer, like everyone else at the time, thought David Williams would be offered the job) would need as long as possible to 'bed in', including bringing in a new coach or two prior to the new season. Yet Stringer had now been gone for nearly a month and the club seemed no closer to having a replacement than they had on the day that Stringer had left.

The man who Chase eventually appointed was, after all the talk of bringing in someone who would be new to the club, an internal appointment, Mike Walker duly following the same path as Stringer and Ken Brown had. Walker, who was famously sacked as manager of Colchester United having led them to the top of Division Four and winning a manager of the month award into the bargain, had been appointed as the Canaries youth team manager in 1987 before graduating to reserve team manager. He therefore knew how the club worked and, importantly, was very familiar with all the players, especially those who'd played for him in the reserve team. Confirmation of his appointment was made on 1 June 1992 with Walker swift to appoint former Canary John Deehan, who'd previously been coaching at Manchester City, as his assistant, along with John Faulkner, once of Sutton United, Leeds United and Luton Town, as his successor in charge of the reserve team.

Walker was anything but the household name that most Canary followers had been hoping for. His appointment even led to Canary fan and writer Kevin Baldwin stating that Walker 'wasn't even a household name in his own household'. Yet it was one that went down well with the Norwich City players, many of whom had a great deal of respect for Walker's coaching and in-depth knowledge of the game. It also helped that he was a very likeable character with no airs and graces who, with his swift appointment of Deehan as his assistant, pulled off something of a masterstroke. Deehan had already been carving out a reputation for himself as a highly capable and innovative coach who, in Ian Culverhouse, would have had someone 'on the inside', Culverhouse having been at Carrow Road while Deehan was still there as a player. If, therefore, Deehan needed someone within the club to speak positively about him to the rest of the playing staff, then it is likely that Culverhouse would have done that, meaning that Deehan would have had a certain amount of respect within the playing staff even before he took his first training session with them.

One of the first issues that Walker had to deal with after his appointment was to sort out the future of Robert Fleck. The ambitious striker had previously stated his desire to leave the club at the end of the 1990/91 season only for a proposed move to Chelsea to be blocked by Robert Chase. In response, Fleck, rather than make a fuss, had agreed to stay at the club until the end of the following season on condition that he could then leave for pastures new with, he insisted, Norwich not standing in his way of signing for a new club, something that Chase, desperate for Premier League football, had readily agreed to. Things were different now. Mike Walker was the new man at the helm and, unsurprisingly, he didn't want Fleck, one of his best players, to leave and made that intention very clear, one that would not have gone down very well at all with Fleck, who was still expecting to move on with Chelsea, rather than Tottenham, who had also expressed an interest through Terry Venables, his favoured option.

One thing that Walker expected of his new charges was that they were fit – extremely fit. Walker was no weakling himself and had few qualms in striding topless around the training pitches at Trowse with his top off, his six pack and all over tan on display for all to see. He was, as the saying goes, 'racked'. It was almost as if he was telling his players, without the need for words, that here he was, long retired and in his mid-forties but he still looked good, still looked after himself and was as fit as any of them, even those that might be half his age. It wasn't too dissimilar an approach to Ron Saunders, who had appeared, like a bronzed Roman god, in front of his players one morning and told them, in so many words, that it was his way or the highway. That was an approach that had appealed to Dave Stringer, who recalls his response to Saunders challenge to his players at the time had been, 'you'll do for me'. Now Walker was laying down the same gauntlet to his squad; he wanted them fit and he wanted them working and believing in themselves as a team, very much an 'all for one and one for all' attitude. For players like Jeremy Goss, who'd got to know Walker extremely well during his time as reserve team manager, Walker's appointment couldn't have been bettered. In his autobiography, Goss recalls:

> Mike Walker getting the job was absolutely the right thing, the best appointment the club could have made ... you can look back now and think what would have happened if Phil Neal had got the job after all? I think for my mates, the club and me, things would have been very different. Mike was great for me. In every sense of the word. He knew me and I knew him, he knew I wouldn't let him down ... I'd have run off a cliff for him. He came in and straight away said to me, 'you're going to be in my team.

I trust you, I like you as a player. You'll be playing. I'm going to build the entire side around you and Ian Crook in midfield. He'll make things happen, you'll help make them happen.

Walker certainly made things happen for the popular Goss. Prior to Walker taking charge, Goss had been a peripheral figure at Carrow Road, one who never seemed to really get a run of games in the side and who was, all too often, the player who missed out, even if the one who was playing in his position on the day – for example, Andy Townsend – was not performing well. Goss recalls knocking on Dave Stringers door and asking – demanding – why he wasn't in the side and, eventually, asking for a transfer.

He nearly left the club twice, with Barnsley and Manchester City both set to sign him at one time. Yet the canny Stringer had talked Goss around on both occasions, promising him that 'your time will come'. It hadn't under Stringer but it did now look as if, finally, it might do under Walker. Perhaps Stringer had been aware that Mike Walker was his replacement in waiting all along?

After a relatively low-key summer the previous year, the summer of 1992 saw the Canaries fly off to Sweden for a preseason tour that would incorporate seven games in nine days as well as some intensive fitness and conditioning work led by Walker. The players were under no illusions that the tour would be anything other than tough – and it was. Yet it was effective and in more ways than one. The Norwich players returned to Norfolk at the end of July as fit as they had ever been in their professional lives, but, as importantly, the squad had bonded and found a real unity and togetherness during that time, something that would have been as equally an important goal to Walker and Deehan as working on those fitness levels had been.

The psychological side of the game was something that Walker knew was becoming an increasingly important factor in professional football the world over. It was no longer adequate to simply get the best eleven players available and to send them out expecting to win the game in the traditional way every time. Norwich would, for much of the pending Premier League season, be playing sides who, man for man, may have been superior to the Canaries in eight, nine, ten, maybe even all the positions on the pitch. So, as the perceived 'underdog', clubs like Norwich needed to have an advantage elsewhere, a hidden quality that would give them a chance of matching their supposedly superior opponents. That secret weapon was self-belief, an inner strength within the collective mindset of the players that, despite all the odds looking to be against them, they could still win. It was the sort of deep inner belief and conviction in themselves as professional footballers and as a club that would soon get a major test, coming, as it did, at half time in the Canaries' first game of the Premier League season.

Results wise, the tour of Sweden had been satisfactory, the Canaries winning four and losing three of their seven games in a loosely put together tournament that featured some lower league sides, a select XI from *Österlen* and two more well-known clubs, G.A.I.S and Trelleborgs FF, who Norwich played in the last game of the tour, winning 2-1. But, as any football coach will tell you, preseason is not about then results in games, it's about performance levels and match fitness. And, as far as that side of things had been concerned, the tour had been a success. Upon their return to Norwich, the Canaries still had four more preseason games to play, one of which was to be a prestigious friendly against Zenit St Petersburg at Carrow Road, but, both in minds and body, Walker knew his players were ready for the challenges that lay ahead.

Sadly for Norwich, the situation regarding Robert Fleck still had to be resolved. Walker had been adamant that he didn't want to lose the striker, but, equally, Fleck was determined to leave and expected chairman Robert Chase to honour the agreement that they had verbally entered into the previous summer. No club can realistically hope to retain a player who wants to leave and, eventually, the Canaries agreed a fee of £2.1 million with Chelsea and Fleck headed off to the bright lights of London to start the latest phase of his career. The deal was finally completed on 12 August, which was just three days until the start of the season, meaning that although the Canaries suddenly found themselves with money to spend on a brand new striker, they only had a limited time to do so. Mike Walker did, of course, have Darren Beckford and Chris Sutton to call upon but, with them being similar types of player, it would not have been practical to pair them together in attack in Walker's preferred (but never obligatory) 4-4-2 formation. He could, of course, have opted to play Ruel Fox as one of two strikers, Fox providing the pace and goal-poaching ability that would nicely complement the more traditional qualities that Beckford and Sutton had to offer. Both were strong and physically imposing players who were good in the air and able to bring others into the game by holding the ball up well. But it would have meant moving Fox from his strongest and preferred wide position in the Canaries midfield.

That wasn't really an option Walker wanted to consider. So, with Fleck gone, the club upped its efforts to bring in a replacement striker and, a little less than twenty-four hours before the season started, they finally got their man, signing Mark Robins from Manchester United for £800,000, usurping, in the process, Dynamo Dresden, who had also been looking to sign him. Robins was, of course, famous at the time for scoring the goal that supposedly had kept Alex Ferguson with the Red Devils in an FA Cup tie at Nottingham Forest two years earlier. Many had tipped him for a bright future at the club after that goal but his career never really took off at Old Trafford and, after scoring eleven goals in forty-eight league appearances from 1988 to 1992 Robins, then still only twenty-two, made the move to Norfolk in order to get the first-team football that had always been just out of his grasp under Ferguson who, a little under six years earlier, had sanctioned the move of another one of his most promising young players, Bryan Gunn, from Aberdeen to Norwich. Ferguson had, at the time, advised Gunn that he should see Norwich as a stepping stone onto bigger and better things in England and it is likely that he would have said the same to Robins, who, it has to be said, had been an impressive signing for Norwich, one that had taken a few pundits by surprise as he had been expected to join a bigger club.

Another new face at Carrow Road that summer was experienced midfielder Gary Megson, who arrived from Manchester City having also had spells with Plymouth Argyle, Everton, Sheffield Wednesday and Newcastle United. He'd even spent a very brief period of time under Brian Clough at Nottingham Forest, one that lasted just under three months as after he had signed for the club, Clough then decided he didn't want him after all and shipped him out again without Megson having made a single appearance for them. Clough was one of thirteen managers that Megson had played under in his career, and, under Walker, his fourteenth, he was expected to bring a little steel to a side that had, to quote one observer, 'stopped caring about conceding goals'. He'd arrived on a free transfer, yet, if anything, it had been a more difficult deal for Walker to bring to fruition than the signing of Robins had been with Robert Chase reluctant to bring a player to the club who had, as far as he was concerned, no resale value. Walker had, however, mounted a strong and passionate argument in response, emphasising how Megson's experience and tendency to talk with his teammates throughout a match (Norwich had become a very quiet side with no player apt to do this during games) would prove to be invaluable. Walker did not, however, select Megson as his captain for the season, with that honour going to another former Nottingham Forest player, the classy and reliable Ian Butterworth.

Two in and one out. A comparatively quiet summer for the Canaries, who went into their opening game of the season, and a challenging one at that, against Arsenal at Highbury as well prepared, physically and mentally, as any Norwich side had ever been at that stage, which was perhaps just as well. Arsenal were going into the season as one of the favourites to win the first ever Premier League title and understandably so with attacking options like Ian Wright, Alan Smith, Anders Limpar and Paul Merson to call upon, the latter three all starting the game with Wright, perhaps surprisingly, sat on the bench. But then so was Robins for Norwich, Walker choosing to start with Chris Sutton as his lone central striker with the wide support coming from David Phillips (one of the most underrated, and, as it turns out, ultimately much-missed players the Canaries have had in recent years), with a revitalised and fired up Jeremy Goss accompanying Gary Megson in the heart of a Norwich midfield that would not be shy in advising the likes of Merson and Limpar they were there and available, at any given time, to relieve them of time, space, and, critically, the ball.

The dawning of the Premier League in England, that 'whole new ball game' (it wasn't) as Sky Sports were so fond of reminding everyone, was given a very low-key introduction in the Arsenal programme for the game with, on page 2, a small headline that stated, 'Welcome to Highbury for our first Premier League match'. On the opposite page to that, the Arsenal manager, George Graham, opened by admitting how he had wanted to make more than one major signing in the summer, lamenting the fact that he had only been able to add Danish midfielder John Jensen to his already expensively assembled squad, going on to name Manchester City (who finished ninth) as his Premier League title winning outsiders. He made absolutely no reference at all to Norwich, unusual and maybe lacking a little bit of courtesy into the bargain, as it is a tried and tested 'tradition' for the home sides manager to welcome his club's opponents and their fans for the day in any club programme.

A small thing maybe but a little sign of the 'me me me' attitude that, over the following years, the Premier League has fostered in its long-standing members. He did, however, have something to say on that subject, not something, perhaps, the suits behind it would have wanted to read by saying:

> I feel the Premier League is new league in name only. I feel the blueprint of the original concept has been watered down and what we have now is little different from last season's First Division.

He was, of course, correct. But it was a dissenting voice, one of a prominent and famous name in the game who was refusing to get carried away by all the hype.

Graham's Arsenal team didn't feel too inclined to get carried away with things either. Aside from a starring role for clean-cut family man Limpar in one of Sky's endlessly played preseason promotional films, they were very much a team that just preferred to get on with things on the pitch, rather than have any dreams of becoming celebrities on it, an accusation that, most certainly, could have been labelled at some of the players from their closest rivals. This down to earth approach was confirmed by skipper Tony Adams in his column for the programme, with Adams claiming that,

> I'm told that Arsenal are 2-1 to win the first-ever Premier League title. That's crazy, before a ball has even been kicked. You won't hear us shouting the odds. That's not our style. But we're determined to bounce back from last season's disappointments, and, with the flair and power we have in attack, we can be entertaining as well as successful.

Definitely understated. Yet, as the travelling contingent of Norwich City fans were left to find out for themselves, the claims of Arsenal being potential title winners as well as those from Adams about the 'flair and power' they had in attack were about to ring true – and, seemingly, at the Canaries expense. The Gunners were devastatingly effective in the game's first half; organised in defence, dominant in midfield and full of pace and variety in attack, so much so that the Canaries were more than fortunate to make half time only two goals down, Steve Bould and Kevin Campbell the scorers. Looking back on that game, Norwich midfielder Rob Newman admitted,

> two down at half time, we were shell shocked as it should have been six. I sat there during the break thinking, 'right, damage limitation', there was no way anyone would have thought we'd turn that around.

No one, that is, apart from Mike Walker. He'd spent the entire summer instilling a sense of self-belief into his players and he wasn't going to let any heads drop now, least of all after just forty-five minutes of a forty-two game season. As Jeremy Goss recalls, 'We were two-nil down at half time. We came in and Mike just told us, "get the next goal".'

Damage limitation? As Newman and his teammates had now found out, 'damage limitation' wasn't a phrase in Walker's vocabulary. His team talk was succinct and to the point, emphasising that the Canaries were still in the game, they hadn't been outplayed and, were they to score first in the second half, then things might just start to get a little interesting. Which they most certainly did. The way the Canaries took Walker's words to heart and emerged for the second half, galvanised and convinced they could turn the game around, marks, for me, the beginning of the most significant half of football any Norwich side has played throughout the club's long and illustrious history. Yes, as Newman had stated, they could have gone for damage limitation, sat back and tried to prevent Arsenal from increasing their lead. But how could they reasonably expect to hold out in such a manner against a side so rich in attacking and creative talent?

Walker knew that his team's best chance of weathering such a footballing assault would have been to mount one of their own against an Arsenal team that might, just might, have been a little complacent over their half-time cuppa, job done and looking forward to their trip to Blackburn Rovers three days later. Ever the realist, Walker also knew his line about scoring the next goal was hugely significant. Had it gone to Arsenal then, for all of the belief he had in his team, he'd have been the first to agree that it would almost have meant game over. If, on the other hand, Norwich scored the next one, maybe a little doubt would creep into the Gunners players' minds, as well as, at the same time, a surge of renewed confidence sweeping its way into the mindset of the Norwich team.

So step forward, Mark Robins, scorer of the game's third goal and the one that not only brought Norwich back into the game but, in doing so, started that famous comeback that ultimately led to the Canaries having one of the best seasons in their history. His sixty-ninth-minute goal was followed up by three more, courtesy of David Phillips (seventy-two minutes), Ruel Fox (eighty-two) and Robins again (eighty-four), his dispossessing of Tony Adams and chip over David Seaman from just inside the Arsenal half one of the many memorable moments in what turned out to be a remarkable season for the Canaries, yet one that may well have never happened had Robins not scored that 'next goal' that Walker knew would be a pivotal one for the team that got it.

Would Norwich have ended up leading the Premier League table (and being the first ever leaders of the Premier League, a plaudit that can never be taken away from them) for much of that season had they not been able to turn around the game at Highbury as they had so emphatically done so? I'll leave that question for you to consider.

The win at Highbury was followed by an equally impressive 2-1 win over Chelsea at Carrow Road, a game that saw Robert Fleck, prevented from playing in it (an opportunity denied to him that he would have cherished and made the very most of), being forced to take on a watching brief from the main stand as goals from Phillips and Robins won Norwich the points after Graeme Stuart had put Chelsea ahead. Six points out of six for Norwich, that feat of winning their opening two league games of the season only the third time they had done so in the top flight since their first season at that level back in 1972. Mike Walker, no doubt satisfied with how his team had started, spoke after the win against Chelsea about those first two fixtures:

Arsenal ... we didn't play well, we played a different system and we weren't on the game and they pummelled us for a while and we had to change the system at half time, Robins came on and scored a couple and that lifted us and we played really well there in a 4-4-2 ... that was a question of tactical and making a bit of a change, obviously we had a few words with them ... tonight, that was a very hard game ... Chelsea competed and made it very difficult for us. We gave away the goal, a bad pass out of defence and they hit us on the break, an excellent goal from their point of view. Half time? I felt as long as we compete, we keep our confidence ... I said "we were 2-0 down at Arsenal, we're only 1-0 down here, it's not a problem, is it?" The important thing is that we didn't capitulate, we had to keep competing with them and I felt that if we did that then we'd get the break. I think the players are beginning to get the confidence that they can score goals.

Walker's final comment was particularly telling. The Canaries had endured quite a few seasons and gone through numerous strikers in an effort to score more goals. Now, with Robins on board and Sutton beginning to flourish, there was, all of a sudden, a real goal threat in the team, especially with Ruel Fox and David Phillips both being encouraged by Walker to make runs into the penalty box themselves in support of the two strikers. It had taken the Canaries six games to score the same number of goals from the start of the 1990/91 season while, from the beginning of the previous campaign, they'd managed to score six goals in their first three games but then went onto draw a complete blank in three of their next four games.

Mark Robins, in particular, had made a big difference to the way the Canaries played. He wasn't solely a penalty-box predator but, rather than that, would look to be involved in the general play, linking up and supporting the Canaries midfield before, at the critical moment, finding time and space to score, that combination of all-round play plus an unerring eye for a chance when it was presented to him typified by his goal against Chelsea when he had stolen into space and lifted his shot over and past Dave Beasant.

Even at £800,000, the second highest transfer fee that the Canaries had ever paid, he was already looking like a bargain with his three goals in just under one and a half games, a total that Darren Beckford had needed fifteen appearances to match from the beginning of the previous season. With Chris Sutton looking more and more impressive by the game and with Lee Power desperate for a chance to impress Walker as well, the pressure was mounting on Beckford, who was now in danger of becoming Walker's fourth choice striker a little over a year after becoming Dave Stringer's marquee record signing for the club.

The Canaries may have been scoring more goals as the 1992/93 season progressed but they were also conceding them with some abandon as well, as a 7-1 thrashing at Blackburn on 3 October ably demonstrated. John Polston had been named as one of the Norwich substitutes for that game, with Mike Walker preferring to switch Chris Sutton back to the centre of the Canaries defence alongside Ian Butterworth. Needless to say, it was the last game that Sutton would play at centre half that season, although, post-match, Walker refused to lay any blame on his players for the capitulation, pointing out, accurately, that Norwich had restricted Rovers to only eight or nine clear-cut chances throughout the match, the problem being that Blackburn had successfully converted seven of them, a chance to conversion ration success that was, and remains, virtually unheard of in top-level football. Alas, on that one day in a blue moon that it did, Blackburn had made the most of it and Norwich returned home chastened but, unlike the press who were now not only writing Walker's side off but also tipping them to now plummet down into one of the relegation places, aware of the fact that, despite that scoreline, they were still a good team. The Canaries went onto prove this fact by winning five of their next seven league games, although there was still time for another heavy defeat, 4-1 this time and at the hands of Liverpool at Anfield.

For many fans of the club, the result that brought to an end any chance that the Canaries might have had of winning the Premier League title was the 3-1 defeat to Manchester United at Carrow Road on 5 April. The real damage had, however, been done much earlier than that. It came during the club's run of games and results from 12 December 1992 through to 16 January 1993, a month that, ultimately, cost Norwich their chance of lifting the Premier League trophy at the end of the season. Six games played, no wins but three draws and three defeats with only one goal being scored for a return of just three point from a possible eighteen-not the sort of form title contenders are expected to find themselves in at any stage of the season. Sadly for Norwich, that spell over Christmas and the new year hit their chances far, far more than the defeat against Manchester United ever did. They'd been top of the Premier League and eight points clear of second placed Blackburn after a 2-1 win over a typically spirited Wimbledon side on 5 December yet, after a 1-1 home draw against Coventry City on 16 January, the Canaries led the table by just one point with forty-two to their name in total with Manchester United, Blackburn Rovers and Aston Villa, in second, third and fourth places, respectively, were all on forty-one points; all had a superior difference with both United and Villa each having a game in hand.

The Canaries rallied, winning their next league game against Crystal Palace 4-2 before winning 1-0 at Everton three days later, a victory, thanks to a Chris Sutton goal, that put them back on top of the Premier League table. Ten days later and very aware of the fact that both United and Villa were continuing to put the pressure on just behind them, Norwich travelled down to The Dell to play Southampton, lost 3-0 and dropped down to third place. That elusive summit was reached again before the end of the season, and very memorably into the bargain, coming after a 1-0 win over Aston Villa at Carrow Road, the goal coming from brand new dad, John Polston, in the eighty-first minute.

Norwich's earlier bad run, however, had meant that, with no points margin to play with, they'd almost certainly have to win all of their remaining six Premier League games to win the title (as it turns out, had the Canaries done exactly that, they would have ended the season as Champions, finishing top with eighty-three points with Manchester United second on eighty-one points), something that even the most optimistic of Norwich fans would have thought an unlikely prospect.

Thus, the damage had been done over that period of time at Christmas and the new year. Even if Norwich had managed a win at Manchester United on 12 December rather than losing 1-0, it would have extended their lead, at that time, over the Red Devils to twelve points, meaning that wins, rather than defeats, at home to Ipswich and away to Sheffield United would have then seen them have more of a buffer, more of a margin of error as the season reached its conclusion, possibilities that might, just might, have ended up seeing Ian Butterworth lift the Premier League trophy that May rather than see the Canaries end the season in third place.

Perhaps, but it is all too easy to speculate and think of what might have been if only certain things had happened and others hadn't. The phrase that comes to mind at such times is the one that relates how, if your auntie was in receipt of a certain bodily organ, then she would be your uncle. The truth of it is that Norwich City enjoyed an exceptionally good 1992/93 season, one that, had they not dropped points at critical times and perhaps had a slightly stronger squad of players for Mike Walker to call upon, could have seen them win English football's ultimate prize for the first time in their history.

The harsh reality that follows is that, in the end, we weren't *quite* good enough to do so. But what a season and what a wonderful ride Mike Walker and his players had taken the club and its fans on, one that will never be forgotten by anyone who was there at the time.

Third place at the end of the very first season of Premier League football then. It was still a remarkable achievement by the club, one that no English team came even close to surpassing until Leicester City performed a far greater miracle by winning it in 2016. There was also the added disappointment once the dust had settled that Norwich hadn't, after the great season they'd had, beaten Aston Villa, who they had done the league double over, to the position of runners-up, guaranteeing, in the process, a place in the following seasons UEFA Cup. Finishing in third place, admirable and wholly unexpected as it had been, still seemed a bit of a last-minute let-down after being no lower than second for nearly three quarters of the entire season. A place in that competition was now dependent on Arsenal beating Sheffield Wednesday in the FA Cup final. If the Gunners came out on top it would mean they would have qualified for the following seasons European Cup Winners' Cup competition, thereby forfeiting their place in the UEFA Cup, which they'd sealed by also winning the League Cup. With England only having two places in the UEFA Cup, Norwich would then, by virtue of finishing third in the League, step up to replace the Gunners, joining Villa in what would be the Canaries first ever campaign to feature competitive European football.

With that in mind, there wouldn't have been a Norwich City fan anywhere who wasn't rooting for Arsenal at Wembley and their joy was unconfined when a former Canary, Andy Linighan, won the trophy for the Londoners during extra time in the replay. One of the most important goals in the history of the Canaries was therefore scored by another club in a game that Norwich weren't even playing in, but at least the scorer used to wear a Canary on his shirt, and it is to be hoped that Linighan got some satisfaction out of scoring and thus guaranteeing his previous club their spot in the European footballing spotlight from the autumn onwards.

One particularly pleasing aspect of the 1992/93 season at Carrow Road was the fact that it saw, after some lean years, the Canaries begin to find their shooting boots again. The previous two league campaigns had been disappointing in terms of the numbers of goals scored with forty-seven (1991/92) from forty-two league games (an average of 1.119 per game) following on from forty-one in thirty-eight (1.078 per game) in 1990/91 and forty-four from thirty-eight (1.157) for the 1989/90 season. In contrast to all of that, the Canaries' goals scored for all league games at the end of the 1992/93 season showed a total of sixty-one from forty-two games, a much more healthy average of 1.45 per game, which was, at that time, the club's highest ever total of goals scored over a single season in top-flight football. Much of the credit for that, of course, had to go to strikers Mark Robins and Chris Sutton, who had contributed fifteen and eight goals, respectively, with midfielder David Phillips scoring nine. Pleasing stuff for a side that had been, for some considerable time, rather goal shy. Unfortunately for Norwich, the goals had also been flying in at the other end of the pitch – and with an even greater frequency – with a total of sixty-five conceded over the season meaning that, astonishingly, the Canaries had just achieved the highest ever league finish in the club's history but with a negative goal difference to go with it.

As well as Robins and Sutton were doing as his first choice strikers, Mike Walker knew he would need some additional options in his squad as the season drew to a close and he was quick to act when his number one target became available, moving swiftly to sign Efan Ekoku from Bournemouth the day after he made space for Ekoku in his squad by allowing Darren Beckford to move to Oldham for £300,000. It had never quite happened for Beckford at Carrow Road, his progress at the club affected by a series of injuries as well as the responsibility of being the club's record signing. He'd shown, without question, flashes of the sort of player he could have been on more than one occasion, moments that included his hat-trick against Everton, a vital goal in the Canaries 3-2 win at Aston Villa in November 1992, and a moment of improvised brilliance in a game at Oldham when an imperious back-heel completely took out half the Oldham Athletic defence and set up a Norwich goal in a 3-2 win at Boundary Park that had seen Mark Robins score a hat-trick of his own. Replacement Ekoku had been signed with the following season and the prospect of playing in Europe in mind and he only started one league game for the Canaries following his arrival, the 3-3 draw at Middlesbrough on the last day of the season, a game that saw eighteen-year-old midfielder Andy Johnson scoring City's final goal of the campaign after sixty-eight minutes. Both players were exactly the sort of professionals that Walker was keen to integrate into his first-team squad with the 1993/94 season in mind – young (Ekoku was twenty-four), hungry for success and fiercely ambitious, attributes that would help them fit in well with the rest of his driven and extremely focused squad. For Walker, his players and, most of all, the fans, the 1993/94 season couldn't come quickly enough with Walker offering a tantalising hint of what he hoped was to come by declaring that he saw no reason why the Canaries could not go onto improve on what they had already achieved within the next twelve months.

Such was the total and utter faith that he had in himself and his players, as well as the conviction in his voice whenever he spoke, you couldn't help but believe him. It was a pity, therefore, when one of the major talking points of that close season was how the Canaries lost influential midfielder David Phillips after failing to agree terms on a new contract with him and, as a consequence of that, losing him to relegated Nottingham Forest for a fee that was fixed by a transfer tribunal. The exact fee paid was never made public but, amusingly, was high enough for Phillips to quip afterwards that Norwich had sold him in order to pay for their recently installed undersoil heating. Funny or not, the whole situation regarding Phillips and his controversial departure from the club came across as being rather small time and smacked, regrettably, of a lack of ambition on the part of the club. Did Norwich under-appreciate Phillips so much that they felt they would be better off without him and was it negligence or arrogance on the part of the club in allowing the contract of such an important player to run down?

Phillips would, of course, have wanted an improvement on the basic terms of his contract; he had more than earnt the right to expect that and it seems almost incredulous now that he eventually decided a move to a club that had just been relegated from the Premier League was a more attractive option to him, professionally and personally, than staying with one that had European football to add onto another season in among the English games elite. Norwich had never been the biggest payers in the league as far as a weekly wage was concerned but the club's bonus structure was so good that, when a few Arsenal players had heard about it in the players' bar after a game against Norwich (contrary to what they may say in public, professional footballers 'compare and contrast' the terms of their contracts with their peers at every opportunity), they had to admit it was far, far superior to theirs.

So, given his importance to the club, why on earth did the Canaries not make more effort to retain Phillips that summer? It feels, in hindsight, as a small and early sign that things were not quite as they should, or could be, at the club, something which, even then, would have been a concern to Mike Walker, whose own contract as Norwich City manager was so modest, he was, by some considerable margin, the worst paid manager in the Premier League. If, as the last nine months had shown, Norwich were capable of developing into one of the country's leading clubs, then the chairman and board of directors had to put down a marker and show some ambition to reflect that objective because one thing was absolutely certain: the club wouldn't be able to sustain the relative success it now enjoyed without substantial investment being made in both the playing squad and the management team. With this in mind, losing David Phillips without, it seemed, much of an effort being made to retain his services seemed careless, bordering on downright negligent. The club surely wouldn't let their well-regarded manager slip away so easily-would they?

The club also committed a bit of a PR faux pas that summer when Robert Chase announced that Norwich City would not be signing up for football's new racial equality campaign, claiming, somewhat naively, that there was no need to. The admirable Lets Kick Racism Out Of Football campaign had been launched by the Commission for Racial Equality and the Professional

Footballers' Association and featured a ten-point plan of steps and measures that senior English clubs were being asked to follow in order to combat racism. Quite why Robert Chase felt the need to publicly disassociate Norwich from the scheme can only be speculated on, but it seems, again, a decision made by the chairman that didn't have the club's best interests at heart, especially as it ended up tainting the club's proudly held reputation of being a family club, one that was a safe and decent place to attend in order to watch football.

Having added Efan Ekoku to his playing ranks towards the end of the previous season, Mike Walker went on to add just two more new faces to his squad before the opening game of the 1993/94 campaign – namely centre half Spencer Prior, who arrived from Southend for £300,00, and goalkeeper Scott Howie, signed from Clyde for the same amount. Prior, who'd made 135 league appearances for Southend over a four-year spell at the club, had also been courted by Wolverhampton Wanderers, who made it abundantly clear they were both prepared and able to offer him a larger salary than that offered by the Canaries. Prior, however, chose to join the Canaries, attracted by the possibility of playing in the UEFA Cup that season, something that would have been an equally significant allure for the highly rated Howie, who, like Prior, had received quite a lot of interest from English clubs. It was a brave choice for the twenty-one year old from Glasgow, who now had the highly unenviable task of usurping Bryan Gunn as Norwich's first-choice goalkeeper, a battle that the popular Mark Walton had been forced to concede, Walton admitting to the *Eastern Daily Press* on 24 April 1993 that he felt he was 'being eased out of the door, I feel the club had turned its back on me'.

Yet another example of a lack of tact within the suits at the club? Walton being disregarded and, eventually, discarded, David Phillips lost to Nottingham Forest, and a very public decision made to not sign up to the Lets Kick Racism Out of Football campaign.

Thank goodness there would soon be some football to look forward to.

As far as playing matters were concerned, the Canaries were soon in action again after that valedictory draw at Middlesbrough on the last day of the season, the entire squad, coaching team and most of the board jetting out to the Caribbean, ostensibly to play in a competition known as the Hampstead Cup but also to let their collective hair down a bit. The Canaries played the Jamaican national side on 12 May, losing the game 2-1 before, four days later lining up against the Cayman Islands, losing 1-0 and ending up at the bottom of their three-team group. No end of season silverware for the Canaries then but it's highly unlikely that anyone would have been too bothered about the club's Caribbean no-show. The purpose of the tour had primarily been to show some appreciation to the players and staff who had worked so hard over the league campaign that had just ended, with the 'serious stuff' set to commence in the middle of July when Norwich would head out to Denver, Colorado, to take part in the Four Nations Cup. That had opened with a much more competitive opening against Danish Superliga champions FC Copenhagen on 16 July, which had ended in a 3-3 draw, Copenhagen prevailing 4-3 after a penalty shoot-out.

Football fans are used to being told that results come quite a long way down the list in terms of what the priorities clubs look to get from preseason tours and friendlies in general. The opportunity for recently signed players to meet and get to know their new teammates is a prime consideration as is the chances these summer rituals will give to players previously considered to be on the fringes of the first team to impress the manager. Then there is the fitness training, the tactical exercises and the personal fitness routines taken on board, bespoke individual plans that would need to be rigorously observed until the end of the season.

Then, of course, there is the annual horror of horror for all professional footballers: getting fit again after the (relative) excesses of a few weeks' holiday, a time when a football is rarely, if ever, seen and the dreaded bleep test is king. So yes, in terms of the football that was actually played, Norwich may have lost to FC Copenhagen, just as they subsequently did, 3-2, to the Colorado Foxes in the competitions third/fourth play-off match. Yet, for all that, the Norwich players were finding, to a man, the whole exercise to be of enormous personal and professional value. Reflecting on that time in *Gossy*, his well-received autobiography, Jeremy Goss recalled it all quite fondly:

We wanted to build on what we'd done, we'd missed out on the Premier League title in the end but look, we were serious about coming back and having a proper go at it the next time around. That meant we had to be prepared to work right from the off, hard work, more hard work and then some hard work to finish it off with. Mike and John Deehan took the lads to a pre-season training camp in Denver, Colorado. We played a couple of games out there in a competition alongside three other teams but the whole purpose of the trip was to get fit. They were, without doubt, the hardest training sessions of my life, Mike literally ran us all into the ground. It was stinking hot and so were we. But it paid off. I was as fit and strong as I'd ever been. And full of confidence. There is one moment I'll never forget while we were out there, we were training, running probably, and I felt great. I was loving it, getting fit, good friends around me, it was a moment of clarity, of knowing I was exactly where I wanted to be, doing exactly what I wanted to do and with the people I most wanted to be with. I couldn't wait for the start of the new season, I was desperate to get started.

Goss, a self-confessed fitness nut, was having the time of his life. If most of his teammates could have said, or even thought, the same thing, then the portents for another successful season at Carrow Road were already being put into place. Mike Walker saw no reason whatsoever why his team could not improve upon their excellent performances throughout the 1992/93 campaign and go a few steps further the next time around. Read through those words of Jeremy Goss again, 'we were serious about coming back and having a proper go at it the next time around...'

He believed they could as did his teammates. Mike Walker and John Deehan certainly believed they could. The biggest obstacle would be persuading Mr Chase to believe it as well and commit to the spending and overall investment required to give Norwich as good a chance as they could possibly have to do so. Sadly, the unprofessional and rather sour way he and his cohorts had dealt with the David Phillips situation tended to suggest that they weren't prepared to do whatever it took to build upon that success. Moreover, as promising a pair of players that Spencer Prior and Scott Howie were, the fact that Norwich's two main preseason signings had joined the club from Southend and Clyde, respectively, rather than, say, Spurs and Chelsea spoke volumes of both the club's perceived ambitions and spending power (i.e. somewhat limited in both scope and imagination).

But the show must go on. And with regard to that particular summer, it did. With stickers from the Caribbean and the USA on their suitcases already, the Canaries' squad now had to prepare themselves for a whistle-stop tour of Sweden that involved four more friendly games to be fitted into a typically no nonsense and very physically demanding schedule that Mike Walker would have enjoyed inflicting onto his players. Walker had now been in the job for a year and had, in that time, got the total and utter respect of all of his squad, a now very tightly knit group of players who knew that they could afford to have a laugh and a joke with him but, at the same time, could never cross the line else, as Jeremy Goss said of Walker, 'he's a big bloke who could give you a hefty clomp if he wanted to!'

Fitness wise, at least, the players would now have been as ready as they would ever have been and it would have shown as they overwhelmed the modest opposition in show in their final two games, for, after a win over Nacka FF (3-1) and hard-earned draw against IFK Vasteras (1-1), they proceeded to sweep aside BKV Norrtalje to the tune of 6-2 before ending the tour with a comprehensive 15-0 over Krylbo IF. The Canaries then wrapped up their preseason preparations with a 2-0 win at Scunthorpe United before winning 3-2 at Birmingham City, whose fans were preparing themselves for the first season in charge of new owner David Sullivan, a football club owning 'new boy' who would, you can be sure, have had the ear of visiting Norwich chairman Robert Chase before, during and after the match.

Having selected Arsenal as their opponents for the first game of the previous season, the Premier League fixture computer chose to give Norwich an equally challenging task for their first game of the 1993/94 season. The visit of reigning champions Manchester United to Carrow Road was immediately selected by Sky for their showpiece Sunday afternoon live game and, with it, and in between the endless reruns of clips depicting the Red Devils front pairing of Lee Sharpe, Andre Kanchelskis and Ryan Giggs ripping their way through Norwich's defence at will during the corresponding fixture just four months earlier, all of the football talk in and around the ground leading up to the match was 'can they do it again?'. This was not a reference to lightning striking twice as far as the Canaries were concerned though, far from it. The interest and debate that was raging at that time was all about if Manchester United could repeat the previous seasons Premier League success with Norwich a mere sideshow, a sacrificial lamb for Alex Ferguson's side to push asunder on their way to more glory.

The Red Devils' 2-0 win on a gloriously hot and sunny Sunday afternoon at Carrow Road was perhaps a deserved one, if only because United had looked just a little sharper than the Canaries throughout. One thing that they didn't do, however, was cut through the Norwich defence with quite the same swagger and panache as they had done in that previous meeting, with both their goals coming through moments of individual opportunism rather than total dominance. The first was a simple chance converted from a rebound off the crossbar by Ryan Giggs while the second came about as the result of an uncharacteristic back-heel from the normally more direct Mark Hughes, the sort of lay off that, nine times out of ten, goes directly to an opposition player. And just as well it didn't, as Alex Ferguson may well have felt the need to have a little chat with Hughes after the match if it had.

Not on this occasion though; Hughes' vision and touch was precise enough to set up Bryan Robson for the second and decisive goal. A disappointing home defeat as a season opener then, yet there was no need for Norwich fans to feel too downhearted. Their team had performed well and only lost because when it came to taking what few chances were on offer, United had been rather more adept at making the most of them. Positive proof that Norwich had lost none of the quality that they had so ably demonstrated throughout the previous campaign came in their next match against Blackburn Rovers at Ewood Park. The Canaries fell behind to an Ian Atkins goal after just seven minutes, equalising right on half time through Chris Sutton. Not to be undone, Kenny Dalglish's side then went 2-1 up when Jason Wilcox scored. Yet, back came Norwich again with Chris Sutton's header back across the penalty area from an Ian Crook free-kick being met by Rob Newman, who headed past Bobby Mimms. Two minutes later, Sutton scored his second and Norwich's third after turning Kevin Moran all shades of inside out on the edge of the pitch before cutting inside and placing a shot beyond the reach of Mimms. 3-2 to Norwich and game over. It had been a thoroughly professional performance, one of their best in the league over those two memorable seasons with Sutton outstanding throughout. There can be little doubt that he would have impressed Dalglish that evening with his demonstration of all-round attacking excellence, his ability in the air allied with deftness of touch and no little skill with it possibly reminding Dalglish of one time Liverpool team mate John Toshack.

Two more wins swiftly followed for the Canaries, a 4-0 romp against Leeds United at Elland Road followed by an always welcome home win over arch-rivals Ipswich Town, the visitors lucky to escape with only that single goal defeat thanks to an inspired performance by ex-Canary Clive Baker in goal, who'd had little chance with the only goal of the game, a typically emphatic strike from Jeremy Goss. Gossy's typically emphatic finish had been the first goal that East Anglia's lesser footballing light had conceded that season as well as the first league match they'd failed to score in since March. For midfielder Goss, those two games marked the beginning of a purple patch of form that, by the end of the season, made him one of the most well-known names in the English game, his decider against Ipswich coming after he had scored a truly stunning volley in that 4-0 win at Leeds, one that was hit with such venom and accuracy that even the normally hard to impress Leeds fans gave him a standing ovation in recognition for that strike, one that, deservedly, won Goss the BBC's Goal Of The Month award for August.

Norwich's next three games saw varying degrees of frustration for the Canaries, the home match with Swindon Town, winless and pointless, on 28 August ending in a 0-0 draw. Four days later Norwich travelled to Hillsborough where, in an astonishing eight-minute spell, Sheffield Wednesday found themselves 3-0 up, courtesy of goals from Chris Bart-Williams (fifty-three minutes), Mark Bright (fifty-eight) and Andy Sinton (sixty-one). Memories of the previous seasons slaughter at Blackburn would have been at the forefront of most Norwich fans' thoughts after Sinton had rattled in the third with still half an hour to go, with the Owls rampant and eager for more. Sadly for them, their enthusiasm for all-out attack ended up costing them the win as Norwich then struck three times themselves, albeit in 'only' thirteen minutes; the Canaries fight back started by Mark Bowen (sixty-two) and Efan Ekoku (seventy-two) with his first goal for the club before Chris Sutton's cool finish three minutes later earnt Norwich a point in a quite remarkable game, one that saw all six goals scored in a shade under twenty-five minutes.

Ten goals in three away games for Norwich then and seven out of nine points to go with it – impressive stuff. It was a pity, therefore, that the Canaries home form didn't even come close to matching it with Wimbledon, a regular nemesis for the home team, the next visitors at Carrow Road, their 1-0 in a dour game being settled by a goal from Lawrie Sanchez. Typical Norwich so far then with thrilling highs neatly juxtaposed against frustrating lows, something that the club's fans had long got used to, a mix of winning against fancied sides like Blackburn Rovers and Leeds before tripping up against the so-called lesser lights like Swindon and Wimbledon. That good away form had, however, seen the Canaries comfortably sat in eighth place in the Premier League after that defeat against the Dons, with two more away league fixtures to come, games that would see Norwich score another seven goals.

But first things first. Because the Canaries now had the rather compelling prospect of their first ever match in European club football to look forward to, a home clash with Dutch Eredivisie side Vitesse Arnhem. Having, through no fault of their own, been denied the pleasures of a UEFA Cup campaign three times since winning the League Cup in 1985, the Canaries had, finally, made it into the competition at the fourth attempt. It was, of course, a very special time and event for the club but was even more so for their hardcore supporters who had followed them, home and away, for many years, hardly ever missing a match, even if it involved a ridiculously impractical trip to one of the games in more remote outposts in the middle of a working week. This was, for example, the case when Norwich had been drawn to play at Middlesbrough in a League Cup third-round match on a Tuesday evening in 1990, a near 450-mile round trip that still drew a fair following of Norwich fans, despite most of them needing to make early starts the next working day. Oddly enough, Arnhem, in the Netherlands, was only another 40 or so miles further distant than Middlesbrough. But that didn't make it any less exotic. A wonderful adventure for both players and fans was about to begin. I asked Norwich fan David Thornhill, better known to all and sundry as 'Spud', for his memories of that long-awaited European campaign for the Canaries:

Looking back to those previous times when we'd qualified for European football and the subsequent ban that first prevented us from competing in the competition, it may have been blessing for me and maybe some other supporters of my age that we were prevented from competing in European football during the 1980s. Norwich first qualified for the UEFA Cup in 1985 following our winning the Milk Cup and the time we would've played our first game in Europe, I would have been just 10 years old. Similarly, following the other two qualification seasons in 1987 and 1989 I was still only 12 and 14 years old, respectively, so I rather suspect I wouldn't have been able go to the games abroad, especially if it had meant my travelling on my own.

I'll be honest. At the start of 1992/93 season, I was only expecting one thing. Another struggle. Especially after only just survived the drop at the end of the previous May. But then one of the great things about being young is that you don't really have many expectations. And definitely not winning the league! Did I honestly believe we could win the, as it was now called, Premier League? No not really. The only time I genuinely thought we might have a chance was after beating Aston Villa at the end of March; after that match, plenty of fans around me in the Barclay were saying the title is ours. But then we went and got beaten in our very next game against Manchester United! Oh well, it was good whilst it lasted. Did I then honestly believe we could finish in at least third place? Not really. Even when I was bouncing up and down at Ayresome Park during our 3-3 draw against Middlesbrough on the last day of the season (and on my 18th birthday), I was just joining in the partying and hoping beyond hope that we would finish in third place, which, thankfully, we did.

But did I think we would get a European place? Not really. No one had ever done the domestic cup double. With Arsenal having recently won the League Cup, beating Sheffield Wednesday in the final, they now had a chance to do that elusive Cup double as they were also in the FA Cup final where they would be meeting Sheffield Wednesday again! So, for me. it was painfully obvious that Arsenal were not going to win that one, meaning Norwich, for all we'd achieved that season, wouldn't qualify for the UEFA Cup. Anyway, I hated Arsenal, primarily because of the infamous brawl between the two sides at Highbury in November 1989, when we ended up getting a heavier punishment than the Gunners! So that was it, decided. Arsenal would lose the FA Cup final just to annoy me. I truly and honestly believed that Arsenal would not win.

I remember watching it the game at my grandparents. Did I believe at half time, even with Arsenal winning, that Norwich would end up going on our 'European Tour' as a result? No, I can't say that I did, even after my Grandad insisting that we would win. No Grandad, Sheffield Wednesday will get back into the game. And they did, it ended 1-1, meaning there'd be a replay. Which Sheffield Wednesday would win. See what I mean? Never expect too much where Norwich are concerned.

The replay was due to be played the following Thursday and my normal negative feelings were kicking in. I was watching the game with a few other Canaries in a pub telling anyone and everyone who would listen that Wednesday would win. On and on the game went, into extra time now and heading for penalties. Just as well I never built up my hopes. But wait, Arsenal have, unbelievably, made the most of the one final chance that's fallen their way. A header from ex-Canary Andy Linighan beats another ex-Canary Chris Woods in goal with a future Canary manager in Nigel Worthington standing helplessly by a post. Goal! 2-1 Arsenal. Only seconds later, the final whistle went and Arsenal had won the cup. More to the point, Norwich were definitely in Europe. The pub duly erupted. The happiest people in there seemed to be the fans who were a lot older than me. They really appreciated it and understood more than anyone what a massive achievement it was for the club.

The draw for the UEFA Cup first round was made on July 14th. I was working at Start Rite Shoes at the time and, as with all the other shoe factories in Norwich at that time, there were set holidays, you couldn't just go and book one when you wanted. Yet, and how good was this, the second leg tie would be played during one of our communal weeks off. You can guess, therefore, what the only thing I was interested in, yes, hoping against hope that the second leg would be played away from home so I'd be free to go to it.

Looking back, I think the draw was made at around about 11 a.m. I wasn't particularly bothered who we got, it could have been some random Albanian side as far as I was concerned. All I wanted was for the second leg to be played away from home. So, when a work colleague approached me and told me we had got Vitesse Arnhem in the first round I wasn't concerned with asking questions about our opponents or looking them up. Nope, not me. I didn't even ask where Vitesse was. Because as that was the first part of teams name, that must have been the name of the city. I was only interested in one thing, asking him if it was home or away in the first leg? Home was the reply. YES!! So I could go to away game. I was buzzing now, I was going globetrotting. Well it felt like I was. It was only a few minutes later than I thought to ask where was Vitesse, what country is Vitesse in? It's not Vitesse I was told, it's Arnhem. And Arnhem is in

Holland. Oh I thought, they do things the other way round in Europe do they? At least Holland wasn't far away, that was something I remembered from my Geography lessons at school.

Reading through the newspapers, it struck me how strict the rules were for English supporters heading off to Europe to watch their teams play. It was, after all, only the fourth season that English clubs had been allowed back after the ban which followed on from the Heysel tragedy. But, yet again, I wasn't bothered, they could be as strict as they liked. We were Norwich and we always behaved ourselves on away trips. The club quickly made arrangements for the game, announcing that the only way to travel to Arnhem would be through the official club travel arrangements. Not a problem. And, as no one from my family or circle of friends would be going, I'd be making the trip with people I'd got to know through Club Canary. So, with travel packages with match tickets going on sale on Saturday August 7th, a day that I didn't have to work, there was only one place I was going to be heading for on that particular morning. One little problem though. Like so many children in those not so dim and distant days, I didn't have a passport as the family only ever took their holidays in the UK. So I had to get that sorted out and headed to Norwich's main post office, in Davey Place, to get that sorted out. It was a lot easier back then, you just needed a couple of passport photos and some ID and that was that, I was now in receipt of a yearly visitors passport. The buzz was now most definitely starting.

Fast forward to August 7th. Saturday morning. I set my alarm for 5:30 in the morning and, before I knew it, I was pedalling towards Carrow Road with £100 in cash, my passport and season ticket, all set to get myself sorted out at the old box office at Carrow Road at the back of the River End where the bookies now stand. I was rather hoping to be first in the queue, but no, there were approximately 20 other Canary diehards who'd had the same idea with some of them still laying there in their sleeping bags, having got there at around 9 p.m. the previous night! At least it was August and it wouldn't have been too cold. Some fans had done exactly the same thing during the 1959 FA Cup run, but that would have meant spending the night on the pavement in January!

By 9:00, the queue was a lot longer but, after the box office had opened and before I knew it, I was being served, handing over no end of personal details and information to the person in the office before being given a piece of paper. We aren't giving out match tickets yet, they explained. You'll need to produce this piece of paper on the evening before the match and that will get you your place on the coach. You'll then travel on that coach over to Holland and, once you're there, you'll get your match ticket. And whatever you do, don't forget your passport. And that was it, I'd sorted everything out and was now cycling home, happy in the knowledge that I was not only finally going abroad but doing so in order to watch my football team.

As a result of all the money I'd needed to spend in order to go on our European tour, I didn't have too much to spend at the start of that season, so I missed our great wins at Blackburn and Leeds with, at the latter, a certain Jeremy Goss scoring a quite wonderful goal. But more about him later. For now, that didn't matter. I was heading off to Arnhem. And, funnily enough, for all the excitement at the time, I don't remember much about the build up to the first leg match. I do remember that we lost to Wimbledon at home on the Saturday before it was played, mainly because I'd taken my cousin Graeme along, his first ever game. Sadly, like we normally did when we played the Crazy Gang, we didn't show up and lost 1-0. One thing I do remember is the disappointing attendance of only 14,851, unbelievable really, considering that, just a few months earlier, we'd finished third in the first ever Premier League.

Four days later, on Wednesday 15th September 1993, Norwich were making club history, playing their first ever competitive European game, a 'mere' eight years after we'd first qualified for Europe, a match that should have been, without any doubt, a sell-out. But no, there was only 16,818 there to witness this fabulous new chapter in the 91 year history of our great club. I sat in the Barclay but even that wasn't full. The fans including myself, who were there, were making plenty of noise with 'On The Ball City' being sung out loud and proud, over and over again. Not too many people seemed to have popped over the water from Holland though. They wouldn't have missed too much though, not in the first half at least, which ended 0-0. Mike Walker later said that Norwich had spent in showing far too much respect to their opponents, he wasn't going to have a repeat of that in the second half and soon had them playing like the team that had performed so well throughout the previous season, giving the Canaries a team talk that clearly worked wonders. Norwich gradually grew into the game and began to dominate Vitesse with Gary Megson and Ian Crook bossing the midfield between them. Six minutes into the second half, Norwich deservedly scored, Efan Ekoku going down in history as the first ever Norwich player to score in a European tie, a fantastic volley via an Ian Crook pass, a goal that won the BBC's Goal Of The Month award for September, the second month running a Norwich player had picked up the prize! Two more goals followed from Jeremy Goss and John Polston, whilst

Darren Eadie made his first-team debut near the end, coming on for Gary Megson. A 3-0 win and a convincing one at that, surely we were as good as in the second round already?

As I left the ground, delighted with both our second half performance and the result, I chatted to a few Vitesse Arnhem fans outside. Quite why there was a heavy police presence post-match I don't know as people in both supporters groups were happy to chat and all the exchanges were really friendly. I told one Vitesse fan I was looking forward to coming over for the second leg, he was impressed to hear that but warned me that their ground was a lot smaller than Carrow Road. That little bit of information disappointed me a bit to be honest but, overall, it didn't spoil the bigger picture, which was Europe here I come.

Norwich now had four consecutive away games to look forward to, starting with a trip to Loftus Road to play QPR before trips to Bradford City in the League Cup and, back in the Premier League, at Everton. I'd already paid to go on the Vitesse trip but still wanted to go to all three of those other games, especially Bradford, as Valley Parade would be a new ground for me. I also liked the ground at QPR, a definite favourite. So that was in. This left just Everton. I did (and do) like Goodison Park but, ultimately, I needed to save money for my European adventure so that was the one I sacrificed.

You can already guess what happened. Norwich drew with QPR and lost to Bradford, who were two divisions beneath us but then went up to Everton and won 5-1, with Efan Ekoku scoring four of our goals. Typical. Still, we'd won and I was going on a European tour so it didn't really matter that much.

On the evening of September 28th I made my usual walk to Carrow Road, getting on the bus as soon I got there. It was due to leave at about midnight. Was I now, finally, after waiting for so long, really about to start the journey? And were we leaving too early? We did leave on time, departing Carrow Road en route to Harwich on what was, to be fair, a fairly uneventful trip, even that part of it made on the boat. But it didn't stop me feeling the buzz of a new adventure, one that increased as we arrived in Holland and made our way, back on the coach, to Arnhem where we arrived at midday, which meant we had around seven hours to wait until the kick-off!

On the coaches we had been told that we were free, in that time, to mingle in and around the streets of Arnhem but to remember that we were representing the city of Norwich, so no troublemakers. I found that warning a little surprising to be honest. I knew I just wanted to enjoy myself and was sure that every other Norwich fan there felt the same, which meant that there would be absolutely no trouble. We were then advised to be back on the coach and ready again by 4 p.m. as we would then depart for the ground, complete with a police escort. Most of the Norwich fans made for a massive shopping centre. All the bars were open, frequented by lots of Norwich fans singing 'On the ball, City'. There was a police presence in the city but there was no trouble. I soon spotted an Arnhem fan and duly posed for a photograph with him before buying a Vitesse Arnhem scarf. I was, by now, really enjoying and getting into the whole European experience but, before I knew it, it was 4 p.m. and I was back on the coach and ready for the police escort to the ground.

Off we went then, destination, the Monnikenhuize, home of Vitesse Arnhem. And, again, we all started to feel excited. It was quite a scenic route there, travelling through an area of Dutch countryside that reminded me of Mousehold in Norwich, with woods on either side of the road. Then, and quite suddenly, we were at the ground. If you are from Norwich and have played in local league football, you'll know there is a football pitch in the middle of Mousehold called 'the Fountain'. Local Sunday morning teams as well as locals play on the pitch there and its nothing really special. Neither was the Monnikenhuize. Indeed, if I'd have closed my eyes and then opened them again, I could easily have been convinced I wasn't in the Netherlands at all, but was in the Zak's Restaurant car park in Norwich looking over to the Fountain.

We got off the coach and went in the direction that was instructed to us by the police. Before long, someone asked one of the Dutch policemen about the bar and where he could get a drink, to which the policeman replied that there would be no beers in the ground. I bought a souvenir t-shirt marking the game as I went into the ground but the lack of a bar and the refreshments that it might have provided did rather annoy a lot of Norwich fans! There must have been around 1,500 of us altogether, the majority of whom were on the terraces. The rest of the ground, though, was totally empty, but then it was still around two and a half hours until kick-off.

At this stage in my Canary supporting life, I had only visited about 25 different grounds, most of them ones in the top flight that I'd gone to with Norwich with the only time I'd been to one quite as ramshackle as the Monnikenhuize being somewhere like Cambridge or Exeter. The Monnikenhuize capacity was only 12,000 but I'd gone along expecting a lot more than this. But it still, small crowd or not, felt as if we were all caged in and surrounded like animals. Clearly, the Taylor Report had not reached the Netherlands yet. Vitesse eventually moved onwards and upwards to a ground called the GelreDome ground in 1998 – it has a capacity of 25,000. I was fortunate enough to visit it in 2000 and it's a world away from their previous ground, being very modern with some superb facilities. Yet, back in 1993, visiting their ground then made Abbey Stadium look out of this world. As for the attendance on the night Norwich were there? Just 9,133.

Whilst we waited for the kick-off, we kept ourselves amused by singing and dancing on the terraces. And that whiled away the time nicely as, before we knew it, it was kick-off time. The omens were good as, apart from the shock defeat at Bradford, Norwich had been flying in our away games with three wins and two draws in the Premier League away from Carrow Road, scoring 17 goals in the process. But this game wasn't anything special, ending up as a dull 0-0 draw, with Efan Ekoku, who couldn't put a foot wrong at Goodison Park a few days earlier with his four goals, missing three great opportunities. Not that it mattered of course, we'd won easily at Carrow Road and were through to next round of the UEFA Cup, 3-0 on aggregate. When the final whistle went, I remember climbing up onto the fence, it was like revisiting my youth on the Barclay terrace when the fences were up there. The happy players came over to applaud us fans and we returned the compliment, delighted to have been part of Norwich City's first ever competitive game abroad.

Unfortunately the police had decided that, after the final whistle, the Norwich fans were going to be cooped up in the pen there for a little bit longer – we'd already been in there for four and a half hours and were now kept waiting for another hour. Yet, in all that time, no one showed any real frustration. At one point I looked over towards the pitch and watched Mike Walker being interviewed, a positive end to a great night and yet another tactical masterpiece engineered by Walker and John Deehan.

Eventually the police released us from the cages of the ground and we made our way straight back onto the coaches and home to Blighty. There were plenty of choruses of the Norwich anthem on the ferry back before we all trooped onto the coach again and towards the A140, en route back to Norwich, getting back to Carrow Road, I think, at around about midday, around 36 hours after we'd left! I was, by now, rather tired! But I'd just witnessed a major part of Norwich City history, which meant all the effort involved in getting a passport and cycling to Carrow Road early on a Saturday morning as well as all the time it took to get to the game and back was well worth it, all so I could have and always remember the 'I was there' moment.

The following day was spent helping my Dad and Stepmother move house. At midday I heard the draw for the second round of the UEFA Cup and finding out we were due to play Bayern Munich with the first leg due to be played at their famous Olympic Stadium. Now they were a special team and I, just as everyone else, had most certainly heard of them. But was I about to head off to Bavaria? Sadly not. As I've already said, I was working in a shoe factory where everyone had to go on holiday when the company said they did, so there was no chance of actually asking for any extra time off. I did raise the subject with my supervisor: was there even the faintest possibility that I could take the time off to go? His reply was simple and to the point. 'Well, if you do go, don't bother coming back to work'. So no, I wouldn't be attempting to make the trip but would, instead, I'd watch the game at a pub near to me called the Branford, which is on the corner of Spencer Street and Branford Road. Surprisingly, it wasn't as packed out as I thought it would have been, which was rather handy as I ended up getting an excellent view of the TV.

Bayern's line up was a bit special and so different to Vitesse Arnhem's. They didn't have any household names whereas Bayern did. West Germany's skipper for a start in Lothar Matthaus, who'd lifted the World Cup only three years earlier. Then there were some more household names, the likes of Ziege, Wouters and Nerlinger. Add to that the fact that they hadn't lost a home match in any competition for a year and that no British side had ever beaten them at their Olympic Stadium in a competitive European match (neither had any French or Spanish side, Ed) and you begin to get an idea of just how much Norwich were up against. The match was being shown by Sky Sports and their pundit, Alan McNally, a former Bayern player, stated that Norwich had no chance of winning. To be honest, I didn't think we had a chance either. Yes, our away record was still pretty good and we had won 2-1 at Chelsea in the league just before this game but, in all honesty, I wasn't expecting anything from this match at all.

The first half of that game still lives on in my mind with crystal-clear recall. After Jeremy Goss had hit the sweetest of volleys I remember jumping up in celebration before the ball had even hit the back of Aumann's net. What a goal that was. Lothar Matthaus, of all people, had headed the ball into Gossy's path after coming under pressure from Mark Robins, Matthaus ending up with his backside firmly planted on the ground as the goal went in. The pub erupted and, as Gossy ran in celebration to the corner of the pitch, I remember someone picking me up as the rest of the team joined him, everyone, that is, apart from Gunny! He'd done what he always did at Carrow Road when Norwich scored and that was heading off towards where the Norwich supporters were; he was one of us and enjoyed the goal celebrations as much as we did. The game was under way again by the time we'd all calmed down and the big question being asked was could we hold onto our narrow lead for the rest of the game? Of course we couldn't, we had the cheek to go 2-0 up instead.

The scorer of our second goal was Mark Bowen, who headed the ball up and over Aumann after running, unchecked and unseen, onto a beautifully placed ball from an Ian Crook free-kick. Yet this time I didn't celebrate. Why? Because I must have been the only Norwich fan in that pub who thought the ball had gone wide and out for a goal kick. By the time I realised it had gone in, I was a few seconds behind everyone else's celebrations.

But were we really 2-0 up at Bayern Munich's Olympic Stadium? We were. It was, as John Motson famously said at the time, 'fantasy football'.

Just before half time Bayern pulled a goal back. This meant that the second half was one of the longest 45 minutes of my life. Could we honestly hold Bayern out for all that time? Of course we could. And mainly down to the heroics of Bryan Gunn. Remember his save from Valencia? I leapt skyward in delight as the ball went the same way, up into the dark Munich night after it deflected away after Gunny's moment of magic. Then there was Ian Culverhouse rousing the team up, you could see him doing it whilst everyone in the pub could hear me doing the same as I shouted at the television, 'Come ON City!!'

The second leg was played a fortnight later at Carrow Road. I got my ticket easily as I was a season ticket holder but ended up being a bit annoyed because, all of a sudden, it seemed as if everyone in Norwich wanted to be there, nearly 21,000 in the end, whereas there'd been 'only' 16,818 for the game against Vitesse Arnhem. Where were the 4,000 or so fans who came along for Bayern when we needed them in the earlier round?

I sat in E block of the Barclay just behind the five young lads who were wearing the t-shirts that spelt out the name GOSSY. And why not? The new hero of the Canary faithful was doing, as it had been said, the deeds whenever needed, scoring either fantastic goals or important ones – and sometimes both! The game started and it started to get a bit nerve racking after just four minutes when Valencia scored to bring the aggregate score to 2-2. Yet, even then, there was no need to panic as we were still ahead on away goals. The ground fell into absolute silence when that goal went in and you really could have heard a pin drop for a few seconds. But then someone started a rousing chorus of 'On the Ball, City' and we were off again, doing our very best to lift the team.

Half time came and we were still 1-0 down. Yet, as had been the case with the home match against Vitesse, some rousing words from Mike Walker at the break were enough to lift the team and, just after the second half started, another round of 'On the Ball, City' thundered around Carrow Road. Five minutes in and, after winning possession, Norwich advanced down the left with Mark Bowen on the ball. Again, I remember all of what happened next as if it was yesterday. The ball was swung over, flicked on by Chris Sutton and, for a brief moment, time stopped altogether as Jeremy Goss – who else – ran through the middle of the Bayern defence to tuck the ball into the net, leaving, again, Matthaus on his backside. I can still remember the roar that greeted the goal; in fact, the whole of Norwich must have heard it. It was loud!

So, 1-1 on the night and 3-2 to City in the tie overall. Amazing. But now Bayern were attacking, looking to score the goal that would have taken the tie into extra time. But they were getting desperate. Matthaus, who seemed to spend as much time on the floor as he did on his feet, then lost his cool with the Belgian referee and got himself booked for his troubles. Then Gunny got involved and he was booked to, it makes me laugh whenever I watch it these days.

Not long after that, the final whistle went and my team, Norwich City, had knocked Bayern Munich, the biggest club in German football and one of the most famous football clubs in the world, out of the UEFA Cup. Cue a massive celebration during which I remember dancing around the seats with the 'Gossy posse' before leaving Carrow Road where the celebrations continued and I ended up driving around the city in my friend's car, windows down, horns beeping and fans in and around all the bars in the city busy celebrating. The intensity of the noise all over the city was absolutely electric.

When the draw was made for the next round that Friday we learnt that yet another famous team, namely the Italian giants Inter Milan, were heading to Carrow Road. Would they go the same way as Bayern Munich, who had left Norfolk with only jars of Coleman Mustard to call their own, not an expected place in the next round of the competition. Could we see Inter Milan off in much the same manner?

This match marked the first time that I found myself being approached by various people asking me if I could get them tickets for the game. My answer was always the same: no chance. The only ticket I would be getting would be mine, especially as those fans who had been so busy asking me for some clearly couldn't be bothered to come to Carrow Road for league games. We'd had yet another poor attendance at Carrow Road for the game against Manchester City just four days before Inter visited, 16,626 came along for that one, where were all of those who came to the Bayern game? My attitude was if people couldn't be bothered to come along for league games, then I couldn't be bothered about helping them get tickets for cup games.

As it turned out, a couple of days before the Inter match, there was a real cold snap in Norwich, which resulted in some doubts as to whether the game would even go ahead. Happily, the undersoil heating that the club had purchased and installed a few months earlier (and which David Phillips claims the money the sale from his transfer to Nottingham Forest raised helped to pay for, Ed) got its first serious test and the game went ahead.

Norwich gave it their absolute all with one fantastic shot from Jeremy Goss hitting the crossbar before Ian Crook hit the rebound over. Norwich were on top and a goal looked certain to come. But it didn't and, suddenly and without warning, Inter's tricky Uruguayan winger Rubén Sosa was brought down by Rob Newman in the penalty area, right in front of me in the Barclay. Now, as a youngster I wore green and yellow glasses and as far as I was concerned, Sosa dived and the referee promptly bought it. I shouted my disapproval but, of course, it made no difference. Dennis Bergkamp took the penalty – he was at the game because it was played before he had developed his fear of flying. He made no mistake and Inter were a goal ahead and an away goal into the bargain.

After the game and as I was queuing up to buy tickets for our match at Ipswich, I remember telling everyone how Sosa had dived and fooled the referee into giving a penalty meaning that we had been robbed. Yet I look back on the incident now and it is the clearest and most obvious penalty decision that you will ever see. As far as the second leg was concerned, I was, again, unable to go because we weren't allowed to take time off for holidays from the dates officially sanctioned by the shoe company. So, whilst those 3,000 Norwich fans who made it to the San Siro for the game have many a tale to tell, I had, again, to stay at home. All I have to contribute from that day is the fact that, as I was at work, I just listened to the radio as the game was an afternoon kick-off. We played well but another late goal by Bergkamp sealed the match and the tie for Inter, meaning that Norwich were out.

That whole experience of Europe, from qualifying in the first place to the anticipation and the games themselves, six in all, might only have lasted for around six months and I ended up missing out on two trips, one to Germany and the other to Italy. But I still have some great memories of that time, memories that so many younger supporters of our club will probably never experience as I doubt we will qualify for Europe again. And, even if we do, would it really be the same, now that it all revolves around group games rather than straight knock out matches?

I'm sure that, when I'm in my old age, I'll still be reminiscing about that time with young Canary fans. From our very first game in Europe to the moment when time stood still as Germany's World Cup winning captain sat on his backside watching as Gossy scored the goal that knocked out the German giants. Good times. And I was there.

Bravo, Win or Die.

The Canaries' memorable run to the third round of the UEFA Cup is now, at the time of writing, something that happened nearly a quarter of a century ago. As Spud points out in his memories of that time, it now feels all the more special as there seems little chance that the club will be playing in competitive European football again anytime soon and, even if it was to happen, certainly not through a high-placed finish in the Premier League. That particular thought would, however, have been far from the minds of Norwich fans as the competition progressed as there would have been some expectation, not that unrealistic at the time, that the club would soon get another chance to compete against the very best that European football had to offer. Not unrealistic? Yes, absolutely. Don't forget that, since 1985, the club had qualified for the UEFA Cup on three separate occasions, only to be denied the opportunity to do so because of the ban placed on all English clubs after Heysel. No one at the time of the Inter Milan ties thought that would be the first and last time that City would play in Europe, especially after just five days on from their exit from the competition in Milan, Norwich faced Leeds United at home, the Canaries' 2-1 win lifting them up to sixth place in the Premier League table on thirty-one points with a game in hand over fifth placed Newcastle (thirty-two points) and two in hand over Arsenal in fourth spot (thirty-four). Even Leeds United, in second place, were only on thirty-six points and the Canaries had two games in hand over them as well.

No need to suspect, therefore, that Norwich would not qualify for the UEFA Cup again on the current evidence, which more than suggested they were quite capable of returning yet again for the following season's competition. The Canaries had found a new home, had found it most enjoyable and now wanted more. With just over half of the 1993/94 Premier League season now to go, the target had to be another top-three finish at the very least, starting at Ipswich Town, just a week before Christmas. But it would not be easy. East Anglia's perpetual second club had inflicted two defeats on the Canaries during the 1992/93 season, painful enough at any time but much more so when you consider that even one win over the Blues that campaign would have seen Norwich finish that season in second, rather than third place. It wasn't to be then and it wasn't to be in this fixture either, which Ipswich won 2-1, an early penalty conversion by John Wark setting them on their way before Mark Bowen equalised before half time. The second half proved to be fairly uneventful until its closing stages when, after receiving his second booking of the game, Norwich striker Lee Power, on as a substitute for Efan Ekoku, was sent off. Norwich hastily reverted to a 4-4-1 formation in response with Ruel Fox playing as a lone and isolated striker but both he and his teammates had been knocked out of their stride by Power's dismissal and, after Ipswich secured a corner late on, Neil Thompson's ball into the Canaries penalty area was headed into his own goal by the unfortunate Gary Megson, meaning Ipswich had won it at the death, their third consecutive league win over Norwich. It was, as it always is, a morale sapping and extremely disappointing result, one that would need a swift response in what would unquestionably be another tough league fixture, the visit to White Hart Lane to take on Tottenham Hotspur.

Injury had kept Jeremy Goss out of the Norwich side that had lost to Ipswich, one that was eventually serious enough to see the midfielder miss seven games. Goss had, through his knack of scoring both spectacular and important goals for Norwich, not least his strikes in both the away and home legs against Bayern Munich, become a cult figure at Carrow Road with curly blond wigs a popular seller in the club shop. He had also, if reports were to be believed, become something of a wanted man in terms of his footballing ability, with Chelsea one of a number of clubs rumoured to be preparing a big-money bid for him. Things then took an almost surreal twist when it was revealed that Portuguese giants Benfica were also interested and were preparing to offer Norwich £400,000 for him, a ridiculously low sum but one that, you assume, would have been enough to pique Goss's interest in a move and set the potential transfer wheels in motion. Goss has since said that the talk of him moving onto bigger and better things, a prospect that had tempted many a big name Norwich City player in recent years, was nothing more than paper talk, adding that he had no intention of leaving the club anyway as he, his teammates and manager all thought the club was close to winning a trophy and, of course, ending the season with another European qualification secured as well.

The club's hopes of another high league finish, dented with that defeat at Ipswich, rose again when, in one of the Canaries best performances of that season, they attacked Tottenham from the off at White Hart Lane, ending the game having made an astonishing fifteen shots on target with a beleaguered home defence struggling to cope with a Norwich line-up that featured three Tottenham old boys as well as the attacking flair, pace and raw power of Efan Ekoku, Ruel Fox and Chris Sutton. The final score was 3-1 in Norwich's favour with Sutton getting two of them, bringing his total of league goals scored for the season up to eleven in the process. He was fast becoming one of the big name strikers in English football and it was becoming more and more clear that, with every goal he scored, interest in him from some of the countries bigger clubs would increase. The hope was, at least in the short term, that for as long as Norwich remained in close contention for a trophy or place in Europe, Sutton could be persuaded to stay for a while longer, a fact later reinforced, somewhat unconvincingly, by Canaries chairman Robert Chase, who stated that, as far as he was concerned, if Sutton wasn't still at the club at the beginning of the 1994/95 season, then he wouldn't be either. Fighting talk from the man at the top, but it fooled no one, least of all Sutton himself. His performance and the two goals he'd scored for the Canaries in their win at Blackburn back in August had gone down almost as well with the Blackburn management team as they had the Norwich one and he was pretty much their number one transfer target from then on in. This was, as it happens, a desire that was shared by the man himself, Sutton later admitting to Matt Tench of *The Independent,* 'as soon as the speculation about me started six months ago I thought that if there was one club I wanted to talk to it was Blackburn. Blackburn was always my first choice. The club is similar to Norwich in terms of the population and area, although it's a bigger club, and I didn't want to move to a big city...'

Sutton scored again two days later in Norwich's next game at home to Aston Villa, putting the Canaries ahead after an error by the normally reliable Shaun Teale had given him enough time and space to beat Mark Bosnich. It seemed, at that point, that Norwich, sixth at kick-off, would go onto seal another important win against the side just below them in the table but Villa equalised via another defensive error, this time courtesy of the even more reliable Ian Culverhouse, whose weak back pass was intercepted by Ray Houghton. Three minutes later, Villa were ahead when Dean Saunders struck a fine shot from all of 25 yards, a goal fit to win any match and certainly this particular one with Ron Atkinson's side holding onto their lead with relative ease to take home the points and leave the Norwich fans wondering quite how their side had managed to lose a game they seemed certain of winning at half time. Not all of the post-match talk was about the result, however, as it had recently emerged that Mike Walker, the architect behind Norwich's remarkable rise towards the pinnacle of the English game, had fallen out with Robert Chase over a new contract, one that he, quite rightly, felt was overdue, given how well he had done since being given the top job the previous August.

What was particularly worrying about this rumour was the fact that Chase, a builder by trade, had a reputation of digging in and not conceding an inch of ground if he thought he was in the right. Unfortunately, this was a character trait that his manager just happened to share. As far as Robert Chase was concerned though, his word on all things had to be final and non-negotiable, especially with regard to transfer fees paid and the terms of players' contracts. Jeremy Goss recalls that, after he had signed a new contract with the club, Chase had told him that he was now the 'best paid player at the club', something Goss knew was patently untrue. Mike Walker, in contrast, was nowhere near being the best paid manager in the Premier League with the reality being that, in financial terms, he would not only be lagging behind all of his peers in the elite but quite a few in Division One (now the Championship) as well. With that in mind, it seemed very reasonable to expect that, after all he had achieved since his appointment and with the Canaries looking to maintain their progress that season, Walker would get the sort of new deal that befitted his status as one of English football's best young managers, rewarding in both terms of an increased salary and the security a longer contract would give him.

Yet there seemed no sign of one coming or a positive announcement about the manager's future being made. Looking back now, Chase's refusal to acknowledge what Walker had done, and was continuing to do, at Carrow Road seems an act that borders on professional negligence. It wasn't as if Walker had 'merely' followed the remit that he would undoubtedly have been given upon taking the job (i.e. to keep the Canaries in the Premier League). Walker had, tongue in cheek, referred to this throughout the 1992/93 season, reminding everyone that, even when the club was still top at Christmas, they now had enough points to stop worrying about any possibility of relegation. Such modest comments hid the fact that he had overseen an unforeseen yet spectacular transformation of the club's fortunes, one that had led to many leading writers and pundits within the game to suggest that Norwich were on the verge of gatecrashing the long-established cartel of 'elite' clubs within the Premier League on a permanent basis.

A scenario that had, ultimately, left Chase and Walker at loggerheads over the latter's long-term value and importance to the club, something that would not have gone unnoticed in a fair few boardrooms up and down the country, places where, you felt, Walker's achievements were much more appreciated than they were in his own. It was clearly a story that was going to rumble on for some time unless a swift and definite resolution came, one way or the other. Yet one wasn't quick in coming, at least one that would have pleased Walker, his players and the fans of the club and by the time Norwich travelled to Southampton on New Year's Day 1994, gossip about Walker's future had gone from being a purely local matter to one that was occupying the hearts and minds of the national media. Norwich's 1-0 win, sealed via an excellent strike from fully 20 yards out from Chris Sutton, was the subject of some cheer but the rumours and speculation soon started up again and, by the time Norwich met Newcastle at Carrow Road four days later, Everton, who'd sacked Howard Kendall at the beginning of December, made it known that they were interested in talking to Walker about the managerial vacancy at Goodison Park, the scene of Norwich's 5-1 demolition of the Toffees barely three months earlier.

That interest would, you suspect, have sparked an immediate response from the Canaries board had they really wanted their highly rated manager to stay, a time, finally, to put an end to all of the speculation about Walker's future and Everton's interest by starting talks on a new improved contract. Yet nothing was forthcoming and as the Norwich players assembled at their Trowse training ground in order to ready themselves for a trip down to play Wycombe Wanderers in the FA Cup the following day, the issue had already reached a point of no return, Jeremy Goss remembering bumping into his then former manager as the midfielder prepared to make the trip down to Wycombe:

We were at the training ground getting ready to depart for an FA Cup tie down at Wycombe. I had just left the main changing room, having originally gone in there to change my boots. The rest of the lads were all up on the main pitch at Trowse. As I walked down the corridor and headed out, I noticed Mike walk out of the staff room there, he came past me and, as he did, I said, 'Gaffer, you alright?'

Mike's answer was the last thing I was expecting – even despite all the gossip that had been doing the rounds over the last few weeks.

'Look, Gossy. I'm pleased I've bumped into you. I'm leaving the football club. I'm going to be the new Manager of Everton.'

It's just the two of us stood there in the corridor. I'm beyond shocked. I say the first words that come into my mind, they spill out of my mouth like a runaway train. 'Well it's brilliant for you Gaffer. But, I tell you what, you're going to leave a big, big hole here. We'll miss you bad, really bad. And this club isn't going to be the same without you.'

I can still recall the moment so clearly. Was I trying to convince him not to go? I don't know. I didn't want him to and I knew that things would change overnight. But then it was a great opportunity for him, you couldn't deny that. He gave me a half smile and made to carry on, saying, 'Come on, it's time for me to tell the rest of the lads'.

From that moment onwards, Norwich City became a different club.

Robert Rosario, particularly rated and appreciated by Robert Fleck. (*Photo courtesy of Norwich City Football Club*)

David Phillips, who claimed the club had sold him in order to pay for the undersoil heating. (*Photo courtesy of Norwich City Football Club*)

Colin Woodthorpe evades the attention of Mike Marsh (right) and Bruce Grobbelaar to put Norwich 1-0 up at Carrow Road on 22 February 1992. (*Photo courtesy of Norwich City Football Club*)

Goalmouth melee versus Southampton in 1992. (*Photo courtesy of Norwich City Football Club*)

John Polston clears the lines ahead of Teddy Sheringham and Gordon Durie (No. 8) in an FA Cup tie on 24 January 1993. *(Photo courtesy of Norwich City Football Club)*

Chris Sutton – centre half turned lethal centre forward. (*Photo courtesy of Norwich City Football Club*)

Darren Beckford, signed from Port Vale for a club record £925,000. (*Photo courtesy of Norwich City Football Club*)

Ruel Fox turned defenders inside out. (*Photo courtesy of David McDermott*)

Mike Walker and John Deehan taking training in the snow. (*Photo courtesy of David McDermott*)

Ian Crook wearing the Donkey of the Day top in training. (*Photo courtesy of David McDermott*)

Jeremy Goss evades a challenge versus Inter Milan as Ian Butterworth looks on. (*Photo courtesy of Norwich City Football Club*)

John Polston clearing his lines in a match against Everton. (*Photo courtesy of David McDermott*)

Manager John Deehan happily shows off new signing Ashley Ward. (*Photo courtesy of Norwich City Football Club*)

Martin O'Neill's Norwich City squad line-up prior to the start of the 1995/96 season. (*Photo courtesy of David McDermott*)

Above: Martin O'Neill keeping an eye on things from the dugout. (*Photo courtesy of Norwich City Football Club*)

Below left: Danny Mills – sixty-six league appearances between 1995 and 1998. (*Photo courtesy of David McDermott*)

Below right: The infamous 'On Loan To Division One' T-shirt. (*Photo courtesy of Christopher Jakeman*)

Gary Megson loosens up some tired limbs at a training session. (*Photo courtesy of David McDermott*)

Jon Newsome powers home a header against Brentford in a 1996 FA Cup tie. (*Photo courtesy of David McDermott*)

Above left: The one and only David Rocastle – a special player. (*Photo courtesy of David McDermott*)

Above right: Looks like Ulf Ottosson is having a problem removing one of his ear studs. (*Photo courtesy of David McDermott*)

Below: Keith O'Neill, Sarah Thomas and Darren Eadie model the new kit in 1997. (*Photo courtesy of Norwich City Football Club*)

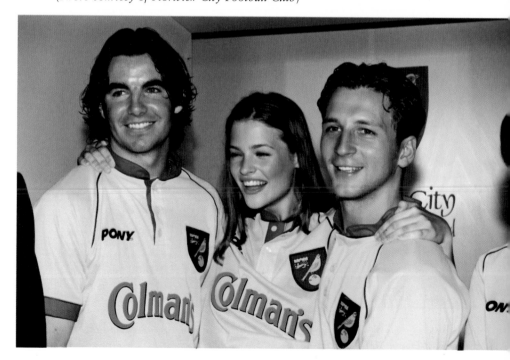

Andy Marshall and Peter Grant doing a spot of publicity for a local company. (*Photo courtesy of David McDermott*)

Bruce Rioch and Bryan Hamilton observing the on-pitch action. (*Photo courtesy of David McDermott*)

The first-team squad line-up for a photo prior to travelling to an away fixture. (*Photo courtesy of David McDermott*)

Erik Fugelstad – the Viking from Viking was a very dependable left-back. (*Photo courtesy of David McDermott*)

Above left: Bruce Rioch with Paul Dalglish and Cedric Anselin. (*Photo courtesy of Norwich City Football Club*)

Above right: Craig Fleming, the best man marker in the game, according to Alex Ferguson. (*Photo courtesy of Norwich City Football Club*)

Below: Tension prior to a penalty shoot-out against Bolton Wanderers in 1998. (*Photo courtesy of David McDermott*)

Keith O'Neill celebrates a goal with some typical dance floor moves. (*Photo courtesy of Norwich City Football Club*)

Iwan Roberts has just knocked Swansea out of the League Cup. (*Photo courtesy of David McDermott*)

Chase's refusal to even talk to Walker about a new contract, together with Everton's very obvious allure as a big club, one with a rich and successful history, large ground, good squad of players and, you assume, more money for a new manager to spend than Walker could ever have dreamt of having at Norwich had done the trick and Walker had resigned. Then, once his departure from Norwich became official, he duly made the Everton board aware of his interest in the role as their new manager, an academic exercise as he knew they wanted him, the confirmation of his appointment being made on the Friday (7 January) before that weekend's tranche of FA Cup matches.

Despite previously having done little to nothing in order to make their manager want to stay and seeming quite content with the prospect that he might simply walk away, Norwich's response to the situation, when it eventually came, was a classic case of too little, too late. Robert Chase had already refused Everton permission to speak to Walker on two occasions before, on the night of 6 January finally meeting with him but, if reports were to be believed, refusing, yet again, to discuss offering him the new contract he wanted. He did, however, attempt some appeasement, promising Walker substantial bonuses at the end of the season even if it turned out to be one not as successful as the previous one.

Content that he had won over Walker with that counter offer, Chase declared the meeting over and the two men went their separate ways. But he hadn't come anywhere near to persuading Walker to change his mind, and the now ex-Norwich boss had just been returning from delivering his letter of resignation to Chase's secretary at Trowse that Friday morning when he'd bumped into Goss. The Canaries' immediate response to his departure was to claim that Everton had made an illegal approach for Walker with Chase going onto claim that he had evidence to support this and was expecting, with that in mind, for the FA to look into the matter via a disciplinary enquiry. As for Walker, his only concerns now was for his new club and, in an interview he gave Trevor Haylett of *The Independent*, he ended up sounding almost dismissive of his old club at the same time as he was, diplomatically, 'bigging up' his new one:

> With a little bit of work and attention I am sure we can return to our rightful place. Everton have always been synonymous with what I call the right way of playing and hopefully it will be a good marriage. I would have liked to have finished amicably with Norwich but you have to make a decision and I am quite happy with it because I know what I wanted. I am ambitious and there was only one decision to make. If I get things right here the sky's the limit. With due respect to Norwich they are a small club and could not give me the possibility of reaching so high.

Walker's first spell at Carrow Road, one that comes complete with some of the most memorable matches and incidents of the club's history, lasted barely eighteen months, during which time he'd been in charge for a total of eighty league and cup matches, winning thirty-six of them. His departure, one that had led to Jeremy Goss's statement that the club wouldn't be the same without him, was treated with a mixture of disappointment and disbelief by Canary fans. I asked one of them, Kathy Blake, for her thoughts and recollections on Mike's time at Carrow Road as well as the long-term aftermath of his shock departure:

> In the days following the departure of Paul Lambert from Carrow Road, there was some debate among City fans as to whether or not he had been the club's greatest manager.

There's no easy answer to that question.

How do you compare his achieving so much with so little at his disposal with Ken Brown's unique achievement of bring meaningful silverware back to the Fine City for the first time? Which is more impressive – Ron Saunders breaking into the top flight for the first time, albeit with a team that didn't really entertain, or John Bond's free-flowing team of the seventies? Both, of course, took us to Wembley.

It's not possible. It's very much a personal thing and it's like comparing apples with oranges.

For my choice, I would look no further than the Nineties and Mike Walker. Here is a man who brought Norwich City to the attention of not only the nation but the whole of Europe. He also winked at me the first time I met him...

Walker had first come into the consciousness of Norwich fans as a big genial goalkeeper with a Burt Reynolds moustache, who we occasionally saw playing for Colchester Utd on Anglia TV's *Match of the Week* on Sunday afternoons. We vaguely knew from the same programme that he had progressed to manage them for a brief spell and was then sacked despite the U's being top of the league at the time. In 1987, he made his way to Norwich City, where he took up a post as youth team coach, and then in 1992, after the departure of interim manager David Williams, he was surprisingly appointed manager.

Like so many of those who came before and after, including Brown and Lambert, he took up his post at City accompanied by no great fanfare. 'Another cheap option – a typical Norwich City appointment' was a familiar reaction from the fans.

But this soon evaporated and was replaced with a huge respect as his team achieved astonishing victories at Arsenal and Chelsea, and amazingly spent such a large part of the 1992/93 season at the top of the Premiership. We continued to challenge Manchester Utd all the way to the title, falling away only in the last few weeks. We eventually finished third, a position which proved good enough to qualify for the UEFA Cup for the first time in the club's history. The accolades poured in for Walker and TV appearances followed, including a first appearance by a Norwich City manager on *BBC Sports Personality of the Year*. We had an affable, Crocodile Dundee lookalike as our manager, who was exceedingly comfortable with the media and, more importantly, was delivering on the pitch. Inevitably, rumours soon started that the 'big clubs' were interested in tempting him away from Carrow Road.

In Europe, the fairy tale continued. A solid first-round victory over euro journeymen Vitesse Arnhem was followed by arguably the greatest result in the club's history when we eliminated one of Europe's heavyweights, Bayern Munich. I remember driving to work on a cloud of euphoria the morning after. To this date, we remain the only English club to have beaten them in their own back yard at the Olympic Stadium.

We were finally knocked out by eventual cup winners Inter Milan. Even then, we didn't let ourselves down. Arriving for the second leg at the San Siro with a weakened side through a mixture of injuries and suspensions, we never really looked like overturning the 1-0 deficit from the first leg. Ian Crook's absence was particularly galling as he missed the game after getting booked by an over-zealous referee at Carrow Road for not retreating quickly enough at a free-kick. But in the end, a goal in each leg from a young Dennis Bergkamp proved too much for the Canaries. Like many others at that time, I couldn't really afford to travel to those games, so I borrowed money to do so. I remember feeling terribly guilty as there were probably things I could have better spent the cash on. This was compounded by the feeling that European trips were going to be a regular thing in the coming seasons. But that wasn't to be the case and we have never reached those heights again. I'm so glad that I pushed the boat out and went as it's possible that I may never get another chance in my lifetime.

Norwich returned to the bread and butter of the league after the cup run, and that was where it all started to go wrong. Walker wanted to push on and make the club even stronger. On several occasions he had gone public with his wish to 'loosen the purse strings', including during a live broadcast of *The Footballers' Football Show*, one of Sky TV's early soccer fanzines. Unfortunately, chairman Robert Chase didn't share his views.

Walker had most of the supporters with him and what followed was one of the stormiest periods in the club's history. The relationship between manager and chairman became more and more strained, and finally ended in January 1994 when Walker left for Everton. I don't think he had any great yearning to go to the Toffees but had become so frustrated that he felt that he had to get away. We were awarded £75,000 compensation. Even in those days, that was a laughable sum for what we'd lost.

Feelings boiled over among the fans. There were anti-Chase demonstrations at games, 'red card' protests and boycotts, and a new supporters' group, the Norwich City Independent Supporters' Association, was born.

It was a defining time for me personally. I went from being a passive fan to being a proactive fan. I felt very strongly that I needed to do something. A massive opportunity had been wasted to put Norwich City on the map, and I joined the new association to show my discontent. Whereas before I'd felt so impotent, now I felt I could make a real difference. It felt good to be with like-minded people. Not everyone agreed and we had our critics. To this day I still encounter those who seem to genuinely believe that Chase did a good job, and the old arguments surface again. Some fans saw NCISA as troublemakers and anti-club. That couldn't have been further from the truth. We were aware that there were fans out there who supported Chase and we always tried to be a platform for debate, rather than simply a protest organisation. Increasingly, though, we became a focus point for the bitterness surrounding the antics of the chairman. NCISA went from strength to strength and our membership grew. It became a feature of the association throughout its existence that membership numbers always grew when things were going badly. One of the unwritten laws of physics is that the membership numbers of a supporters' association is always inversely proportional to how well the team is doing.

Meanwhile, things were not going well at Everton for Walker. Like Saunders, Bond and, more recently, Paul Lambert, he found that transferring the success he'd had at Norwich to a new club was easier said than done. The pressure cooker of Goodison Park expected immediate success and when that failed to materialise, his days were numbered. He was eventually sacked after just ten months. I sometimes think that, like players, a football manager just clicks at a certain time at a certain club and nowhere else. Again, Lambert springs to mind.

Perhaps illogically, I was very angry when Walker was sacked. It felt like having a car you are very fond of stolen and then the thieves torching it. It seemed that the big clubs felt that they could just come along and take away something very special from my football club and then discard it when it was no longer required. I remember feeling similar emotions many years later when Aston Villa sacked Paul Lambert. I appreciate that this is a very naïve view, and what they did was no different from us recruiting managers from lower league clubs.

Back at Carrow Road, John Deehan had taken over as manager but he was always on a hiding to nothing. Vultures from the bigger Premiership clubs began picking over the carcase of City's UEFA Cup team and favourite players left without being replaced. The team became weaker and weaker, and eventually (and inevitably) we were relegated to Division One at the end of the 1994/95 season. Deehan departed and Gary Megson briefly took over before; he, too, left the club just two months later.

Chase enjoyed a brief respite from the vitriol in 1995 with the appointment of fans favourite Martin O'Neill as manager. It wasn't long, however, before O'Neill also became frustrated with the financial constraints set by the chairman. He tried long and hard to sign Dean Windass from Hull City, famously saying, 'I would like to sign the player and I would like to sign him before the end of the century.' The long drawn-out saga tried O'Neill's patience to the limit and, like Walker before him, he walked away.

From the heady heights of the Olympic Stadium just over a year earlier to this. It was at this point that I reached my lowest ebb as a City fan.

With the club on its knees, morale-wise and financially, Chase finally resigned in April 1996. It was a JFK moment for me. I can remember exactly where I was and what I was doing when I heard. I'd often imagined that moment and wondered what I'd do. Throw a party? Laugh? Cry? When it finally happened, I didn't do any of those things. I just felt numb. I didn't feel anything. There was nothing to celebrate. It was too late and the damage had been done.

Geoffrey Watling bought Chase's shares and sold them to Delia Smith a year later. She soon endeared herself to fans by fetching Walker back. We were all delighted. It felt as if things had turned full circle and we'd emerged out of a dark tunnel. But it never worked out and he was sacked (on the back of two 5-0 home wins, oddly enough). I actually think he should have been given more time. Many others since have been dealt with far more leniently by the board.

Possibly he should never have returned in the first place, given the weight of expectation on his shoulders. They say you should never go back and this was a good example. I often think of this when fans crave Lambert's return. Sometimes it's better to stay away and retain your legendary standing.

I'm not quite sure why it didn't work out for Walker second time around. Some say the team he took over in 1992 had been inherited from Dave

Stringer and was pretty special and that the hard work had already been done for him. He'd also suffered personal tragedy with the loss of his wife Jackie to cancer in 1997, and that might have been a factor. I just wonder if he'd become cynical about football after all he'd been through and that he'd lost his hunger for the game?

So the manager once lusted after by the Premiership's big boys and who had achieved so much here disappeared into football's wilderness. Apart from a brief spell with a Cypriot club, he never managed again. I felt something had died and we'd lost something very special, the likes of which we may never see again.

I still believe that Norwich City Football Club was at a crossroads in 1993, and what happened then defined the future of the club for a long time. It's not so much what happened then as when it happened. At the time, football was just about to change forever. There was a gulf between the biggest clubs in Europe and everybody else, but it wasn't the yawning chasm that exists today. We had the chance to grab a sizeable piece of the fame and fortune that has become a feature of the modern game. The events of the mid-1990s defined which side of the divide we would end up on, possibly forever.

Some might say we would have 'done a Leicester' and sunk as quickly as we had risen. Maybe. But it would have been nice to find out.

Walker's shock exit from the club was hardly the best preparation for the looming FA Cup tie at Wycombe for which Walker's assistant, the popular John Deehan, had been asked to assume the role of temporary manager. Temporary or not, the smart money was already being staked on him being asked to take on the role permanently. It would, if confirmed, be a decision that might have seemed tainted with risk, given the fact that Deehan's only previous managerial experience had been a two-year spell with former Canary Mel Machin at Manchester City, where he'd worked as the Blues' player coach. Machin, who was now in charge at Barnsley, was another who was being connected with the role, together with thirty-six-year-old Mark McGhee, who was gaining a very respectable reputation for himself as manager of Reading. The countless rumours now had to be put on hold, however, as the remaining coaching staff, led by Deehan, had that very tricky FA Cup match at Wycombe to prepare for. Wycombe's own manager, Martin O'Neill, someone who had already enjoyed two spells at Carrow Road as a player, was another obvious frontrunner for the role, a man who was now heading into one of the biggest matches in his clubs history with plenty of speculation surrounding his future and people wondering if he was about to take charge of his present club for the last time in a match against his next one.

Deehan may have had no experience at the top level as a manager but he was football savvy enough to know that he didn't need to impose himself onto his players or stop being the 'Dixie' they all knew and highly respected as an innovative and progressive coach. His mantra would have been business as usual with the club carrying on in exactly the same manner as it had, and would have continued to do so had Walker stayed. To that end, he named the same starting XI players for the Wycombe game that Walker had chosen for the league match against Newcastle a few days previously, showing his faith in the players and system that had, for now, rarely let the club down. Walker's departure had, however, created a little bit more interest in the match than what might have been expected, interest enough for the BBC to choose it as one of the games they would show extended highlights of on that nights *Match of the Day*, hoping, it would seem, that a little bit more yellow and green blood was spilled at Adams Park.

Yet Norwich City do not do things according to the script. If the final page is set to tell of a stirring victory then only mediocre capitulation will follow. Likewise, many an anticipated defeat has been followed up with a shock win. In short, Norwich City are very definitely a side that delights in doing precisely NOT what it says on the tin. So if anyone was expecting the Canaries, still reeling at the departure of their charismatic manager, to offer up a meek surrender down in leafy Buckinghamshire, then they were going to end up disappointed as Deehan's side put in a consummate performance against the newly promoted Division Three side and the vast majority of the 7,802 who had come to witness the giant-killing. Two goals from Chris Sutton, one in each half, won the game for Norwich, a win and display that clearly told the club's board that they, much like Deehan and the team, didn't really need to change things around too much, the end result of that being confirmation of Deehan's appointment as the club's new manager prior to the Canaries' next league game against Chelsea at Carrow Road on 15 January.

In hindsight it is far too easy to say that the appointment of Deehan as Walker's replacement was a poor one. Yet, in doing so, the Canaries were simply repeating that long-established policy of promoting from within whenever a new manager was needed, one that first been seen in 1980 when Ken Brown had succeeded John Bond. Brown had, subsequently, been replaced by Dave Stringer in 1987 with Mike Walker a third consecutive internal appointment in 1992. Now, two years later, the board were repeating a now well-established trend with Deehan. And you can understand the logic in their thinking. Brown, Stringer and Walker had all been relatively successful appointments so was there any reason to think that Deehan wouldn't carry on in much the same manner?

Liverpool had, after all, seen years of unprecedented success by adopting the same policy themselves with regard to their managerial appointments and if it was good enough for them then surely it would be more than good enough for Norwich? It's certainly one that the club stuck to for many years. John Bond had been an outside appointment when he took over at the club in 1973 but it took the Canaries another quarter of a century to recruit a new manager from outside the club again, the man in question being Bruce Rioch, who, like Bond, had absolutely no previous playing or coaching connections at Carrow Road to call upon when he accepted the job in 1998.

As far as Walker was concerned it was a case of 'the King is dead, long live the King' with the club's upward trajectory in English football expected to continue unabated with Deehan's smooth transition into the manager's role. But was it one that would prove to be as equally inspiring as those that saw similar promotions for Brown, Stringer and Walker or would it be the one that demonstrated that while lightning might strike in the same place once, twice or even three times, expecting it to do so for a fourth time in a row, as Liverpool had found to their cost with Graeme Souness, who'd followed on at Anfield from Bob Paisley, Joe Fagan and Kenny Dalglish as the Red's fourth successive internal managerial appointment, one that hadn't been a success and would see him resign three weeks after Deehan took charge of Norwich, was a case of stretching your footballing luck just a little bit too far?

Deehan was, of course, on a hiding to nothing at Carrow Road. Had he done well it is likely that any plaudits that did happen to come his way would be tempered by reminders that he had succeeded Walker's team and was basking in the reflected glory of another man's work. If, however, he had struggled, there would have been accusations that all the progress that has been made under Walker and Dave Stringer was now being wasted. On reflection, it is unusual that Walker did not look to take Deehan with him to Goodison. The two of them were a managerial partnership who worked well and prospered together; indeed, neither were very successful in their consequent careers without the other at their side. Walker chose, however, to appoint former Canary player and coach David Williams as his assistant at Everton indicating, perhaps, that he'd never had any intention of asking Deehan to join him there.

You cannot help but wonder how the career trajectories of both men might have changed, quite possibly for the better, had Deehan joined Walker on Merseyside and, with that, how things might have been at Carrow Road had Chase and his directors appointed the best man available as his successor, which, if that meant looking outside the club, may well have led to a Mark McGhee, Mick McCarthy or Tommy McLean making his way to Carrow Road.

Having passed his initial test at Wycombe with flying colours, Deehan now had two league games to contend with, drawing 1-1 with Chelsea at Carrow Road before sharing the points again in a thrilling 3-3 draw against West Ham under the Upton Park floodlights and in front of the Sky Sports cameras on 24 January. It was a game that had, at the very least, showcased Deehan's football philosophy, one that wasn't so far removed from Walkers and based on the Canaries trademark pass-and-move style with the ball constantly going forward and to feet at every opportunity.

Remarkably, those two draws in the league were followed by five more, these being against Liverpool (2-2), Arsenal (1-1), Swindon (3-3), Blackburn (2-2) and Sheffield Wednesday (1-1), meaning that Deehan's start as Norwich manager had coincided with a seven-game unbeaten run in the Premier League, as impressive a statistic today as it was then and one that meant that, even without a win in that mini-run, Norwich were sat in a comfortable ninth place at the beginning of March. It was a position that a good run in March and into April could only be improved upon with, of course, the undoubted highlight being the return of Walker and his Everton side to Carrow Road on 21 March, a game that the ubiquitous Sky Sports had already selected as the must-see game, portrayed as the 'grudge' clash between the Canaries and their former boss.

Worryingly, the first two games in March saw Norwich fall to two consecutive defeats, the first time that the Canaries had lost two games in a row for nearly a year. The first was at Wimbledon where a tiny crowd of just 7,206 saw the home team prevail 3-1, despite Norwich opening the scoring after just six minutes when a poor back pass from Warren Barton was intercepted by Efan Ekoku, who shot past Hans Segers with ease. Norwich's lead lasted for around half an hour with Robbie Earle equalising in the thirty-seventh minute before putting the Dons 2-1 up in the sixty-fifth minute, Dean Holdsworth adding the third five minutes later. It was Deehan's first taste of defeat as Norwich manager and only the Canaries second loss in ten games, but the manner of it was the most worrying thing as, aside from a bright opening, Norwich had never really been in the game at all and had, at times, been out played by their energetic opponents, who had taken the game to Norwich and reaped the rewards for doing so. It was a similar approach that was taken by QPR at Carrow Road a week later, Ekoku again giving the Canaries hope with an early goal, a lead that Norwich hung onto until the forty-ninth minute when Simon Barker equalised. Ekoku then scored his third goal in two games to retain the lead for Norwich only for Gavin Peacock and Gary Penrice to make the score 3-2 in the visitors favour, Devon White making it 4-2 with six minutes to go, a late 25 yard strike from Chris Sutton coming too late to make any real difference to proceedings.

Much had been made of Deehan starting his reign at Norwich with a seven-game unbeaten run. However, that run could now be turned on its head via the fact that Norwich had now gone ten Premier League games without a victory, a run stretching back to the 1-0 win over Southampton on New Year's Day. In terms of where they sat in the Premier League, it had not done the Canaries much harm; indeed, they were still ninth in the Premier League table and only four points distant from Leeds United in sixth place. So no real harm done? That depended, ultimately, on your outlook at the time. Had, for example, Norwich been able to register four wins during that run, with one of those being in either the Wimbledon or QPR game, form and an ability to get results and points that certainly hadn't been beyond them in the last eighteen months or so, that would have been an extra nine points in total, which would have seen the Canaries in fifth place and only a point behind Newcastle and Arsenal in third and fourth. If, however, things had gone the other way and the Canaries had lost four of the games they'd ended up drawing, they'd have been down in eleventh place, mid-table and battling it out with the likes of Ipswich, Coventry and Wimbledon for mid-table mediocrity, something that may have been acceptable a few seasons ago but was now seen as tantamount to failure.

The Canaries' next Premier League fixture, following the high-scoring defeat in West London, had ended up being taken up for live coverage by Sky Sports as it featured the return to Norwich of prodigal son Mike Walker with an Everton side had started life under his stewardship with a 6-2 win over Swindon Town but had since followed it up with the sort of inconsistency that supporters at Goodison Park had long since become accustomed to – two wins, two draws and two defeats. Eager to boost his striking options and maybe relishing the chance to spend the sort of money that had never been available to him at Carrow Road, Walker had acted swiftly in making Brett Angell's initial loan spell at the club a permanent deal, signing him from Southend United for a fee reported to be in the region of £500,000. Angell had, reportedly, been a one-time target for Norwich, the forty-seven goals he had scored in 115 league games for the Shrimpers suggesting he may well have been able to make the step up to the Premier League.

What, however, might have been a good signing for the Canaries may not have been quite so well regarded on Merseyside and, for a club that had been spoilt on the qualities of strikers like Joe Royle, Bob Latchford, Graeme Sharp, Gary Lineker and Andy Gray, the arrival of Angell might have seemed rather underwhelming to most Everton fans. He arrived at the club having just had a major surgery on his left leg, something that the Everton hierarchy must have been aware of considering his prior loan spell at the club, but that didn't deter Walker, who duly made him one of his first-choice strikers, Angell being slotted into a traditional two-man strike force at Goodison alongside Cottee.

Cottee and Angell duly took the field at Carrow Road on 21 March in a game that was taking place during the same week that Everton's alleged illegal approach for his services was being investigated by the Premier League. If he had arrived in Norfolk expecting a warm welcome from his one-time adoring support, then he was to be disappointed as the Norwich fans gave full vent to their anger at his sudden departure, much as it might have been precipitated by Robert Chase, who, for once, was not the focal point of concentrated yellow and green discontent. His rumbustious reception was repeated by his former charges, who played with the sort of attacking verve and freedom that had long been missing in Norfolk, chalking up a 3-0 win that saw two of the goals come from the club's full-backs, Ian Culverhouse and Mark Bowen, the former's fortieth minute strike only his second goal for the club in 360 appearances.

Well beaten and suitably chastised, Walker took his leave of the Carrow Road pitch, but only after taking time to congratulate some of his former players on a performance that had his trademark of total football written all over it. One or two of those players might have, justifiably, been wondering if Walker was set to give them a call about joining him at his new club, among them Jeremy Goss, who half expected to be given the opportunity to leave Norfolk to join him but, for whatever reasons, it never came and, once the excitement of that game had died down, Norwich City, fans, players and current management alike were able to finally move on and put the entire episode of his departure behind them. His eventual legacy at Everton was not one that will stick in the memory of Evertonians; his brief tenure at the club saw them avoid an unlikely relegation from the Premier League on the last day of that 1993/94 season after a last gasp 3-2 win over Wimbledon while, of his signings, Brett Angell was later described by goalkeeper Neville Southall as having a 'first touch like a tackle'.

The win elevated Norwich up to eighth place in the Premier League table, a remarkably satisfactory state of affairs for a club that had gone into that match on a run of ten games without a win. John Deehan was, slowly (and maybe too slowly for some Norwich fans) beginning to bring his own style of football to the club, one that, while it didn't neglect the passing game that Walker had preached, was adding a little directness to the Canaries' game, this being typified by Deehan's first signing for the club, winger Neil Adams, who arrived from Oldham Athletic for just £250,000. Deehan also gave debuts to goalkeeper Scott Howie and striker Ade Akinbiyi before the end of the season, the latter being seen as a powerful and uncompromising attacking option who would be expected to benefit from the crosses provided by Adams and Darren Eadie. The purchase of Adams for such a low fee would certainly have met with the approval of Robert Chase, who had, in early February, sanctioned the departure of another wide player, Ruel Fox, to Newcastle for £2,250,000, leaving the Canaries £2 million up on the two deals. Manna for Chase, perhaps, but a disturbing sign of things to come for the Norwich support, aware that interest in Chris Sutton from other clubs was increasing on an almost daily basis, while a report in the *London Evening Standard* had linked Mark Bowen with a return to Tottenham.

Such was the way in which the Canaries had seen off Everton, most of the club's fans might have been forgiven for thinking that the club would now push on and put together a decent run of results in their remaining nine league games in order to finish in as high a league placing as possible. The top ten places in the Premier League were considered the expected standard, yet the top six was a more than realistic proposition, especially as Norwich's run-in included games against clubs that were, for one reason or another, struggling at the bottom of the Premier League, including Southampton, Sheffield United and Oldham, of which, the latter pairing would end up being relegated.

Yet, frustratingly, the opposite was the case as the Canaries stuttered their way to the end of the season, the home defeat to Sheffield United on 23 April the low point. It was the Canaries' eighth home league defeat of the campaign (they'd lost just two the previous season) and had now won just two league games out of the eighteen that had seen Deehan in charge.

Typically, Norwich followed up that seasonal nadir with an unexpected but deserved 1-0 win at Liverpool in their penultimate game, Jeremy Goss marking both the game and the occasion (it was the last match to be played at Anfield in front of the famous standing Kop) with one of his now trademark strikes from long distance.

Norwich saw out the season with a tame 1-1 draw against Oldham Athletic at Carrow Road, Robert Ullathorne's seventy-second minute goal set up by a typically pinpoint cross from Latics old boy Adams. It meant a twelfth place finish in the Premier League for the Canaries, one that, in previous seasons, might have been considered a satisfactory conclusion for their efforts. Yet, given the club's achievements throughout the previous campaign and the high profile European exploits that had followed, twelfth place was now seen as a considerable disappointment.

Walker had raised the Carrow Road bar to unforeseen heights. The pressure was now very much on Deehan to lift it even higher.

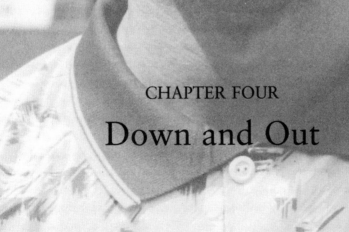

CHAPTER FOUR

Down and Out

The tried and tested gag about some football clubs needing revolving doors was increasingly one that could be applied to the Canaries.

Andy Johnson, scorer of Norwich's sixty-first and final Premier League goal in the 1992/93 season. (*Photo courtesy of Norwich City Football Club*)

One of the many high points of Norwich City's remarkable start to life in the FA Premier League had been the steady rise to fame of striker Chris Sutton. Nottingham-born striker Sutton, the son of former Canary midfielder Mike, had joined the Canaries as a schoolboy, making his youth team debut for the club in a match against Millwall in April 1989 shortly after his sixteenth birthday. A little over two years after that, Sutton made his senior Canary debut against Queens Park Rangers at the tail end of the 1990/91 season, the first of thirty-one league and cup appearances he would make for Dave Stringer, during which time he contributed five goals, three of which came in the club's run to an FA Cup semi-final that season.

At 6 foot 3 inches, Sutton had originally been seen as a centre half, his powerful physique and standout ability in the air making him an obvious candidate for such a role. However, both Stringer and, later on, Mike Walker had seen something more in the way he was able to play the game; an ability to find a pass, make space for both himself and his teammates and to be clearly comfortable with the ball at, or played to, his feet, illustrating that here was a player who would be comfortable in most positions on the pitch but who would, ultimately, excel in an attacking role. Proof positive of that came in one of those FA Cup games, a 3-0 win over Notts County at Carrow Road, which saw Sutton, paired with Robert Fleck in attack, score two goals, a neatly placed shot from close range plus a brave diving header.

Clearly, Chris Sutton was a centre forward who could also do a job in the back four, rather than a centre half who could do a job in attack and, although Mike Walker later played him in the Canaries' defence during the 1992/93 season, those decisions were driven by injury to one of his first-choice centre halves rather than a preference to play him there. Sutton was a natural centre forward and Walker knew it, underlining that fact by electing to start him in the Canaries' opening game of the 1992/93 season at Arsenal in the number nine shirt. He went onto score ten goals for the club during that campaign, making himself, by the start of the following season, an automatic first-team choice in the club's attack, benefitting, and, no doubt, thoroughly enjoying playing alongside the likes of Ruel Fox, Darren Eadie and Efan Ekoku, all of whom possessed, in abundance, the one asset that Sutton didn't possess in his armoury: pace. It certainly paid dividends for Norwich, who still ended a disappointing season having scored a total of sixty-five league goals, thirty-nine of which had come in the club's away games, a total only eventual champions Manchester United exceeded with forty-one. Sutton ended the campaign with a total of twenty-five league goals for the Canaries, a club record in the top flight, which still stands to this day. Thus, with only Andy Cole (thirty-four) and Alan Shearer (thirty-one) scoring more league goals for their clubs that season than Sutton, Norwich's prize asset ended the season as a man who was very much in demand, the resultant transfer speculation that was now surrounding him bothering Robert Chase so much that he felt compelled to make his now famous claim to the Norwich fans that Sutton wasn't for sale and that if he wasn't at the club at the beginning of the following season, then he wouldn't either. A brave statement to make but also a naive one as the Norwich fans easily saw it for the hyperbole that it clearly was, resigned, as they now were, to the fact that he would be on his way later that summer; it was only a question of where he would end up and how much it would cost the buying club to prise him away from Carrow Road.

Sutton certainly had a few options open to him. He ended up entering initial talks with Manchester United, Liverpool, Arsenal, Tottenham, Leeds United, Chelsea, Newcastle, Sheffield Wednesday and Blackburn Rovers, nine suitors in all, of which, two, Arsenal and Blackburn, ended up making definite offers of £5 million to Norwich for him, with Alex Ferguson and Manchester United offering a million pounds less and, in the process, suggesting to Mike Sutton that Chris spent another season at Norwich, something which would have more than suited the Norwich fans and a possibility that might have already been discussed at boardroom level that went onto prompt Chase to make his statement about Sutton not going anywhere that summer. Unfortunately for the Canaries, however, and as much as a move to Old Trafford might have appealed, Sutton's mind was made up: he wanted to move that summer, and, given the choice between Arsenal and Blackburn, opted for the latter with, not unnaturally, the prospect of linking up with Alan Shearer the following season one of the deciding factors in his choice.

Thus, for the second time in three seasons, Norwich City had sold their star player and leading goalscorer in the close season, Robert Fleck having departed Norfolk for Chelsea in the summer of 1992. The Canaries had been fortunate enough to find a quality replacement for Fleck in Mark Robins and would, no doubt, hope to do so again. Unfortunately for them, the fee that Blackburn had paid for Sutton meant that Norwich were now seen as a club that had money to spend, the inevitable consequence of it being that if any club chairman knew it was the Canaries on the other end of the phone, the asking price for any player would automatically be upped by around 25 per cent.

Norwich's preseason arrangements prior to the 1994/95 saw the Canaries tour Holland and Belgium, playing a total of four games in nine days including a return game against Vitesse Arnhem, the team they'd met in the UEFA Cup nine months earlier, Vitesse getting the upper hand on this occasion with a

2-0 win. Victories over Den Bosch (2-1) and Royal Antwerp (2-0) followed before the tour ended with a 0-0 draw against Mechelen. Norwich then beat Peterborough United 2-1 at London Road before accepting an invitation from Progresul Bucureşti in Romania to meet them in a final preseason game, one that Norwich lost 1-0 and a game that they might well have done without, the match and long trip to Romania coming only a week before the season started. Friendly matches of this nature could be financially lucrative, however, and with Norwich still known as the 'plucky' English side that had seen off Bayern Munich on their own patch, Norwich still had a little international allure they could rely upon in such matters, so, even if the game did end in defeat, it did at least mean a bit more money in the bank.

John Deehan had been busy in the transfer market during the summer, with some of the funds raised from the sale of Chris Sutton being put to good use with Jon Newsome turning out to be the most significant of his four purchases, the Leeds centre half arriving for a club record fee of £1 million, becoming, in the process, the first ever Norwich player to cost the club a seven-figure transfer fee. Newsome was joined at Carrow Road by another defender in Sheffield United's Carl Bradshaw (£450,000) and Oldham Athletic midfielder Mike Milligan (£850,000), a competitive trio that would, it was hoped, quell the growing suspicions that, as good as the football that Norwich played was, there was a lack of steel in the side, a tendency for Walker and now Deehan's sides to be too 'nice' in their approach. With two defenders and one midfielder brought in, all that remained for Deehan to do now was to source a replacement for Sutton, not something that would have been easy for either the Norwich manager or whoever he signed as, naturally, the player in question would immediately have been labelled as 'the replacement for Chris Sutton' with all the attendant pressure and expectation that would have brought him. Mark Robins had, at least, the knowledge that, as popular as Robert Fleck, the man he replaced at Norwich, had been, he had never been a prolific goalscorer during his time at the club. A goal maker? Yes. A fiery character liked and respected among his teammates and fans alike? Definitely. But a striker guaranteed to get you twenty plus goals a season? Robins had ended the 1992/93 season with fifteen Premier League goals to his name but that had come from thirty-four starts so it is quite likely he would have topped twenty had he played more games.

He was never going to be a Carrow Road legend in the manner that Fleck had been, but he knew where the goal was – and that was more than enough for the Norwich fans, a demanding group who had been raised on a diet of goal-hungry strikers right back to the 1950s when the likes of Johnny Gavin, Ralph Hunt and Terry Bly had been their goalscoring idols at Norwich.

This rich tradition had continued through the sixties, seventies and into the eighties with names such as Terry Allcock, Ron Davies, Hugh Curren, Ken Foggo, Ted MacDougall, Justin Fashanu and Kevin Drinkell. Even the 'gaffer' himself, John Deehan, had an excellent record as a consistent goalscorer for the Canaries, as his record of seventy goals from 194 senior appearances shows. Whether Robert Fleck and Chris Sutton would be regarded with the same sort of affection in years to come remained to be seen. What was more important is that the Canaries needed another striker before the start of the 1994/95 season, especially as questions were now being raised about Mark Robins' long-term future at the club.

For Robins, the 1993/94 season had been a frustrating one. He'd started it as Mike Walker's first-choice striker and had been named in the starting line-up for the Canaries' opening six Premier League fixtures, yet had, on three of those occasions, been replaced by Efan Ekoku. Furthermore, he'd failed to make the score sheet in each of those six games while Ekoku, ambitious and eager to start matches, had come on in place of Robins in the Canaries' game at Sheffield Wednesday and scored Norwich's second goal in the 3-3 draw. His reward was a starting place in the Canaries' next four games, of which both his and a seasonal highlight would have been the four goals he scored in Norwich's 5-1 win at Everton, a feat that established him, very firmly, in John Deehan's mind as the perfect strike partner for Sutton. Ekoku's place in the side was cemented further when Robins suffered a long-term injury that October, one that was serious enough to keep him out of the side until the following April.

The player Deehan chose to strengthen his attacking options was twenty-two-year-old Mike Sheron, who joined the club from Manchester City for £1 million. It was a signing that, on that great leveller paper at least, looked to be a good one. Sheron had made thirty-eight Premier League appearances for Manchester City during the 1992/93 season, playing against Norwich for them in both fixtures and scoring the Sky Blues' consolation goal in their 2-1 defeat at Carrow Road on 20 February where, in tandem with Niall Quinn, he had been dangerous throughout and had all the makings of a quality player in the years ahead. His ability and potential had already been noted at international level where he had been capped by the England U21 team on sixteen occasions between 1992 and 1993, games that had seen Sheron play alongside Andy Cole and Steve McManaman. He'd scored four goals in that time, including two in an impressive 3-0 win against Holland on 27 April 1993 where, ironically, his strike partner had been Chris Sutton. Sheron had now arrived at Norwich as Sutton's replacement and the pressure on him, as it would have been on any incoming striker at that time, was enormous.

Norwich commenced the 1994/95 season with a disappointing 2-0 defeat at Chelsea, a game and Norwich team that, after 369 appearances for the club, was lacking the classy and reliable Ian Culverhouse at right-back for the Canaries, new signing Bradshaw taking his place. Cully, as he was fondly referred to by teammates and supporters, had fallen foul of both his manager and chairman during negotiations for a new contract to such an extent that, in a rare sign of unity between a Norwich manager and Mr Chase, he was dropped from the first team and pretty much ostracized from all first-team activities. Sadly for Culverhouse and for the club, he hadn't been the first player to have entered negotiations for a new contract with the Canaries only to find the club reluctant to offer him anything like acceptable terms in return for his commitment to the cause. The same thing had happened to David Phillips and would, in time, also bring a sour note to the end of Mark Bowen's time at Carrow Road. Thus, with Bradshaw seen as a cut price and reliable replacement who, in addition, would have been on nothing even close to the money that Culverhouse was on at Norwich, he eventually joined Swindon Town on loan before signing a permanent deal for the club just after Christmas 1994.

Walker had gone, as had Phillips, Fox, Sutton and now Culverhouse. It was becoming clear that things were never going to be quite the same at Carrow Road as, following that opening-day defeat at Chelsea, Deehan had, by the time the two sides met for the return league game at Carrow Road on 10 December, given another six players their senior debuts, a total of eight since the start of the season.

The eight in question were, alongside summer signings Bradshaw, Newsome, Sheron and Milligan, Johnny Wright, Keith O'Neill, Jamie Cureton and Ashley Ward. The first three players had been promoted from the youth ranks plus, in Ward, a new purchase. Ward had been signed from Crewe Alexandra for £300,000 as a replacement for Efan Ekoku, who, after scoring seventeen goals in just forty-five appearances for the Canaries, had been sold to Wimbledon for approximately three times that amount. Ward went onto make a very encouraging start to his Norwich career, scoring twice on his debut as Chelsea were soundly beaten 3-0, Cureton scoring the other goal just twenty seconds after he had come on as a replacement for Mark Robins.

Ward proceeded to follow up his fine start at the club a week later when he scored the only goal in Norwich's 1-0 win at Crystal Palace, a goal made via a wonderful 50-yard run from Darren Eadie, who was now, as supporters had feared, attracting a lot of interest himself from other clubs. The win, Norwich's eighth of the season, was enough to see the Canaries head into the festive period in seventh place, and one of only three clubs in the Premier League still to be unbeaten at home.

Vindication, surely, for the club's underpressure duo of Robert Chase and John Deehan? The increasing amount of criticism that had been directed at the Canaries' chairman had been relentless, despite the club's respectable showing over the first half of the season, pressure that was now, slowly, beginning to be levelled at Deehan as well, seen by some as nothing more than a lackey happy to carry out whatever instructions were demanded of him by Chase. Deehan was, however, very much his own boss who wanted to do things his way and he would have not welcomed the summer sale of Chris Sutton to Blackburn. On the other hand, the £5 million that Norwich had received for Sutton had been put to good use by Deehan, whose summer recruitment looked to be paying off handsomely with Carl Bradshaw and Jon Newsome effortlessly slotting into the Canaries back four, one that had now kept a clean sheet in seven Premier League matches including an almost unheard of run of four consecutive games and seven hours of play elapsing between Paul Furlongs goal for Chelsea in the seventy-fifth minute of the opening defeat at Chelsea and the forty-fifth-minute penalty scored by John Wark for Ipswich a month later.

Newsome was, in particular, looking to be a good signing. He'd come from Leeds United where the ten appearances he'd made for them in the 1991/92 season had earnt him a medal as part of Howard Wilkinson's title-winning squad. He wasn't content, however, to forever act as cover for the club's first-choice defensive partnership of Chris Fairclough and Chris Whyte, especially as, during the following season, his one-time Sheffield Wednesday teammate David Weatherall started to get games ahead of him, so he had more than welcomed the chance to move to Norwich and first-team football. Newsome had slotted straight into the Canaries' starting XI as a replacement for former Captain Ian Butterworth, who'd suffered what turned out to be a career-ending knee injury while waterskiing, an injury severe enough to mean that he didn't feature at all for Norwich during the 1994/95 season. The unfortunate and hugely underrated Butterworth eventually left Carrow Road in November 1995 by accepting a role at non-league Kings Lynn before moving onto play in the US with the Colorado Rapids.

Phillips, Fox, Sutton, Culverhouse and now Butterworth gone with Adams, Bradshaw, Milligan, Newsome, Sheron and Ward in. The tried and tested gag about some football clubs needing revolving doors was increasingly one that could be applied to the Canaries. Yet the club was riding out the storm with no little élan. Seventh in the Premier League and in the quarter finals of the League Cup by Christmas 1994 with, of the new signings, Newsome and Ward particularly impressing.

Then there was the growing presence of the Canaries younger players, determined to make the very best of the opportunities that Deehan was only too willing to give them and match the impact that Darren Eadie had made on the club and English game over the last couple of years. This included Johnny Wright, Keith O'Neill and nineteen-year-old striker Jamie Cureton, an England U18 international of whom great things were expected.

Cureton had made his senior debut for the Canaries in the 3-0 win over Everton on 5 November as a second half replacement for Mark Robins. He went on to make two more relatively low-key appearances from the Norwich bench before doing so again for the third time in four matches against Chelsea on 10 December, the game that saw Ashley Ward score two goals on his Norwich debut. The game is best remembered for Ward's immediate impact at the club with his two well-taken efforts the highlights, but it shouldn't be forgotten that Cureton had again impressed after replacing Robins ten minutes into the second half, scoring with a header just twenty seconds after coming onto the pitch for his first ever senior goal in professional football, one that, at the time of writing, continued up until the end of the 2016/17 season for Farnborough in the Southern League Premier Division for whom he signed a short-term contract in April 2017. Twenty-two years and counting, therefore, since his first goal for the Canaries – impressive stuff by any standards and a tribute to his professionalism and love of the game.

But, of all the fledgling Canaries ready and willing to make their mark at the club during the 1994/95 campaign, it wasn't Jamie Cureton who ended up making the biggest impression. That honour surely belongs to goalkeeper Andy Marshall, whose sudden and unexpected elevation to regular first-team football coincided with a run of results throughout the second half of that campaign that was as disappointing and frustrating as those for the first half of the season had been encouraging.

Marshall had, by the start of the season, superseded Scott Howie as the club's second choice keeper, a tribute to the faith placed in him by Deehan who saw the nineteenth-year-old former trainee as a better bet than the much more experienced Howie, a Scotland U21 international who'd joined the club from Clyde in 1993 and had made the bench in each of City's UEFA Cup games the previous season. Such was Deehan's confidence in Marshall, however, that he opted to let Howie return to Scotland to join Motherwell that October, leaving Marshall as the established number two to Bryan Gunn.

Paul King, a Norwich fan who attended his first match in 1971 and who now estimates he has seen a total of 1,800 Canary matches home and away, took time out to look back at that 1994/95 season for me, the first part of his account below concluding with that unexpected call-up to the Norwich first team for Marshall:

After the euphoria of the previous season – the UEFA cup run, victory at Anfield in last game in front of the Kop and our best away record in the Premier league to date (winning nine and only lost four) – there was plenty of optimism amongst the fans prior to the 1994/95 season, with many people confident, not unreasonably, that the Canaries would further be able to consolidate ourselves as a top-10 Premier League team that campaign.

John Deehan was starting his first season as manager with Gary Megson as his assistant. Chris Sutton had left for Blackburn Rovers and Ian Culverhouse would eventually leave to join Swindon Town. In came our first £1-million signing from Leeds, centre half Jon Newsome plus tough tackling defender Carl Bradshaw from Sheffield United and sought after striker Mike Sheron from Manchester City. With Mark Robins back to fitness and Efan Ekoku upfront, it was exciting times – or so we thought...

Sadly, however, although the first five games produced six points, we only scored one goal, that goal coming courtesy of Mark Robins' winner at home to West Ham in late August. Our next goals came in a strange local derby at Portman Road. The game itself was fairly comfortable and we ran out 2-1 winners thanks to goals from Rob Newman and Carl Bradshaw with John Wark replying for Ipswich. The oddity in that game surrounded the pitch. Quite simply, there was no visible penalty area marked out at the North Stand end. This caused great consternation among the officials (and indeed Sky TV) as both Wark's and Bradshaw's goals were from penalties and the referee had to consult with his linesman to confirm that both fouls were actually in the area. From my point of view, Ipswich's was but to this day I'm still not sure about ours!

This started a run of three wins, one draw and one defeat in our next five games; amongst those teams we beat were Blackburn Rovers, for whom the returning Sutton scored after just four minutes before goals from Mark Bowen and Rob Newman won it for us, plus a superb game and comeback against QPR, which saw us win 4-2. Whilst all this was happening, Efan Ekoku was sold to Wimbledon and he returned the favour by scoring against us in a 1-0 defeat at the end of October.

November brought a return of only five points whilst December started with a very unlucky 1-0 defeat at Old Trafford, which saw ex-Red Devil Mark Robins score for Norwich only for the goal to be ruled out for offside. A week later, Ashley Ward, who'd signed from Crewe as a replacement for Ekoku, someone who would soon become a fans favourite, made his debut against Chelsea and scored twice. At that time, Crewe had a well-deserved reputation for producing quality players, and this proved to be the case with Ward as it would a decade later when we signed Dean Ashton from them.

As with Ashton, the reward for being decisive and signing Ward whilst other clubs stalled was immediate. He was the 'proper', no nonsense centre forward who we'd badly needed since selling Chris Sutton, who following those two debut goals continued by scoring the only goal at Crystal Palace. Things were looking good but, as is often the case with Norwich, a touch of bad luck was just around the corner with the Christmas features turning out to be the seasons pivotal moment. We were drawing 0-0 against Nottingham Forest at the City Ground on December 27th when, after saving a shot from Ian Woan, Bryan Gunn collapsed in obvious pain, bad enough for Stuart Pearce, who was nearby, to immediately call for a stretcher to be brought onto the pitch for him as it was clear, even then, that Gunny had broken his leg. His replacement was debutant Andy Marshall, a former trainee who was just nineteen years old and one of the least experienced players in the entire squad...

John Deehan would not, of course, have even considered naming Andy Marshall as his substitute goalkeeper if he didn't think the teenager was up to the task. It is likely, however, that the selection of Marshall above that of the now departed Scott Howie and, prior to Howie, Mark Walton (who actually played a total of twenty-eight matches as Gunn's understudy in his first spell at the club between 1990 and 1992) was more about the club saving money on players wages. Even if he was 'only' a second-choice goalkeeper, both Walton and Howie would have earnt considerably more than Marshall, the sort of sums that a cash conscious Robert Chase would not have been too eager to pay players who, ideally, hardly ever made a first-team appearance. Marshall was therefore highly regarded as someone who had a lot of potential to go places in the game. That didn't make, however, an unexpected debut in a top-ten clash at Nottingham Forest the ideal way to introduce him to first-team duties, or, for that matter, a back four who were used to playing in front of Gunn but who would now be expected to 'nursemaid' the raw young teenager through his first few games for the club.

To make matters even worse, after just five minutes of the second half and following a Nottingham Forest corner, Marshall came out for the kick, taken by Lars Bohinen, misjudging the flight of the ball as he did so and, along with his back line, had to watch as the ball sailed over him and into the goal to give Forest the lead. The combination of conceding such a soft goal, combined with having to witness the popular Gunn be stretchered off in some pain, was too much for the Norwich players, who never regained their focus for the game as a result, meaning Forest were able to comfortably hold onto their lead and close the match out.

The unfortunate Marshall was, inevitably, the focus of most of the post-match debate. Had, people wondered, Norwich erred in not having a more experienced second-choice goalkeeper to call upon if required? Marshall was an extremely capable young player, something he would go onto prove throughout his senior career, which saw him make over 400 league and cup appearances for several clubs and only calling time on his playing career in 2014 when he was thirty-eight. Yet, here he was, a first-team rookie, still in his teens and barely four months into his first season as a member of the Canaries' first-team squad being expected, with no warning, to cover for Gunn in a vital Premier League match.

But not only that because, in doing so, he would, then and into the remaining matches of that season, be expected to form a quick working relationship with a defence that was used to playing with Gunn, one which, in the unrelenting heat of Premier League football, would have little to no time to bed him in.

Gunn's injury and that subsequent promotion into the first team for Marshall that followed has long been identified as the main reason why the Canaries' respectable start to the 1994/95 campaign (they were comfortably sat in seventh place prior to the Forest game) so rapidly and irrevocably fell apart during the second half of that season and ultimately ended in relegation. But here's a question: is that assumption cum accusation fair on Marshall or is there a bigger picture to take into consideration when considering the Canaries' spectacular fall from top-flight grace that season? In order to try and see if that was, as I believe, the case, I spoke to Norwich's captain and record signing, Jon Newsome, who was only too pleased to talk to me about that time and his career in Norwich as a whole.

I started by asking Jon if he'd been surprised at getting the opportunity of a move to Norwich when he was, at the time, building up his career at Leeds United where he won a First Division Championship medal less than three years earlier.

I was at a stage in my career when I wanted to play regular first team football and, to be fair, it wasn't really happening for me at Leeds where I was still in and out of the side along with another centre half, David Weatherall. We'd both been part of a very good youth team set up at Sheffield Wednesday, so we knew Howard Wilkinson from his time as manager there and ended up being two of his first signings for Leeds. I was very keen to establish myself there as we had a great side with some good players in it like Gordon Strachan, Gary Speed and, for a while, Eric Cantona. I knew Howard was after some more players as well, players who he'd obviously want to have in his first team. Carlton Palmer was one of them, although he joined the club after I'd signed for Norwich. So that was pretty much it for me at Leeds really, there had been some talk that summer that Norwich were interested in me and, although it went a bit quiet after the initial speculation, Norwich came in for me again once Palmer had arrived and I was more than happy to travel down to Norfolk to talk to them.

Why? It was an easy decision. Norwich were one of the up and coming Premier League sides at the time, they'd also had that good run in Europe and, for a while, everyone was talking about them and their players. Plus I wanted to play and when I met John Deehan, he made it clear that I would not only be playing every week but that they'd want to appoint me as the club's new captain. It helped, I suppose, that Gary Megson was at Norwich at the time; I'd known him when he was at Sheffield Wednesday and he had some good things to say about the club and area. Norwich really made me feel wanted. I was given the red carpet treatment as soon as I arrived at the club, the chairman (Robert Chase) was very accommodating with me and everyone there was very confident about the coming season and the role I'd be playing and, in the end, I was delighted to sign for them.

I was also impressed about the plans the club had for the future. They didn't want to rest on their laurels and live off what they'd accomplished over the past couple of years, they wanted to push on. There were big plans in the offing for the new training complex at Colney and at the time I signed, Norwich had one of the best young players in England in Chris Sutton, although I'd been advised that I wouldn't have the chance to play alongside Chris as he was due to be sold, which was a bit of a disappointment. But, regardless of that, I was still really happy to be in Norwich. Being a Sheffield lad, it was a bit of a novelty for me to living so near to the coastline! I initially bought a place in Thorpe St Andrew before settling down in Eaton, which was handy as it was very close to the training ground. We settled really quickly as well as everyone had gone out of their way to make us feel welcome, everyone at the club, naturally, but also all of our neighbours.

What were your first impressions of your new teammates?

When you're playing the game you inevitably get a bit of a pre-conceived idea about other players, either by playing with or against them, or training alongside them for your club. So I had a few ideas about my new teammates and what they'd be like at the time. However, as soon as I started training with Norwich, those early impressions went up quite a bit, they seemed different players from what I had seen and been used to, there was a lot of quality in the squad. And it was a very friendly one. Right from the off they all made me feel very welcome. We'd all socialise together after games, there was an enormous players lounge at Carrow Road so we'd all be in there after a match, and, as each of us would get about ten tickets each for friends and family, it would usually be full and we'd all stay behind for about two hours, something that was made easier as there was a crèche provided for the kids. One of my best mates at the club was John Polston, we did a lot together including doing a car share for getting into training.

You know that John now runs a series of fitness camps in the Reading area?

Yes, I'd heard about his boot camps. It's quite funny that, as John was never the best of trainers. In training we used to have an old orange vest that the worse trainer had to wear, and more often than not, it would be John that ended up wearing it.

But that was all part of the relaxed attitude at the club. There was a lot of pressure and expectation placed on the players at Leeds, so much so that Howard Wilkinson ended up taking down all the pictures of that great side of the '60's and '70's that were hanging up everywhere. It was nothing like that at Norwich, the club went about everything in the right way and that translated onto the pitch where we were relaxed and felt confident enough to play our own game and let the opposition worry about us.

It helped, strangely enough, that Norwich was such an isolated place. This meant we didn't really have much of a choice other than to do a lot of things together as a squad and that helped form a very strong bond between all of the players. We enjoyed each other's company and that showed in training and on the pitch.

And we all wanted to play! I missed a game early on in that 1994/95 season (against Aston Villa) as I'd snapped some little bones at the base of my spine. John Deehan was, however, eager to get me back in the side as soon as possible, it was a game against QPR and he was at me, saying, 'you've got to play, you're the only player we've got who'll be able to cope against so-and-so (probably Les Ferdinand, who missed the game anyway!) in their side'. So I played and that wasn't a problem, when your manager makes you feel that wanted and important, you're going to play, injury or not.

You wouldn't have joined the club expecting your first season at Norwich to culminate in relegation. Looking back at that time, the popular consensus is that Bryan Gunn's season-ending injury was the catalyst for the run of poor results that eventually saw Norwich go down, looking back, is it really as simple as that?

Yes, Gunny's injury did play a big part in our poor second half of the season. He was a quality goalkeeper, no doubt about that, the sort of goalkeeper that a defence loves to play in front of. He had hardly any weaknesses in his game and that gave us an enormous amount of confidence in him. He was very vocal, he came off his line to take crosses, and he was good with the ball at his feet, everything you wanted from your goalkeeper at a top club.

Marsh, to be fair, struggled at first. He wasn't very good with the ball at his feet and his kicking wasn't as good as Gunny's. Plus, of course, he wasn't used to playing with us and neither were we with him. And he was never going to be as vocal as Gunny, if anything, he needed us to be talking to him, not the other way around. So yes, we had less confidence in him as a goalkeeper than we did with Gunny, but that's hardly surprising, he was a young player who was still finding his way in the game, it would have been the same with anyone who came in as Gunny's replacement. John Deehan brought in Simon Tracey on loan from Sheffield United to give Marsh a bit of a break but that never worked out and Marsh was soon back in the side.

But, as big a part as that injury played, you can't pin it down as the determining factor in our relegation. We'd started that season with Mark Robins and Efan Ekoku in attack, two very good forwards who'll get a decent amount of goals for you. Yet, as the season progressed, both were sold and, apart from Ashley Ward and Mike Sheron, we had to rely on two more young players, Jamie Cureton and Ade Akinbiyi to get amongst the goals whenever they were called upon. It was as difficult for them as it was for Marsh. They'd come into a side that had previously had Mark and Efan in it, and, before them, Chris Sutton. That's a lot of expectation to place on a young player's shoulders and, as we began to struggle to win games, you could see that they were finding it difficult.

John Deehan resigned after we lost 3-0 at Newcastle and Gary Megson was appointed as caretaker manager. What were your thoughts on that appointment, coming at a crucial time with only five games left to play?

I had a lot of time and respect for Gary, he was, like me, a northern lad and we pretty much sang from the same hymn sheet. He was a no nonsense type character and he came across that way as a manager as well as being a quality player. Meggy gave it everything but it wasn't enough to save us from going down and he left the club at the end of the season with Martin O'Neill, who'd done so well at Wycombe, coming in as the club's new manager. I found Martin a real up and down character. One minute he'd be telling you that you were the best player in your position in the country, good enough to play in a World Cup and all that, out would come the wine and we'd all have a drink together with Martin extolling our virtues.

Then we might suffer an unlucky defeat and it was like the end of the world as far as Martin was concerned. He'd give you a lot of stick and get on your back a bit and, from that point of view, he was a real 'old school' type manager, an arm around your shoulder one moment, a bollocking the next, But, for all that, we got on well enough.

Norwich started that season well enough but the club's financial difficulties were soon going to become apparent and, as one of the more high-profile players at Carrow Road, there was always going to be speculation about your future.

Yes, and it started when Martin was still the club's manager and not long after he'd been appointed. He called me into his office as there had been some talk that Aston Villa were interested in signing me. His question to me that summer was to the point: do you want to stay at Norwich? I had no hesitation in answering yes, I had been part of a side that had gone down and wanted to play my part in getting us back up to the Premier League at the first attempt. So I stayed and we started the season, under Martin, reasonably well. There was constant talk of other clubs being interested in me as the season progressed but nothing that concrete and it didn't worry me too much as I still wanted to stay.

Then Martin left the club and Gary Megson came back, this time as full-time manager. The rumours about me moving didn't go away and, eventually, I was notified by the club that Sheffield Wednesday had made a bid for me and that it had been accepted. It was on my day off and I'd been preparing to spend it with a friend but, of course, all that changed and I went into the club to have a meeting with Robert Chase about it. He played hardball, the club needed the money and, as part of that, he wanted to pay me as little of the loyalty bonus that I was due as possible. Meggy was not happy about it but admitted that the club had no choice, the finances were in a mess and they had to let me go. I wasn't the only one as Ashley Ward left at the same time, the club badly needed the money and we were considered two of its best assets. It helped that I was going back to Sheffield to play for the club that I'd initially left in order to join Leeds as I am a Sheffield lad and that will always be home. Despite that, I have, and will always have, a very soft spot for Norwich and Norfolk, I enjoy going down there whenever the opportunity arises and my daughter is, of course, a Norfolk girl as she was born whilst I was at Norwich.

A thoroughly enjoyable part of my career spent playing for a special club where I played the best football of my career.

Despite Jon and his Norwich teammates' best efforts, the Canaries endured an appalling run of form following that defeat at Nottingham Forest. With Gunn ruled out for the rest of the season, Andy Marshall took his place in goal for their following match, a 2-1 win over Newcastle at Carrow Road, the three points secured through goals from Neil Adams and Ashley Ward with both strikes from the Norwich new boys coming in the opening ten minutes. Marshall's performance was good enough to draw post-match praise from Magpies manager Kevin Keegan while, in front of Marshall, the Canaries' own version of 'Captain Courageous' in Newsome played for the whole ninety minutes despite having a broken nose.

A win and performance that was hardly indicative of the dreadful run of results that was to follow. Yet that match, played on New Year's Eve 1994, was Norwich's penultimate Premier League success of that season as, in the twenty league games that followed, the Canaries contrived to lose twelve of them, ending the season two points adrift of Crystal Palace in twentieth place and relegated, a depressing end to a briefly promising campaign, which Paul King continues to reflect upon below:

Andy Marshall later became the Norwich No. 1, but undoubtedly had the game of his career on New Year's Eve when his heroics kept out a Newcastle front line of Beardsley, Peacock and Fox, which resulted in a 2-1 win for Norwich. It was fairly evident despite his heroics that more experienced cover was needed and this was provided, so we thought, in the loan signing from Sheffield United of Simon Tracey. Unfortunately it was a complete disaster including gifting Dion Dublin a goal for Coventry and in his next match, also against Coventry in the F.A. Cup, the biggest cheer was when he was stretchered off. Tracey never played for us again.

In early February after a home draw against Southampton, it suddenly dawned that we were drawing a lot but not winning many of our league games. This was mainly down to the good cup runs we were having in both cup competitions with five of those games squeezed into little over a month in the new year as well as four league games in the same period, nine matches in all during that period. In the League Cup we reached the quarter-finals before losing at eventual finalists Bolton Wanderers whilst in the F.A. Cup we got to the 5th round before going out at Everton. By the time March came it was clear we were going to be in a relegation fight. We were 2-0 up at West Ham before having Rob Ullathorne sent off in a case of mistaken identity with Spencer Prior, which gave the Hammers the confidence to fight back and rescue a point in a 2-2 draw, whilst, four days after that, we lost 2-0 to QPR meaning we'd taken just nine points from a possible total of 42 with a visit from Ipswich to come on the following Monday night that would be covered by Sky Sports, who would, undoubtedly, relish the label of 'East Anglia's relegation six pointer' that they would attach to it, given that Ipswich were in even worse trouble than us at the time.

Fortunately we looked very comfortable in our 3-0 win in a game that saw John Wark sent off for taking out Darren Eadie, who was one of the scorers in that win, Jamie Cureton and Ashley Ward getting the others. Room for optimism, therefore, with three consecutive away games coming up, including one at Highbury against an Arsenal side who were, prior to kick-off, only five points adrift of us themselves, despite having some big name players like Tony Adams, Ian Wright and Paul Merson to call upon. They saw us off 5-1 on April Fool's Day with their first two goals coming in the opening six minutes, one of them from Lee Dixon. We were able to recall Gary Megson for the game at Leicester that followed, he pretty much ran the show from midfield but it wasn't enough as we lost 1-0 with all the talk following the game focused on whether or not John Deehan would still be in charge by the time we went up to St James Park to play Newcastle three days later. That talk wasn't so far out. We lost 3-0 and Deehan resigned immediately. afterwards. Gary Megson was duly appointed as caretaker manager for the rest of the season with another on loan goalkeeper, Andy Rhodes, who'd joined us from St Johnstone, stepped up as his assistant.

Unfortunately, there was to be no 'new manager bounce' with Megson as we lost our first game with him in charge to Nottingham Forest, which was followed up by a 1-0 defeat at Tottenham for whom Teddy Sheringham scored. That result saw us drop into 20th place and was the cue for more very loud protests against Robert Chase to kick-off, notably so prior to and during the match at home to Liverpool on April 29th. Chase had countered this by placing speakers in strategic places around the pitch pre-match under the guise that the loud rock music that they played out would motivate the crowd to get behind the team. We'd be doing that all season however and knew that the real reason for their presence was to drown out the protests that were being directed at him from all areas of the ground, the Norwich fans now completely fed up and disillusioned by his apparent lack of concern at the situation we were now in. It led to a terrible atmosphere and another defeat, Liverpool winning 2-1 with Ian Rush scoring the winner with just over five minutes to go.

Yet, even now, after a sixth consecutive league defeat, all was not lost. We had to go to Leeds for our penultimate game knowing that, if we managed to get a win there, we'd be in with more than a chance of saving ourselves at home to Aston Villa in our final game. We started well and began to play as we knew the team could, taking a first half lead through Ashley Ward and looked good until the 79th minute when Jon Newsome was very harshly penalised for what looked like a perfectly timed challenge on Tony Yeboah, who'd clearly dived as was made very apparent on the consequent TV footage. Gary McAllister scored from the resultant penalty and we went to pieces, losing the game in the last minute when Carlton Palmer scored the winner. The final whistle went to a chorus of boos and jeers from the Norwich fans, all aimed at Chase, whilst the players all slumped to the ground unable, it seemed, to be able to take in what had happened at the end of a season that had, at one point, seen us go to as high as sixth place in the Premier League. The season ended with a half-hearted 1-1 draw against Aston Villa at a very subdued Carrow Road and we all went home wondering what the summer would bring...

Paul's pessimism at the end of that depressing season is well placed. Norwich had, in the space of three seasons, gone from finishing third in the Premier League and winning plaudits both at home and throughout Europe for their performances in the 1993/94 UEFA Cup competition to dropping out of the Premier League, manager-less and, it seemed, now penniless, after winning just two games in the second half of the 1994/95 season while, steadily but inexorably, losing many of the players that had played such a big part in their initial success, including David Phillips, Chris Sutton, Ruel Fox, Mark Robins and Efan Ekoku. For anyone looking for even the slightest glimmer of a silver lining among all the gloom and doom around Carrow Road there was none to be seen. There had been desperate times at the club before yet, even then, there seemed something to hold onto, a glimmer of hope. But not this time.

The normally intransigent Chase was now under tremendous pressure from the club's fan base. Calls for his resignation had been resolutely ignored, the embattled chairman now determined to turn things around in order that, when the time did come for him to finally leave the club, it would be on his terms rather than those of the club's support. His first task in the summer of 1995 would have been to appoint a new manager, the club's fifth in four years after Gary Megson had departed in the wake of the Canaries relegation. As was usually the case, speculation as to who the new man in charge at Carrow Road would be was rife with several names being mentioned as possible contenders, one of whom was, intriguingly, former boss Mike Walker, who'd left Everton the previous November. Given that Chase was still at the club, however, the notion, no matter how attractive, seemed fanciful at best and it is almost certain that he would not have entertained a return at that time in much the same way as Chase would not have offered him his old job back.

A non-starter then. But there were plenty of other possibilities, so many in fact that, according to Chase, the club received around fifty applications and enquiries from interested parties during the early part of that summer. The list might have included Danny Wilson, David Webb or Mick Wadsworth, all of whom were impressing at Barnsley, Brentford and Carlisle, respectively, while in Scotland, Alex Miller was doing exceptionally well at Hibernian. Then there was ex-Canary Steve Bruce.

He'd just completed his eighth season at Manchester United, making a total of thirty-five Premier League appearances during that campaign but he was fast approaching his thirty-fifth birthday and was known to be wanting to eventually move into a managerial position. His name would almost certainly have been raised at some point during the Canaries boardroom sessions that summer as a possible player manager, a former club icon who the fans would almost certainly rally around. Finally, there was Jimmy Nicholl, the initial front runner and red-hot favourite for the job, so much so that Norwich fans had almost accepted his appointment as a fait accompli that was just awaiting the formal dotting of i's and crossing of t's before Nicholl, bedecked with a large yellow-and-green scarf, appeared on the Carrow Road pitch alongside a smiling Chase.

Nicholl's elevation to overwhelming favourite for the Norwich job was certainly not one that came, as more recent managerial appointments at Carrow Road have been, a left-field one. After making nearly 200 league starts for Manchester United from 1974 to 1982, he'd had playing spells at a number of other top clubs including Sunderland, West Bromwich Albion and Rangers before being appointed as player manager of Raith Rovers in 1990 where he enjoyed some notable successes, including guiding the team to the 1994/95 Scottish First Division Championship and Scottish League Cup, a notable double by any standards. It was widely expected, therefore, that he would now accept a new challenge at Norwich, regardless of the fact that he had a UEFA Cup campaign to plan for in the 1995/96 campaign with Raith, something that might just have tipped the balance, as far as he was concerned, in staying put. In any case, the much expected approach from Chase to Raith never took place as, with his normal single-minded determination, the Norwich supremo, who'd been very much swayed in his thinking by vice-chairman Jimmy Jones, had only one man in mind for the job that laid ahead, and that involved Martin O'Neill, then manager of Wycombe Wanderers.

O'Neill was, like Bruce, a former Norwich player who'd enjoyed two separate spells at Carrow Road, inspiring the Canaries to an unlikely promotion during the second one, which took in fifty-five league appearances from February 1982 to August 1983, becoming, in that time, the first Norwich City player to appear in the final stages of a World Cup when he played for, and captained, Northern Ireland during the 1982 finals in Spain. He had subsequent spells with Notts County, Chesterfield and Fulham before moving into his first managerial position with non-league Grantham Town in 1987. He took over at Shepshed Charterhouse in 1989 before being appointed as Wycombe Wanderers manager a year later.

O'Neill was an ambitious young manager who identified with the level of ambition that Wycombe chairman Ivor Beeks had for a club that had little to no football history or tradition. Beeks had played a huge part in getting the club relocated to a new stadium 2 miles west of the town centre with a capacity of 6,000, a move made with full-time football very much on the agenda as part of the club's future. Wycombe finished sixth in O'Neill's first season in charge before ending the 1991/92 campaign as runners up to eventual champions Colchester United. They were eventually promoted at the end of the 1992/93 season, following that up with a second consecutive promotion via the Division Three play-offs at the end of the 1993/94 season with a 4-2 win over Preston North End at Wembley. They nearly went up again at the end of the season after that, just missing out on the Division Two play-offs and finishing that campaign in seventh place just three points adrift of Huddersfield Town.

O'Neill, who had also led the club to two FA Trophy wins during his time at Adams Park, found out about the Canaries interest in him after Robert Chase made a telephone call to the club with the intention of speaking to Beeks. However, with Beeks away on holiday in Portugal, Chase found himself talking to Wycombe director Graham Peart, who gave the Canaries permission to speak to O'Neill about the managerial vacancy at Carrow Road, much, you tend to believe, against Chase's initial expectations. O'Neill, who was also on holiday, nevertheless took time out to contact Chase and agreed to meet him at Heathrow Airport upon his return to London on

7 June 1995 where he more or less immediately accepted the offer that was made to him by Chase, all of this happening while Beeks was still on holiday and unable to speak with his manager.

However, it seemed that most of the Wycombe hierarchy had pretty much accepted at the end of that season that O'Neill would now be on his way, with Beeks later admitting to the local press that O'Neill's departure was 'a disappointment initially because we had seen off Leicester and Nottingham Forest but now we had to deal with Norwich and that was too much of a mountain for us to climb'.

One of the reasons that O'Neill gave for his decision to accept the Norwich offer was the financial constraints he was regularly confronted with at the club, something he would soon discover would equally impede his desire for progress at Carrow Road. But that was yet to come as he arrived at the club full of the spark and vigour that went on to characterise his long and successful spell in the game as a manager, although, as Canaries midfielder Jeremy Goss recalled in his autobiography (*Gossy*, Amberley Publishing, 2014), first impressions of the new man in charge were not always favourable:

It was whilst I was out on one of my pre-preseason training runs that I felt something go in my leg – if you want to be technical, it was my soleus muscle, which is at the back of the calf. Ping and gone. Not good. I arranged to meet up with Tim Sheppard at the club's new training complex at Colney, and, before long, I was laid out on one of the physio's benches with Tim working away on that muscle for me. We're chatting away, and, naturally enough, the subject of the new manager comes up.

'As a matter of fact' said Tim as we talked, 'I think Martin's in here today.'

Right on cue, Martin O'Neill walks into the room. Were his ears burning? I don't know. But I'm pleased to see him and offer him my hand, awkward as it is to do so, as I'm laying, face down, on this bench. But I'm sure he'll appreciate the gesture.

'Gaffer, congratulations. Welcome to the football club. What a fantastic appointment, I'm sure you're going to do some really great things with us. It's good to see you here.'

All this time I'm laying there, arm outstretched, waiting for him to shake my hand. He knows who I am after all – it wasn't that long ago that he'd praised me after we'd beaten his Wycombe side in the FA Cup. But he doesn't shake my hand, he just stands, looks at me and starts shaking his head. I could swear he might even have been tutting as he was doing so.

'Gossy, Gossy, Gossy. What the f*** have you done, why are you here, before preseason, getting treatment?'

'Gaffer, I was out on a run, I always train throughout the summer – just felt a little tightness in my calf so Tim's just giving it a once over, nothing serious.'

'You train throughout the summer? Well now, that's a nightmare isn't it? Anyway. We'll have to wait and see what happens with you Gossy, we'll have to wait and see.'

I'm a bit shocked at all this. There's no 'hello' back, no handshake, no banter. And it gets worse. He then walks over to where the front of the couch is and puts his hands on my head before rubbing and roughing up my hair, making a right mess of it. And I have to say, I was, and remain, sensitive to people touching me around my head, my face and hair. I don't like it. Yet here he is, standing there, playing with my curly barnet as I'm laying there on the couch.

And it was a big old curly mop back then! The fans were great with it, they used to get curly wigs and wear them at games, a wonderful, even humbling thing to do. I loved that. But I don't love being prone here whilst the new gaffer plays with it. It's embarrassing for a start. Tim is there, I also think there was a young lad near-by getting treatment as well.

And then the new gaffer walks out. Not another word. I'm now trying to put all my hair back in place because it looks like a force 10 gale has blown through it, talking to Tim as I do so.

'Bloody hell Tim, that was a strange thing to do. What was all that about?' Tim, lovely bloke, can't answer that. So he carries on treating my calf. In silence.

Fortunately for Chase, who had been reeling under constant demands from the club's support for him to quit his position, the appointment of O'Neill came as something of a masterstroke, which, even if it didn't put him back on a positive footing with Canaries fans, certainly gave them something else to talk about, be excited and look forward to. His first full day in charge at Carrow Road was on 13 June 1995, a month before Norwich's preseason plans began in earnest with a five-game tour in his native Northern Ireland followed by a trip to the west country, two modest trips indeed in comparison to those made in previous summers, which had included trips to the USA, Kenya and the Caribbean.

The club, in retrospect, were already cutting their coat according to the very modest financial cloth that they now had, one that had been seriously depleted by the £200,000 that was now payable to Wycombe as compensation for O'Neill. He had, however, been promised further funds to allow him to strengthen his squad by the chairman, a statement that former Norwich manager John Deehan advised needed to be to be treated with caution, adding that he fully expected O'Neill to find it difficult to get the funding he clearly needed, regardless of any promises that had been made to the contrary. There was, however, one summer arrival, namely West Ham midfielder Matthew Rush, who arrived for a fee of around £350,000 just after the start of the season. Other than that, however, it was very much a case of 'as you were' at Carrow Road with O'Neill seemingly content to fully evaluate the squad he had inherited before making any changes that he deemed necessary.

There was, however, one other new face to be seen in the Canaries line up for their opening league game in Division One, that of nineteen-year-old right-back Danny Mills, who'd worked his way up the playing ranks at Carrow Road from schoolboy level and from whom big things were expected. Mills proceeded to have a quietly impressive debut, marred only in part when he hauled down the Hatters' Bontcho Guentchev early in the second half, giving away a penalty in the process that Guentchev was only too happy to convert. It was a goal that briefly gave Luton some hope of getting a result; they'd been a goal down thanks to a strike from Jon Newsome and been largely outplayed with it. Fortunately for Norwich, Newsome, leading by example, had other ideas and regained the lead for Norwich two minutes later before, with sixty-nine minutes gone, a 25-yard strike from Neil Adams sealed the win for the visitors in what had been a consummate and very promising display by Martin O'Neill's new charges.

It seemed, even at this early stage, that the preseason optimism generated by O'Neill's appointment seemed justified. The new man at the helm had fashioned together a side that had pace in abundance as well as, in Mike Milligan and Ade Akinbiyi, no little physical presence, qualities as essential for any side wanting to get out of the second flight of English football as they are today. Thus, with O'Neill still expected to be provided additional funds if required, the Norwich fans prepared to sit back and enjoy the ride. But would they? Paul King now looks back at the first half of that season from a fans perspective:

After the disappointment of the previous season's relegation there was still an air of discontent around Carrow Road. Season ticket sales and attendances were down, confidence in chairman Robert Chase was at an all-time low, as was shown later in the season by the post-match demonstrations and to counter act this a new supporters group, The Independent Supporters Group, was set up to try and get change at the football club.

It was imperative that the club got the right man in as manager and this definitely seemed to be the case when it was announced that former fan favourite Martin O'Neill, along with former City defender Steve Walford, Paul Franklin and one-time Nottingham Forest winger John Robertson would be the new management team.

O'Neill had initially been signed by Ken Brown to try and help to fight off relegation at the end of the 1980/81 season, with a view that if we were relegated then he would be allowed to leave. Sadly we were and although it was clear he didn't want to go, John Bond signed him for Manchester City. It was fairly evident that he wasn't happy there and in February 1982 it was announced that he had returned.

For supporters of a certain vintage this will bring about memories of that amazing end of season run where we went from 13ᵗʰ to 3ʳᵈ and clinched promotion on the last day of the season at Sheffield Wednesday. For those supporters too young to remember him playing, think of a combination of Wes and Hucks and that was Martin O'Neill. Ironically when he first signed, Steve Walford was signed on the same day, the two of them forming an immediate friendship that has endured, professionally and personally, to this day.

O'Neill's appointment had engendered plenty of optimism amongst the support that we'd be able to mount a serious promotion challenge and return to the Premier League at the first attempt. Unfortunately, this misguided faith that we'd go straight back up again turned to over confidence when hoards of T-shirts bearing the message 'On loan to the Endsleigh' appeared and they sold in their hundreds. By the time the players ran out first game of the 1995/96 season on a sunny Sunday afternoon in Luton everyone thought this was the case and that promotion would be a formality, a belief that was backed up by an excellent performance by a new look, attacking and very vibrant Norwich side that beat Luton 3-1, courtesy of two goals from Neil Adams and one from Jon Newsome.

That initial optimism was briefly tempered by a 0-0 draw at home to Sunderland that was followed by a 3-1 defeat at Birmingham, a game that I, and many others, will remember as, due to some strange fixture scheduling by the Football League, Ipswich were playing at West Brom on the same day, their locality in the immediate vicinity providing much 'fun' on the A14 and at all the services stations en route.

Following a 2-1 midweek victory over Oldham, it was announced that Robert Fleck had returned, initially on loan but with a view to being signed permanently. Fleckie wasted no time at all bolstering our attack and quickly made his mark, scoring our second goal in a 2-1 win over Port Vale.

We then had two away games that would prove memorable for different reasons.

Firstly a 2-1 defeat at Sheffield United that I'll never forget as it featured, for me, one of the worse refereeing performances I'd ever seen. Ashley Ward had put us 1-0 up and we were coasting. However, due to some very strange decisions from the referee, United were steadily getting back into the game and this culminated in injury time at the end of the first half when they equalised through a goal from Nathan Blake that was clearly offside, a contentious decision that resulted in our players confronting the referee as the teams left the field at half time, the culmination of which saw Bryan Gunn given the red card for apparent dissent! This meant Rob Newman had to go in goal for the whole of the second half, with Fleckie, who'd come off for Ade Akinbiyi, later red carded from his place on the bench.

The following Wednesday we went to Wolves, which was never the friendliest of grounds to visit as it proved after the game. Match wise, it had been great as goals from Andy Johnson and Ashley Ward saw us get our first ever victory over them at Molineux.

Things started to boil over near the end after Steve Bull was sent off for headbutting Ward in an off the ball incident, a decision that enraged the Wolves support. Needless to say, they took their frustrations out on us and several coach loads of Norwich fans had a cold trip home as quite a few windows were smashed afterwards.

A draw against Millwall and 6-1 first leg League Cup victory over Torquay followed and then it was Grimsby away.

It was a lovely sunny September morning when three Club Canary coaches left for Cleethorpes but only one arrived on time, the coach I was on. We'd already noticed we were two coaches short by the time we got to Sutton Bridge but, in the era before mobile phones, we had to wait until we'd arrived before we found out that the other two coaches had crashed near the Garden Centre at Necton. It later transpired the first coach stopped behind a car waiting to turn right and the back coach went into the back of the front one. Luckily no one was seriously hurt and both coaches arrived just in time for kick-off to witness an exciting game that ended in a 2-2 draw that saw Darren Eadie sent off.

Norwich were now, slowly but surely, starting to get the season on track and in one home game in October at Barnsley a future City player was in the opposition team. Former Liverpool player Jan Molby was in the Barnsley midfield that afternoon. Molby had such a large girth it was rumoured that the shirts he wore on the pitch had to be made by sewing two normal ones together! We won the game 3-1 but Molby ran the show from midfield to such an extent that, soon after his loan stint with them was finished, we signed him ourselves and he went onto make five appearances, scoring a wonderful goal direct from a free-kick in a League Cup match at Birmingham in what turned out to be his last game for us.

In November there were rumblings that something was going on behind the scenes and in the League Cup replay at Bradford it was rumoured that Martin O'Neill had resigned. The game itself was, for me, a reason why replays shouldn't have been abolished. The first game was a boring 0-0 draw but this was an absolute classic. City went in at half time 2-1 up having been 1-0 down and then the fun began. In an all action end to end attacking second half with the Bradford keeper having probably the game of his career, Bradford went 3-2 up. Norwich piled on the pressure but looked like being kept out. Then in the dying minutes a clear penalty on Darren Eadie was turned down. That was it or so we thought. Man of the Match was then announced as the Bradford keeper and all of a sudden, deep into stoppage time, we were awarded a very tame penalty. The view at the time was that the referee knew he had got it wrong and made amends. Ashley Ward duly slotted it away and extra time loomed. It took Norwich 20 seconds from kick-off to take the lead and from then on only one team were going onto win, which we did 5-3. If that had been on Sky would probably still be being shown.

After a 1-0 win over Crystal Palace on 11 November, we readied ourselves for the visit of rivals Ipswich Town a week later in a game that seemed cut and dried when Robert Fleck put us 2-0 up in the 72nd minute. But it was not to be that simple. John Wark made it 2-1 from the spot and then, with only two minutes left, Alex Mathie tumbled over dramatically enough to make up referee Kevin Lynch's mind for him and he duly awarded them another penalty, much to the annoyance of all the Norwich players, who very vociferously demanded he speak to his linesman, something which is usually a pointless effort as refs never change their mind and, in this instance, the ball was already on the spot with Wark ready to take it. Much to our collective surprise, he listened to the protests and reversed his decision, claiming that Mathie had been offside.

To say Ipswich players, management and fans weren't happy is possibly an understatement.

But the result stood with the win consolidating our position of sixth in the table, a handily placed one on the run up to the Christmas and New Year fixtures.

We followed this up with a couple of good away wins at West Brom and Watford but, despite the win at Vicarage Road taking us up to second place in the table, it was still very obvious that all was still not well behind the scenes. Martin O'Neill had long wanted to strengthen the club's attack with Dean Windass, then at Hull City, his prime target and available, we were led to believe, for around £600,000. O'Neill worked hard on the deal and eventually persuaded Windass to join Norwich with the fee agreed before, quite unexpectedly, the transfer was cancelled with Robert Chase apparently claiming that Hull had reneged on the deal and wanted more money, a claim which, it is claimed, was proven wrong when O'Neill was shown a fax confirming that the Tigers were happy with the initial amount of money involved. He then went to see Robert Chase who supposedly told him that the club couldn't even afford to pay the initial £600,000 agreed and that the club had absolutely no money to spend on incoming transfers.

Matters finally came to a head on December 17th at Leicester. As we were getting off the coaches, a rumour flew around the ground that O'Neill had resigned. As the game was being shown live on ITV, we all went round to the main entrance to find out if this was indeed the case, hoping that it wasn't but soon discovering that it was and that Steve Walford and Paul Franklin would be in charge for the match, one that saw us go 2-0 up only to lose 3-2, with the Leicester winner being scored, ironically, by a certain Iwan Roberts.

I bumped into Martin O'Neill a few years later at an away game and had a chat with him. He admitted that he knew as soon as he had resigned that he had made a mistake and did everything he could to persuade Robert Chase that he wanted to stay in charge but the chairman would hear of it and that was that, Martin O'Neill's brief time at our club was at an end. It was one which had brought some very entertaining football with O'Neill admitting that, on occasion, Norwich could be too entertaining, saying, 'We could be 4-1 up against someone and still expect a draw'.

Walford and Franklin stayed in charge for a League Cup fourth round replay win over Bolton before leaving the club and rejoining O'Neill in his new job as manager of Leicester City. As for the new man in charge at Norwich, we didn't have that much time to speculate who it might be as Gary Megson was reappointed, this time on a permanent basis, in time for the match against Portsmouth at Fratton Park on December 23rd, a game we lost 1-0. It was pouring with rain when he came out for the first time but we ignored that to cheer him and sing his name.

But he chose to ignore us.

Martin O'Neill's sudden resignation as Norwich manager prior to that vital league game at Leicester City on 17 December was prompted by weeks of growing disharmony between him and Robert Chase with O'Neill particularly aggrieved at Chase's refusal to provide him with sufficient funds to sign Dean Windass from Hull City. His letter of resignation, which was given to Robert Chase on the morning of the Leicester game, was immediately rejected out of hand by Chase, who, nonetheless, would have known that rejection to have been nothing more than a symbolic one, well used and acquainted, as he would have been by then, by O'Neill's stubborn streak.

Did O'Neill quit only, as Paul King writes, to later regret that decision and tell the chairman that he had changed his mind and wanted to stay in charge at Norwich? As characters go, O'Neill's was strong but he had, on this occasion, met his match in Robert Chase, a self-made man who didn't take fools gladly and would have regarded O'Neill's wish as a betrayal of the faith he had put in him as well as the funds that O'Neill had already been given – £350,000 for Matthew Rush and £650,000 on Robert Fleck, who'd rejoined the club on a permanent basis after initially joining on loan from Chelsea. That made a total outlay of £1 million on top of the £200,000 that had been payable to Wycombe when O'Neill was appointed, a lot of money by any standards at the time, especially one that was as short of ready funds as the Canaries were.

What made matters even more complicated was the fact that Leicester City, Norwich's opponents in that Sunday afternoon clash, were widely reported as being O'Neill's next managerial destination, something that came as a bit of a shock to another former Norwich manager, Mike Walker, who had been widely tipped to take over at Leicester himself and had been at the match as one of ITV's commentary team, having been interviewed for the job that Friday. He would now be as confused as everyone else as to what exactly was going on but could only sit and wait to see how the whole situation at both Norwich and Leicester would now play out.

What mattered the most for the Norwich fans who'd travelled to the match was that they had not only lost a highly regarded manager but also a crucial game, and in the cruellest of circumstances, leading 2-0 and, despite all the managerial furore, debate and speculation that surrounded them and the club on that particular day, looking good. Leicester's accomplished comeback to eventually win 3-2 therefore came as an additional body blow on what was already turning out to be a very bad day.

It didn't take long for Robert Chase to appoint O'Neill's successor even if his eventual choice was, perhaps, a curious one. The man in question was Gary Megson, the very same Gary Megson who had, as caretaker manager, overseen the club's relegation from the Premier League at the end of the previous season; a man who had, as a consequence, not been deemed as good enough to be given the job on a full-time basis and had been disregarded in favour of O'Neill, and was now considered good enough to come in as his permanent full-time replacement.

Perhaps, as far as Chase was concerned, it was a case of 'better the devil you know' with regard to Megson's return. He knew the club and the players and would have been more than aware of the strengths and weaknesses of each. He'd also be entirely familiar with his chairman's attitude when it came to spending money – i.e. there wouldn't be any available. The return of Megson was, for the Norwich board, as safe and comfortable an appointment as they could make, a man who wouldn't rock the boat or make excessive and unrealistic demands of his superiors but one who would just get on and work with what he was given. He'd been assisting Chris Kamara (now a pundit on Sky Sports) at Bradford City but would now take over at Carrow Road as a man who wouldn't rock the boat or make excessive and unrealistic demands of his superiors but just get on and work with what he had, grateful, no doubt, to have his first full-time managerial appointment in England and content, unlike O'Neill, to keep his head down and maintain a low profile.

Megson made two changes to the Norwich side for his first game, a trip down to the south coast to play struggling Portsmouth, Mike Milligan and Darren Eadie stepping down from the starting XI in favour of Andy Johnson and Neil Adams. It came to nothing as a clearly disjointed Norwich side wasted three good chances to open the scoring before succumbing to a goal from John Durnin early in the second half. A third consecutive league defeat followed on Boxing Day, this time to Southend at Carrow Road, who won 1-0 thanks to a goal from Gary Jones, the defeat sending the Canaries down to eleventh place in the table, the lowest position the Canaries had been in at that time of the season since 1981.

What would have been particularly troubling to the board at that particular time would not have been that defeat and the post-O'Neill slump that the Canaries now found themselves in but the atmosphere in and around Carrow Road on that Boxing Day afternoon. Football fixtures over the Christmas and New Year period are usually played in front of a large and good-natured crowd that would still have been enjoying the remnants of any festive largesse enjoyed on the previous day, but this was anything but that with the anger shown to Chase loud, extremely hostile and coming from all sides of the ground.

And, on this occasion, there were no strategically placed speakers in the ground to drown out the supporters' very clear and obvious anger. Three arrests were made after the game while two policemen were injured in ugly post-match scenes that saw a very vociferous anti-Chase demonstration held outside Carrow Road. Would Chase cling on to power? As far as he was concerned, there was no question that he'd do exactly that.

Another post-match demonstration was held in the wake of the 0-0 draw against Sheffield United at Carrow Road on 28 February, a game that saw a gate of just 10,945, many of whom spent the game chanting 'what a load of rubbish' in addition to venting their collective spleen on the players as well as the chairman. It was an anger that, maybe justifiably, was shared by Gary Megson when, in the lead up to the game against Reading at Elm Park on 16 March, two of the club's better players, Jon Newsome and Ashley Ward, were sold to Sheffield Wednesday and Derby County, respectively, for a combined fee of £2.6 million, a paltry sum for two such important players that spoke, in no uncertain terms, of a fire sale.

Somehow, steeled perhaps by Megson's resolve to beat the odds, Norwich won the game 3-0. But it was far too little too late as all of the damage had long been done and left its mark. The Canaries saw out the campaign with just three wins from their final ten league games to finish the season in sixteenth place and just five points shy of a relegation place, a fact that alarmed the Canaries' hierarchy so much that they promptly, and perhaps unfairly, sacked Gary Megson at the end of the season, a fate that Megson had perhaps expected ever since he had publicly criticised the board in the wake of Newsome and Ward's departures, assuring the clubs now incandescent supporters that 'I was not party to this'. Chase's response to the players' departures had been to say that the club's bankers had demanded that borrowing be reduced by 50 per cent and that he had no choice but to sanction the sales.

Yet, as is very often the case, it was in these very dark hours in the club's history that a glimmer of light would, finally, be seen. And it was to come from an eighty-three-year-old one-time jazz impresario and transport magnate, who also just happened to have a long-lasting and very deep love of all things Norwich City.

CHAPTER FIVE

The Return of the Mike

But now, with his nemesis removed, the path was clear for the 'silver fox' to return to Carrow Road, an appointment which was pretty much driven by the demands of the club's long-suffering support as much as anything else.

Matt Jackson with the 1997/98 Player of the Year trophy. (*Photo courtesy of Norwich City Football Club*)

The Canaries' last game of the 1995/96 season was a trip to south London to play Crystal Palace, an away fixture that has, for a number of reasons – not all of them football related – been greeted with a fair amount of trepidation by many Norwich fans.

Yet the pre-match atmosphere prior to the clash with Dave Bassett's side saw a large, colourful and very vocal Norwich presence at Selhurst Park, all of them buoyed and in good voice for one simple reason, the return to the club of a man who had originally joined the club as a newly appointed director in 1957, one who had, just as he had done nearly forty years previously, been only too ready and willing to come to the club's rescue when the proverbial knight in shining armour was most needed: Geoffrey Watling.

If the Canaries should ever succumb to the fashion of commissioning a statue of one of the club's greats to stand outside the ground as a lasting legacy to their time at Carrow Road, then Watling would almost certainly have to be near the top of a very short list. He was a member of the new Canaries board that was elected after a lengthy meeting of club shareholders on 4 February 1957 and went on to be named as the chairman of the club. The football club were going through a particularly dark period in their history at that time, needing an urgent injection of finances just to carry on trading with Watling pledging that everything possible would be done to raise the £25,000 needed to do that. It's a sum of money that, in the context of the modern game, now sounds extremely modest but consider this: it is roughly equal to £600,000 today. Imagine how difficult it would be for the club to quickly raise that amount by having no other option but to turn to its supporters and beg for it, with no sponsors, no TV money and no oligarch benefactor to call upon for help in their hour of need.

It would virtually be a mission impossible. Yet, somehow, Watling and the new Canaries board raised the amount needed by the end of the 1956/57 season and all was well again – at least for the time being. Now Watling was being asked to step in and save the club from financial ruin again, something he did not hesitate to do.

In the week prior to the Crystal Palace match a three-hour-long board meeting had been held at Carrow Road during which discussions had taken place about a proposed purchase of Robert Chase's 34 per cent majority shareholding by Watling. The proposal received swift backing and was officially passed the next day, with Watling taking control of the club after Chase had resigned. When the news of this startling but very welcome development became official, it became a source of much joy and celebration among Norwich fans with some describing it as the club's very own 'JFK moment' – that instant in history where you always remember exactly where you were and what you were doing when a significant piece of news breaks.

This was, of course, a moment in the club's history that raised hardly a ripple of interest outside of Norwich and Norfolk but, as far as Canary fans were concerned, it was a good excuse to party and, three days after Watlings takeover had been confirmed, a massive travelling army of Norwich fans made their way down to Selhurst Park to celebrate the much desired 'changing of the guard' together.

The fact that Norwich won the game didn't seem to matter as much as it could. In truth, the colour and energy displayed on the terraces that afternoon was far superior to the fare being offered up on the pitch as a tired and thoroughly lacklustre match went through the most basic of emotions, Norwich prevailing 1-0, thanks to an own goal from David Hopkin after just five minutes. Norwich's starting XI featured six youth team products (Andy Marshall, Johnny Wright, Robert Ullathorne, Danny Mills, Jeremy Goss and Jamie Cureton) with a seventh, Daryl Sutch, replacing Wright in the second half. Regular 'home grown' line-ups were, in all likelihood, going to be the way ahead for the Canaries in seasons to come but some comfort could be afforded in the fact that if any of them ended up having as successful a time at the club as Jeremy Goss, now just days away from his thirty-first birthday, but a one-time Norwich City youth team player himself, then the future of the club, at least on the pitch, would be in relatively safe hands.

Looking back at the Chase era now in the twenty years that hindsight grants us, it is, perhaps, a little easier now to find some sympathy for the man who, at the peak of his power, drew so much hatred and venom from the club's support with that anger, at one time, being so acute and physical in its nature that mounted police were famously seen to be making their way down Carrow Road in an attempt to control and disperse protesting fans. I was as vocal an opponent of Robert Chase at that time as anyone, yet, amid all that rancour, it cannot be denied that he did do some very good things at the club including the purchase of land in and around the stadium as well as the long overdue development of Carrow Road itself, the acts of a businessman who wanted to enhance the assets of his business in the only way he knew how, by investing in its infrastructure.

Sadly, that all seemed to come at the detriment of the playing side of the business, something that Chase admitted may have been the case when he gave an interview to Richard Balls of the Norwich-based *Eastern Daily Press* in 2006, responding, when Balls asked him about the accusations he sold the club's playing assets all too easily without looking to replace them, especially with regard to the injury to Bryan Gunn that had seen Andy Marshall thrown into the first team:

> Perhaps with the benefit of hindsight we should have strengthened earlier. Yes, I think that's a fair comment. But it's easy to be wise after the event, isn't it? No one thought at Christmas that we were in any danger at all, but there, that's what makes football the marvellous game it is.

Once the celebrations relating to Chase's departure had subsided, the Canaries' happy supporters were confronted with the harsh reality of the club's growing debt, which stood at £5 million. It was a figure that, as you'd expect, was met with disbelief from many, especially given that the club had, during Robert Chase's time at Carrow Road, generated around £26.5 million from outgoing transfers while spending just half of that on replacements. Where had, as people still tend to say now, all the money gone?

The harsh truth of the matter was that running a football club was becoming an enormously expensive undertaking, especially for one as, relatively speaking, modest in size and outlook as the Canaries. Prior to the club's relegation at the end of the 1994/95 season, Norwich had enjoyed nine consecutive seasons in the top flight of English football in all of its respective guises and out of the twenty-three league campaigns that had come and gone since the Canaries had first won promotion to the then Division One in 1972, they'd maintained their place among the elite for twenty of them, a remarkable achievement. But, season by season, the cost of doing so was only going one way and that was up, up at the sort of angle and speed that would make even the pilot of an F-35 Lightning pass out.

Those far-off days of the sixties and seventies were still, just, a time when a footballing town's local car dealer or scrap-metal merchant could afford to buy and run its local football team. With stadiums and facilities in and around football in a near permanent state of decay with little to no thought given to the welfare and safety of supporters, the game and the people who ran it and the clubs had become complacent, so much so that it needed the triple tragedies of Heysel, Hillsborough and Valley Parade to wake up both football's administrators and club owners to the fact that attitudes needed to change and that they needed to start running their clubs as a business rather than a hobby. That's not to say that Robert Chase ever saw Norwich City as a hobby. If anything, he was rather more foresighted that many of his peers, recognising the need to invest and improve both Carrow Road and the club's training facilities long before doing so became fashionable. Even when it did, many clubs just chose to abandon their ancient, peeling, rotten old stadiums and move into custom-built new ones who countered the character of their predecessors with a very special kind of blandness.

Moving to a new stadium at this time for Norwich was never a likely option. The club chose to fully redevelop its existing ground on Carrow Road, starting with a new River End Stand in 1979. This was followed by a new City Stand in 1986 (though through necessity rather than choice, following a devastating fire that completely destroyed the old stand), a new Barclay Stand in 1992 and, finally, an impressive new South Stand in 2004. In addition to all of this, the club also relocated from its old Trowse training ground to a custom-built new facility in Colney in 1994.

All of which, plus the legal requirement to turn Carrow Road into an all-seater stadium, would have cost the club a considerable amount of money, much of those costs being incurred when neither the TV (the two-year contract for television rights in 1983 was worth just £5.2 million) or sponsorship deals were remotely near the levels they are at today. This meant that clubs had to pretty much finance themselves through ticket sales and incoming transfer deals, which was exactly how the 'Chase model' at Carrow Road worked. It was effective for a time, not least during the mid- to late 1980s when the Canaries were, briefly, one of the leading teams in England. Yet, especially after Sky's involvement in the game began pushing both expectations and costs (including wages and transfer fees) in the game to hitherto unknown heights, men such as Robert Chase and his peers simply could not cope anymore.

The game had, in effect, left them behind. But they couldn't just walk away from it, they had to try to survive within that brave new footballing order. And they struggled. Robert Chase was by no means the only football club chairman to suffer the wrath of his club's support at that time. But, despite all of that and the games steady rise, from then into the out-of-control monster it has become today, he tried, in vain, to carry on but, sadly, hung on to power for too long and, for him, the purchase of his shares by Geoffrey Watling must have come with as much relief and joy for him as it did the Canaries' support at that time.

So, the king is dead, long live the king. And Geoffrey Watling was keen to get on with things, just as he had four decades previously, stating that it was time to 'cut out the cackle and get on with the job'.

Unfortunately, takeover or not, the Canaries were still in debt and the necessary savings were going to have to be implemented by the new regime. This involved making several members of the club's backroom staff redundant as well as releasing eleven players from the senior squad, all of this happening in the few short weeks between the end of one football season and the commencement of another. Among the players leaving the club at that time were a few very well-known names, notably Mark Bowen and Jeremy Goss, both of whom were released, joining West Ham and Charlton Athletic,* respectively, as well as Robert Ullathorne and Jamie Cureton.

But what of the manager? Maybe to his surprise, Gary Megson was given a vote of confidence by the new board in the early part of the summer before being sacked less than a fortnight afterwards achieving, in his departure, the distinction of being made redundant by the club in successive summers. He went on to join Blackpool as manager while his former assistant, Mick Wadsworth, a man whose complicated training routines had completely confused the Norwich players on an almost daily basis, had been appointed as the manager of Scarborough.

All of which meant that the Canaries were now looking to make their sixth managerial appointment in four years, a shocking statistic for a team that had once very much been the watchword for keeping their faith with the man in charge, with John Bond, Ken Brown and Dave Stringer, the three men who had preceded that revolving door policy racking up a total of nearly twenty years between them at the club. Managerial appointments at football clubs are always critical moments in their history but Norwich now seemed, after a long period of stability, to have succumbed to a succession of, with perhaps exception of one, poor or ill-advised choices and paid a heavy price.

If the one inspired choice from that long list of names who had followed on from Dave Stringer was Mike Walker, then it seemed to make a lot of sense that, with one prodigal son returning to the club in Watling, Walker should be the other. It was a return that could never have been made while Chase was still the Norwich chairman. He had, for example, allegedly banned Walker from attending a match at Carrow Road as a TV summariser, a somewhat petty attitude to take when it should be remembered that it was Chase's refusal to reward the stunning progress Walker made in his first spell at the club by awarding him a new and improved contract. But now, with his nemesis removed, the path was clear for the 'silver fox' to return to Carrow Road, an appointment that was pretty much driven by the demands of the club's long-suffering support as much as anything else.

Walker's choice as assistant was John Faulkner, a man who'd first come to the attention of the wider footballing world in 1970 when, after appearing for non-league Sutton United in an FA Cup tie against Leeds United, he

---

* Goss had only been at Charlton for a few days before realising he had made a mistake, asking Charlton manager Alan Curbishley if he could be released from his contract. To his credit, Curbishley agreed and Gossy joined Hearts, also on a free.

so impressed Leeds manager Don Revie that he promptly signed him as cover for Jack Charlton. Faulkner went onto play for Luton Town before heading out to the United States where he played for Memphis Rogues and California Surf before ending his career playing indoor football with the latter. He had since taken up coaching and now, at forty-four, he was another man commencing his second period of gainful employment at Carrow Road, having first worked with Walker as reserve team coach during his first spell at the club.

But Faulkner was not the last Norwich old boy to make a return to the club under Mike Walker's 'second coming' as manager. Not only did he bring back club legend Duncan Forbes as chief scout but also, much to the delight of the Canaries fans, persuaded midfield maestro Ian Crook to turn his back on Ipswich Town and also make a return to Carrow Road only weeks after Crook had been released. Crook had signed a contract with Ipswich on 26 June 1996 and had even attended a press conference at Portman Road. Walker had, however, spotted a potential loophole that he could work to his advantage, the fact that, with Crook's Norwich deal not set to expire until 30 June, he was, technically, still a Norwich player and could, as a consequence, be retained by the club if Norwich made him a new offer. The Canaries did and Crook was delighted to recommit to the club where he'd made his footballing name rather than start on the long and sometimes painful road to professional obscurity at a lesser club 40 miles down the A140.

The Canaries' preseason schedule in the summer of 1996 saw them travel to the Republic of Ireland for three fixtures in four days as Mike Walker saw to it that all the members of his, for him, much changed squad got a chance to impress. Three games and three wins, against Kilkenny City (4-2), Home Farm Everton (2-1) and Bray Wanderers (2-0), were followed by five more preseason friendlies in England, the last of which was a rather disappointing 2-0 defeat to Luton Town at Kenilworth Road. It had been a particularly gruelling preseason for Walkers new-look team with seven games in eighteen days, more than enough action for fitness fanatic Walker and his team of Faulkner and newly appointed coach Steve Foley to know what the strengths and weaknesses of the Canaries squad was as the season opener at Swindon Town fast approached.

The changes to the Norwich playing squad in the two and a half years since Walker had originally departed Norwich for Merseyside were reflected in the team he selected for that match against Steve McMahon's side, with only three players from that famous 4-2 win at Highbury, Walker's first match as Norwich manager, starting, namely Bryan Gunn, Rob Newman and John Polston. Walker did, at least, have the luxury of being able to select

Robert Fleck, the player he had reluctantly seen move to Chelsea in the early days of his first spell at the club, and Fleck didn't let him down, scoring the Canaries' second goal in a comfortable 2-0 win, Andy Johnson having the privilege of scoring the Canaries' first competitive goal with Walker back at the helm.

Norwich's preseason title odds going into the 1996/97 campaign were as high as 28/1, a rather generous offer from the bookies given the impressive way in which they had seen off Swindon with Crook excelling in his new position as sweeper. No new players had joined the club in the summer so it was a case of Walker having to 'make do' with the squad that had been bequeathed to him by Gary Megson, one which was, with finances stretched to the limit, very much dependent on the club's schoolboy and youth player policy delivering players ready for first-team football, a tall order at any level.

Six of them featured in the Swindon match, namely Danny Mills, Darren Eadie, Andy Johnson, Keith O'Neill, Ade Akinbiyi and Daryl Sutch, with goalscorer Johnson a stand-out performer in that game. Walker had given the Bristol-born midfielder his Norwich debut in the 3-3 draw at Middlesbrough back in May 1992 and must have been very pleased to note that he was still at the club just as he would the ever-effervescent Eadie, another player whom he'd awarded a senior debut. Eadie had made his senior Canaries bow in the UEFA Cup match against Vitesse Arnhem in September 1993, a game he later looked back on reflecting that, 'I just came on and ran about a lot'. He'd made giant strides in the game since then, making thirty-one league appearances for Norwich during the 1995/96 campaign and going on to start in forty-two out of the forty-six league games that Norwich played in Walker's first season back at Carrow Road.

Another young Canary who received some wider attention at this time was Keith O'Neill, who signed for the club from Home Farm when he was eighteen, having started his club career at Dublin-based Tolka Rovers when he was just six years old. O'Neill had been on the wanted list of several clubs in England but was persuaded, eventually, to join the Norwich School of Excellence in 1990. He proceeded to sign trainee forms in July 1993 before becoming a full-time professional a year later as Norwich looked to do all they could to fast track him into first-team contention before any of their rivals could spirit him away, such was his reputation, even at that early stage of his career. He made his Norwich debut in November 1994, coming off the bench to replace Rob Newman in a 1-1 draw against Southampton at The Dell but then had to wait for nearly a year before making his first start, having been selected by Martin O'Neill (no relation) in another 1-1 draw, this time against Stoke City at the Victoria Ground; a game that had seen another one of the Canaries up-and-coming youngsters, Ade Akinbiyi, score the Norwich goal. O'Neill went onto make twenty-five league and cup appearances for the Canaries during the 1995/96 season, scoring his first goal for the club in the 3-0 win at Reading on 16 March, a game that was, sadly for him, completely overshadowed by the pre-match controversy and reaction of the Norwich fans to the sudden sale of Jon Newsome and Ashley Ward.

Now under Walker, O'Neill was getting a run of games for the Canaries, becoming, in the process, one of the club's most talked about players and an increasingly important one in a team that played their football the 'Walker way' – a quick-paced passing game with much of the attacking initiative coming from the flanks, an approach that suited O'Neill's game perfectly. Unfortunately for him and the Canaries, he was never able to put a consistent stretch of games together over the full ninety minutes; of the twenty-three Division One games that he started that season, he had to be substituted in seven of them while the most number of consecutive games he was able to start and finish was just six during the early part of the season. This on-off-on start to O'Neill's professional football career partially stemmed from a medical condition that he had suffered from since he was a child known as Spondylosis – a broad term given to degeneration and, over time, general wear and tear of the spinal column, which can, in its most severe cases, cause undue pressure on the nerves and lead to, among other things, muscle weakness in the limbs and very acute pain. It is, in short, a condition that, if you are making a living as a professional athlete of any kind, is going to hamper your development and career no matter what you do to try and combat it.

In O'Neill's case, it seems fairly certain that he would have played a lot of games for Norwich while in some considerable pain and having to take whatever treatment he could, post- and pre-match, to try and help alleviate some of the symptoms. It would, therefore, be rather unfair for him to be labelled as an 'injury-prone' player as the condition he suffered from had been with him for most of his life and would have been an issue even before he set out to become a professional footballer. It was, perhaps, with the awareness that his career could be curtailed at any moment if the condition had worsened that led to O'Neill making the very best of his career for as long as he could, which meant, contrary to some of his monosyllabic and somewhat dull peers in the game, he looked to enjoy himself and, in the process, neither take himself or the game too seriously. It was a refreshing attitude that, nonetheless, led to him upsetting some of the Canaries support when he responded to a question asking him what the best thing about

Norwich was with the quip that it was 'the road to London' – a typically humorous quip from O'Neill, which, nevertheless, did not sit very well with a lot of Norwich fans.

He later admitted that, even as a young player with Norwich, the effects of the Spondylosis had been so severe that, quite often after a game, he'd literally had to drag himself out of the bath while the rest of his teammates were still able to 'jump around', adding that of all the games he was ever selected for, he only ended up playing in around a fifth of them. In a 2003 feature about him in *The Times*, the physiotherapist of Coventry City, one of the clubs that O'Neill went on to play for after he had left Norwich, admitted that his condition was the worst that he'd seen in fourteen years working in professional football, one that, even after O'Neill had quit playing, frequently led to him having appointments with a chiropractor that involved his having to lay on his side while the specialist quite literally pushed his sacrum and pelvis back into its correct position in the body.

Having played so well in Norwich's opening game, O'Neill duly featured in an unchanged Norwich starting line for their next two fixtures, starting with a midweek visit to the Manor Ground to take on Oxford United for a League Cup first-round, first-leg tie. This would be the first of at least four matches due to be played between the two sides that season, Oxford having ended the previous campaign as runners-up to Swindon Town in Division Two and being promoted. In Denis Smith, the former Stoke City centre half, a man who'd played for Stoke against the Canaries in their very first season of top-flight football (1972/73), they'd put together a strong squad of players that included Nigel Jemson, a striker who'd played under Brian Clough at Nottingham Forest, winning a League Cup medal in 1990, and Joey Beauchamp, a midfielder who'd famously left them for West Ham for £1.2 million in 1994 only to decide, soon after signing, that he couldn't manage the daily commute to London from his Oxford home and asked to rejoin the U's. That hadn't, in the first instance, been possible, so he'd signed for Swindon Town only to rejoin Oxford in 1995.

His actions in wanting to quit the Hammers almost as soon as he had joined them had made somewhat of an easy target for both the press and media who perceived him as being a 'spoilt' footballer, yet, underneath all of that, Beauchamp was a quality player, who would have relished the opportunity to prove himself again against sides like Norwich as well as some of the other bigger clubs in Division One that season.

If Beauchamp and his teammates were up for the match then Norwich, perhaps a little overconfident after their win and performance against Swindon, didn't seem to take the match in quite the same way. Yes, their quick pass-and-move game, which was being honed again under Walker, was very much in evidence and, at times, the U's were in danger of being passed off their compact little pitch. But passing the ball is one thing, putting it into the net was another and, as the match developed and even at this early stage of the season, it became clear that, as had been the case earlier in the decade, the Canaries were in some need of a proven goalscorer, someone who would be on hand to convert the myriad chances that the likes of Keith O'Neill, Darren Eadie, Neil Adams and Andy Johnson were crafting. The Canaries did have the benefit as well as a lot of worldly wisdom back in their ranks with the presence of Robert Fleck, but, as hard working, energetic and passionate for the cause as Fleckie was, he needed someone alongside him to share the role and responsibility. When Norwich did eventually make the breakthrough on twenty-nine minutes, it was Fleck who was the provider, his clever through ball being seized on by Johnson, who was quick enough to clip the ball past U's keeper Paul Whitehead.

For the Norwich fans at the game, that should have been that with the onus now on Oxford to press for an equaliser meaning that the Canaries could afford to sit back, soak up the pressure and look to hit their opponents on the break, something they were more than capable of doing with so many players of pace in their side, notably Darren Eadie, so fleet of foot, who could run the skin off a cooling milk pudding. Yet it didn't happen and, with the Canaries players' minds briefly off the job in hand, Jemson made the most of some space to head an equaliser past Gunn just two minutes later with, following his goal, Oxford quite content to see out the game and take themselves to Carrow Road for the second leg with a good chance of a result with Norwich's best chance falling to Eadie, whose solo run ended with his shot hitting the post.

Disappointing. But it was early days yet with Mike Walker happy to keep to the same starting XI for the trip to the preseason championship favourites Bolton Wanderers four days later. And, just as they had done in the week, Norwich started well only for an uncharacteristic error from Bryan Gunn to give Nathan Blake a second opportunity to score after his first effort had been dealt with. Then, a minute into the second half, Norwich conceded another soft goal when Michael Johansen made it 2-0, the timing and the nature of the goal adding to the all-round collective misery of the Canary fans who had made an exceedingly wet trip north and were now all getting soaked on the large open terrace for their troubles. A combination of silk and steel then combined when Darren Eadie (silk) capitalised on Mike Milligan's (steel) through ball to score and, all of a sudden and with just over half an hour to go, Norwich were back in it and looking good again. They had numerous opportunities to equalise and maybe would have done towards the end when Keith O'Neill found himself clean through on goal only to be crudely body checked by a home defender who, unfeasibly, escaped any sort of sanction from referee Terry Heilbron, the resulting free kick, despite being in a dangerous position, coming to nothing. It was a decision that seemed to knock any remaining fight out of Norwich and it came as no surprise to anyone when a fast Bolton break ended with Blake scoring his second of the game to secure a 3-1 win for the home side.

That temporary blip on the 'On Loan to the Endsleigh' road show was swiftly put to rest by three consecutive wins in the league, an early season tonic that came with the refreshing extra of no goals conceded in that run. Those wins, over Oxford United (0-1), Wolves (1-0) and Bradford City (0-2), saw many of the Canaries' former youth team prodigies put in some excellent performances with Danny Mills, Daryl Sutch, Andy Johnson and Darren Eadie all outstanding as Mike Walker's trademark passing game began to bed in. The win against Wolves, one which saw another young talent in Adrian Forbes make his debut, was settled by a twenty-first-minute penalty from Neil Adams.

That spot kick, contentiously awarded at the time by referee Rob Harris, was the first Norwich had been awarded in a league game for over eighteen months and seemed, at the time, indicative of the way the club's fortunes were, slowly, turning under Walker. His team were now, following the win at Bradford, up to second place in Division One, a mini run of four wins out of five league matches that masking the disappointment of an early League Cup exit at Carrow Road after Oxford United won 3-2 in extra time in front of just 7,301 fans, whose evening's entertainment had been enlivened by the rare sight of witnessing two Norwich players sent off in the same game, namely Robert Fleck and Darren Eadie.

The Canaries remained unbeaten in the league until 19 October when goals from Nigel Clough and Paul Dickov gave Manchester City a 2-1 win at Maine Road. Prior to that game, Norwich had, at times, been playing some delightful attacking football, no more so than in the wins at Grimsby Town (1-4) and in the East Anglian derby against Ipswich Town on 11 October, the 3-1 win being nicely set up by two first half goals by Andy Johnson. It had, as usual, been a typically feisty clash between the two sides with the travelling blue contingent feeling particularly hard done by on this occasion as, in addition to seeing their side being completely outplayed, they'd also been witness to a substitute appearance by Ian Crook, who, remember, had all but signed for them that summer before changing his mind and returning, tempted by the return of Walker, to the Carrow Road fold.

Things seemed to be on the up and up within the confines of the club's boardroom as well when a new look board that included Delia Smith and Michael Wynn Jones was announced by the club in the lead up to the match against Birmingham City on 30 November. Smith and Wynn Jones were two of four new directors that had taken their places on the Canaries' board with the famous TV cook and her husband said to be injecting around £2 million into the club, a vital and much needed financial lifeline at a time when, with the arduous Christmas and New Year fixture list fast approaching, Mike Walker was beginning to feel the inadequacies of his squad when it came to both depth and quality, especially with reference to experience.

Walker had already seen Jamie Cureton depart the club in order to join Bristol Rovers in a deal that had come as a surprise to most Norwich fans as big things had been expected of Cureton, a former England youth international who had scored eighty-two goals in ninety youth team matches before notching up a not too dissimilar record for the club's reserves, scoring his first senior goal for the club just thirteen seconds after coming on as a substitute in the Premier League game against Chelsea in December 1994. Cureton's all too brief flirtation with the Canaries at this, the beginning of his career, saw him play under four different managers – John Deehan, Gary Megson, Martin O'Neill and Walker. Yet, for all his promise, he never seemed to convince any of them that he was worth a long run of games in the first team. This inevitably meant that, when his hometown club came in for him, initially on loan, it was an easy decision for Cureton to take his leave of Carrow Road. He prospered with The Gas scoring a total of seventy-nine goals in 198 league and cup appearances before joining Reading in 2000.

His surprise departure, together with a string of injuries affecting many of the side's first-team regulars, meant that, following their bright start to the season, the Canaries subsequently went on a run of ten games without a win, a dreadful run of form that reached its grim conclusion with consecutive away losses at West Brom (1-5) and Port Vale (1-6), the latter result and performance bad enough to draw criticism from the normally mild mannered *Eastern Daily Press*, which labelled it as an insult to the supporters who had made the 400-plus-mile journey to Burslem just four days before Christmas. In truth, with a makeshift back four that featured midfielder Rob Newman and the still inexperienced Johnny Wright, the fact that City lost the game was not so much of a surprise as the margin by which they had lost it. Norwich slipped down to tenth place as a result of this defeat, one that firmly put an end to the brief honeymoon period Walker had enjoyed upon his return to the club.

The fact that Norwich's defence had leaked eleven goals in just two games would have been enough for even the Canaries' normally prudent board to realise something needed to be done about it and you suspect that Walker's pleas for funding in order to go out and strengthen that defence would have been received by more than willing ears. The fact that £450,000 was immediately found in order for Walker to sign centre half Matt Jackson from Everton in time for him to make his debut against QPR on Boxing Day was refreshing in itself, as was Jackson's humorous answer pre-match to the inevitable question of whether he felt he was under particular pressure, coming into a team that had conceded so many goals in recent matches. Jackson's retort was that even if Norwich conceded just four on his debut, it could be regarded as a positive. Smiles all round at Carrow Road, although, as it turned out, Jackson's quip came uncomfortably close to reality as Norwich still contrived to concede three against the Hoops, losing 3-2, their tenth game without a win and now fourteen goals conceded in just three matches.

No one was wearing their 'On Loan to the Endsleigh' T-shirts now.

Tempers were running high at Carrow Road two days later after a touchline fracas between Mike Walker and his opposite number at Bradford City, Chris Kamara, now more famous, of course, for his catchphrase of 'unbelievable' as he mixes punditry on Sky Sports with promotional work for a betting company. Kamara had a lot of quality to choose from within the Bradford ranks with players like Chris Kiwomya, Mike Duxbury and Chris Waddle in his first-team squad yet, despite naming all three in his side to face Norwich, Bradford were passed off the pitch in a much-needed 2-0 win for Norwich courtesy of goals from a Neil Adams penalty and Keith O'Neill.

With their bad run now at an end, the Canaries saw in the new year by beating Portsmouth 1-0 at Carrow Road, new signing Jackson scoring a late goal to secure the points in an otherwise dull game that briefly sprang to life again when, from only 5 yards from the opposition goal and completely unmarked, Ade Akinbiyi somehow managed to put the ball over the bar. The young striker, whose chance to play himself into the first team had come about following the departure of Cureton, was much liked by Walker who brought him off the bench on nine separate occasions in the league throughout the 1996/97 season as well as giving him three starts, the sort of self-belief that any young player wants to repay with goals. Sadly for Ade, he was, like Cureton, unable to fully justify Walker's faith in him and, just five days after the Portsmouth game, joined Gillingham for a club record £250,000, scoring seven goals in the nineteen appearances he went onto make for them up until the end of that season.

With Cureton and Akinbiyi now gone, Walker knew he had to freshen up his options in attack and did so by bringing in Swedish centre forward

Ulf Ottosson on loan from Norrkoping. Walker had also, four days prior to bringing in Ottosson, pulled off something of a coup when he persuaded former England international David Rocastle to also join on loan, Rocastle coming in from Chelsea where he'd been struggling to get games. He had been, and unquestionably still was, a player of the very highest calibre, one who'd won two league titles at Highbury as well as being named in the Professional Footballers Association's team of the year in 1987 and 1989, quite an accolade when you consider such a team is picked by a players' fellow professionals rather than fans or journalists. Rocastle had also played fourteen times for England before, much to the surprise of just about everyone in the game as well as a lot of anger and disbelief among Arsenal fans, he joined Leeds United in the summer of 1992. That move had never really worked out for Rocky as had subsequent moves to Manchester City and Chelsea and it would have been with getting his career back on track in mind that he would have joined Norwich, heartened, no doubt, by Walker's reputation for playing good football.

Rocastle made his Norwich debut against Grimsby at Carrow Road, a game that Norwich won 2-1 despite going down to a twentieth-minute goal from Jack Lester. John Polston and Daryl Sutch replied for the Canaries, who followed up that fixture with a trip to Stoke three days later, winning by the same score with, on this occasion, Keith O'Neill and Darren Eadie the scorers. It was a consummate team performance against a side who were notoriously difficult to beat at home but who were, on this occasion, found wanting at the back for both Norwich goals as the pacy Eadie and O'Neill found to their advantage, seizing on long passes from the Norwich defence (Walker clearly happy to 'mix it' on this occasion and play a more direct game) to race clear and score. With Norwich's defence further strengthened by the presence of Kevin Scott, signed by Walker from Tottenham for £250,000 a day earlier, the win was the Canaries' fourth on the spin, good enough to lift them up into the play-off places and lift the mood at the club from one which had been at near rock bottom following the capitulation at Port Vale to one of optimism with a chance of automatic promotion certainly not being ruled out and a place in the play-offs regarded as a near certainty.

You couldn't blame the Norwich fans for the renewed faith they'd invested in their team. The signing of Matt Jackson had not only considerably strengthened the Canaries' defensive options but had also, as had the signing of Rocastle, been a statement of intent by the club's board. Both Jackson and Rocastle were proven Premier League players with, at the time they had signed for Norwich, a total of around 400 top-flight appearances between them as well as international experience with England, albeit, in Jackson's case, with the England U21 squad. In short, they were both quality players who both had lots of other clubs keen to sign them but had, despite Norwich being in a league beneath the one they were more used to playing in, had no qualms about dropping down a level and being part of Walker's squad, testament to the high regard that the Norwich manager still had within the game.

The arrival of Jackson and Rocastle meant that Ulf Ottosson had been able to commence his own loan period at the club with little to none of the attention that was normally meted out to new signings at Carrow Road, especially when, as was the case now (and often), the club needed to account for every penny spent. Ottosson's loan fee from Norrkoping had been negotiated as the Canaries committing his wages while he was at Carrow Road with the intention that his parent club would yield the benefits of such generous terms when Norwich committed to buying the player at the end of his loan spell. Ulf didn't do his chances of signing permanently any harm when he found himself in the right place at the right time to convert a cross from Robert Fleck in the game against Sheffield United at Bramall Lane to put Norwich 2-1 up in game that they went onto win 3-2. Yet, despite that, Mike Walker didn't feel that Ottosson offered anything better than what he already had, and, after just three more appearances for the Canaries, two of which saw him substituted, Ulf was packed off home to Sweden where he went onto join Ljungskile SK.

Disappointing but no disaster. The real bright spot of the season so far had been the form of Norwich's rich seam of youngsters, especially Darren Eadie, a relative 'veteran' now of twenty-one, and Keith O'Neill. Another who had excelled and who would have been benefitting from the presence of Ian Crook and David Rocastle alongside him in the Norwich midfield was Andy Johnson, who'd been a stand-out figure during the first half of that season. Whether his head had been turned by outside sources or not is debatable but one thing is certain, his growing importance to the side had been noted and Johnson soon declared that he wanted out, this following what is colloquially known as a training ground 'bust up' with assistant manager John Faulkner. The result of that was a clearly piqued Johnson submitting a written transfer request to the club, one that, either he or his representative ensured, was first seen by a local radio station who broadcast the news of his desire to leave before most people at the club had any idea that the letter even existed.

Unsurprisingly, Walker was furious, especially as Johnson had also found himself in trouble with a local taxi driver, which had led to both him and Carl Bradshaw having assault charges being filed against them. Johnson played his last game for the club against Reading at Elm Park on 3 March but didn't see out the game and was replaced by Ian Crook midway through the second half, a sad denouement to a career that had initially promised so much with Johnson going onto join Nottingham Forest in the summer for around £2.2 million.

If only Johnson had followed the example of David Rocastle, sold by Arsenal against his wishes and reduced, in the process, to becoming a bit-part player at Leeds, Chelsea and Manchester City. If Rocastle thought he deserved better then he never showed it, choosing instead to give everything to the Canary cause during his loan spell at the club, one that was proving to be so successful that there was hope that the club would make an effort to sign him on a permanent basis, a forlorn hope, sadly, given the fee that Manchester City would be looking for him as well as the large wages Rocastle would have been on. Mere details to the player affectionately known within the game as Rocky. That match at Reading, played on a heavy mud heap of a pitch on a cold and wet night in an antiquated stadium, saw Rocastle at his very best, gliding over the pitch with ease as if it was Wembley or the San Siro rather than Elm Park.

It was a delight to witness for any of the hardy Norwich fans, myself included, that stood, exposed to the elements, and looked on as Norwich, who'd initially gone 1-0 down, fought back to equalise through a Neil Adams penalty only to lose the game late on when the same player gave away an own goal, hammering the ball into his own net while trying to clear his lines.

Not a good night unless you were David Rocastle, who had excelled throughout and didn't only not deserve to be on the losing side but, realistically, also deserved to be somewhere a little better than a frigid corner of Berkshire on a wet Tuesday night.

The Canaries were now struggling to put any sort of good run together. Four days after that defeat at Reading, Port Vale were the visitors to Carrow Road and came away with a 1-1 draw despite being under pressure for much of the game. Rocastle, playing in the last game of his loan spell, had set up Matt Jackson for the opening goal from a corner after just eleven minutes, a goal that should have given the Canaries the confidence to go on and win the game by two or three goals but, agonisingly, and just as it had on several previous occasions that season, several chances came to nothing and it wasn't a surprise to anyone at Carrow Road when Jon McCarthy equalised for the Valiants a quarter of an hour later. Two consecutive defeats, at Crystal Palace (for whom future Canary Leon McKenzie scored in a 2-0 win) and at home to runaway leaders Bolton Wanderers followed, their 1-0 win and the disciplined way they went about protecting their lead after Scott Sellars had opened the scoring in the twenty-fourth minute leaving few, if any Canary fans, convinced that their side were still promotion contenders as Norwich slipped down into eighth place in the Division One table.

The defeat at Selhurst Park had at least given the Norwich supporters a chance to see two more of the club's young players make their senior debuts, namely Craig Bellamy and Drewe Broughton, who came on for Shaun Carey and Keith Scott, respectively. Bellamy, then just seventeen, might well have been expected to be nervous when he came on but, such was his self-belief, even at that early stage, that he was soon in both the oppositions and his teammates faces in the same confident and cocksure manner that the supporters of all eight of the clubs he played for during his long career would become familiar with – and love him for it. Bellamy's eventual successes as a player in a career that saw him score 170 goals in 540 league and cup appearances were in direct and very stark contrast to that of Broughton, who had shared the day and a senior debut alongside him. He made just nine league appearances for Norwich before, after a brief loan period with Wigan Athletic, going onto join Brentford, one of the twenty-two clubs in England that he ended up playing for in a playing career that eventually came to an end in 2012. He is now a performance coach and motivational speaker.

Norwich won just two more league games that season, an impressive 3-0 win at Swindon (convincing enough in its execution to make the travelling support wonder why they hadn't seen a little bit more of the Norwich they witnessed that day earlier in the season) that included a 30-yard thunderbolt from Darren Eadie and a 2-0 win over Stoke City at Carrow Road that saw one of the quickest goals to ever be scored at the ground after Keith O'Neill's opener just twelve seconds after kick-off.

Occasional flashes of brilliance that had been all too rare in a season that had started well before sinking into mid-table mediocrity. Not an untypical season for a club whose support had been weaned on stories of how their team seemed to have a unique ability to seamlessly bind the sublime with the ridiculous-and nevermind over the course of a season but, all too often, in just one half of one game. The problem with that was, for many, the fact that the Canaries had gone through some genuine and well-deserved highs over the last decade or so, meaning that the club's 'new' support (i.e. those in their late teens and early twenties) had become somewhat accustomed to high league finishes, quality football and quality players.

This meant that scratching around for two consecutive seasons in Division One and ending up those campaigns with finishing positions of sixteenth (1996/97) and thirteenth (1996/97) was not going to be regarded as acceptable, something that the new young wave of Norwich supporters would, in time, come to make perfectly clear to the club's board.

There had, of course, been some high points during the 1996/97 season. Darren Eadie, voted as the club's Player of the Year at the end of that campaign, had put in some sublime performances throughout, ending the campaign as the club's record goalscorer with seventeen in the league. Some of those goals, such as his fierce strike into the top corner of the net at Bradford and his 30-yard wonder strike at Swindon, had been outstanding efforts, the hallmarks of a confident player who seemed to have it all – pace, a fierce shot, the eye for a pass and a good understanding of the game. Something, therefore, for the Norwich fans to celebrate even if they knew, deep down, that Eadie's rise to prominence would, sooner rather than later, start to get the attention of bigger clubs – if it hadn't already.

There was also cause for optimism with regard to the club's ownership and long-term future. Geoffrey Watling's largesse had seen off Robert Chase whilst the club now had, in addition to the statesmanlike Watling, the added presence of Delia Smith and Michael Wynn Jones as newly appointed directors, who had already invested part of their fortune into the club. Smith's presence on the board had also, inevitably, seen the Canaries get a little bit more national press attention than they might have normally expected with lingering shots of her sat in the directors box at Carrow Road now a prerequisite for broadcasters and commentators, while newspaper editors, remorseless in their quest for a naff headline, would contrive to bring Delia into the story no matter what was happening at the club. This meant that Norwich fans had long been accustomed to and were now thoroughly bored of banner headlines like 'Delia's Norwich Cook Up A Storm' and 'Delia's Recipe For Carrow Road Success'.

Finally, there had been the return to the club of Mike Walker. He'd initially departed Carrow Road in the wake of some of the club's greatest ever triumphs in order to seek out bigger and better things at Everton. It had been a parting of the ways that had not gone down well with some sections of the Canary support who routinely referred to him as 'Judas', going on to let him know exactly what they felt about the perceived betrayal when Walker had returned to Carrow Road with his Everton side late on in the 1993/94 season. Walker must have felt, in the wake of his team's convincing defeat on the day as well as the reaction he drew from a lot of the home fans, that he could never go back and that, as far as Norwich City were concerned, bridges had been well and truly burnt.

Yet, despite all that, here he was a season in to his return and now, far from being considered a Judas, was now seen as a potential messiah, a label he had done little to tarnish with some of his side's polished performances in the early part of the season, not least the 4-1 win at Grimsby Town on

1 October that had lifted Norwich to the top of the Division One table, a position they'd strengthened ten days later with the equally convincing 3-1 win over Ipswich Town.

With Walker in charge, fast and free-flowing football on show at Carrow Road and the Canaries top of the table, it could have been the 1992/93 season all over again. And it might have been if the season didn't have, at that point, another seven months to run.

The reality of the situation was that, unlike back in the summer of 1992, when Walker had inherited a squad rich in playing quality, one that had been carefully and meticulously built over a number of years by Dave Stringer, he'd found himself in charge of one that was short on quality, bereft of confidence and in no position to be improved by a visit or two to an already inflated transfer market. Many of the young players in the Norwich squad at that time had been drafted into first-team contention when, ideally, they would have either been left to continue their development in the youth and reserve sides or, given the fact that some of those who ended up in the first team were soon deemed not to be up to the task, loaned out, sold or even released, with Drewe Broughton, Karl Simpson and Johnny Wright three players who fell into that category.

Walker had also needed to rely on the loan market rather more than he might have wanted to. The surprise acquisition of David Rocastle had been something of a coup and the player had performed well during his time at the club but, given that he was never going to sign a permanent deal with the Canaries, it seemed to be more of an placatory gesture made to the club's support, a chance for them to see a big-name player in a Norwich shirt, if only for a short time. Ulf Ottosson had come, scored one goal and been packed off back to Sweden, while in Neil Moore, a defender signed from Everton, Walker's previous team, made just two appearances before the Norwich manager decided he was no better than what he had already got and was duly returned to sender.

The variety of weaknesses in the club's playing squad had ultimately been the Canaries' downfall in the 1996/97 season. Norwich used a total of twenty-eught different players during the campaign from which twelve made less than ten league starts. No wonder the Canaries season had fallen away so spectacularly; as soon as key players became injured or unavailable the ones picked to cover for them had simply not been good enough and that, as a consequence, promotion had never been a realistic goal. It was clear that if the club was ever to retain any hope of returning to the Premier League that the squad would, somehow, have to be significantly improved in the summer if the second coming of Mike Walker was not going to end in disappointment.

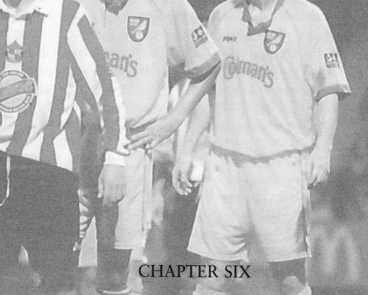

CHAPTER SIX

Designer Disappointment

Most Norwich fans were already a little sceptical about the new strip, mostly because the shorts were now yellow rather than the traditional and long-established green.

Iwan Roberts worrying the Sunderland defence. (*Photo courtesy of David McDermott*)

Norwich's first preseason signing prior to the 1997/98 season was one that no one was expecting; a cultured and world-renowned leader in his field who had, prior to his affiliation to the Canaries, worked alongside some of the most well-known and famous names in the industry.

Only he wasn't a footballer, he was a fashion designer. Enter Bruce Oldfield, who, at forty-six, was at the peak of his design powers, the man who the club had commissioned to redesign the club's strip, one that, according to Oldfield, had looked like a 'sack of potatoes' prior to his getting his hands on one of the most well-known and iconic football strips in Britain. Oldfield's brief had been to make the club's strip look smarter, neater and more contemporary, a fashion item that could as easily be worn on a night out as it could for an afternoon at Carrow Road. The new shirts were, as a consequence, smaller and more fitted than the previous ones, great if you were a professional athlete whose tightly sculpted body would best show off the new 'clutter-free' kit, but not so good, perhaps, if you were a fan who wasn't quite as disciplined about their body shape and how it might look in a football shirt that had a tendency to fit to the body rather than, as had been the fashion, shapelessly hang from it.

The club's new strip, designed by Oldfield and manufactured by US-based brand Pony, was officially launched, alongside the club's new shirt sponsors, Coleman's, in London, with some of the Norwich players dutifully making an appearance in the kit. One of those players had been Darren Eadie, who'd learnt a few days previously that he had been called up for the full England squad for the Tournoi tournament in France that was to take place that June, a fitting reward and recognition from England coach Glenn Hoddle for an outstanding season. Also present at the launch was Norfolk-born model Sarah Thomas, who'd flown back from Australia to model the shirt in exchange for season tickets for herself and Peter, her father. Not surprisingly, she was the focus of attention throughout the event but, as a lifelong Norwich fan, preferred to champion the new strip rather than the team's chances of promotion, claiming that the shirt would be regarded as a 'fashion statement' even though most Norwich fans were already a little sceptical about the new strip, mostly because the shorts were now yellow rather than the traditional and long-established green.

Preseason duties for the club saw them head up to Scotland for a three-game tour, the new strip receiving its first official airing in a 2-0 win over Hibernian at Easter Road. Norwich went onto draw 2-2 at St Mirren before a disappointing 3-2 defeat at Dumbarton brought the tour to an end. Two days after that game, the Canaries were in action again during a testimonial game for former player Bill Punton, now the manager of non-league Diss Town, who he'd taken to the Wembley for the 1994 FA Vase final with the Tangerines emerging triumphant after a 2-1 win over Taunton Town in front of 13,450 spectators. The testimonial game was a much deserved tribute to Punton, who'd been a great servant to football in Norfolk since joining Norwich in 1957, the high spot of his time at Carrow Road almost certainly being playing and scoring in the 1962 League Cup final as Norwich beat Rochdale over two legs. He later spent twenty years in charge at Great Yarmouth before taking over at Diss and a large and appreciative crowd were at Brewers Green Lane on the night to see his side give the Canaries a good game.

Norwich's final game of a busy preseason schedule saw them welcome Arsenal to Carrow Road on 4 August, a high-profile match that gave Mike Walker a final chance to decide on his team's line-up for the first match of the season against Mark McGhee's Wolves. They'd missed out on automatic promotion by just four points at the end of the previous campaign and were now, along with Nottingham Forest and Middlesbrough, one of the pre-season favourites for promotion. It was a fixture that would have shown Walker how far he and his rebuilt side were progressing, and, with the prospect of three new faces in the line-up, the Arsenal game draw an optimistic crowd to Carrow Road, many of whom were quietly confident that the Canaries would have enough about them to win the match. This turned out to be brave but slightly misguided optimism as Arsenal proceeded to put on a virtuoso show in winning 6-2, with Ian Wright, despite the very best attentions of Kevin Scott, scoring a hat-trick.

Walker's three new faces were central defender Craig Fleming, signed from Oldham Athletic, midfielders Peter Grant, signed from Celtic, and Spaniard Victor Segura, who'd arrived from Spanish Second Division side Lleida. His arrival had generated a lot of interest among the Norwich fans as, aside from being the first Spaniard to sign for the club, he also had a fairly impressive footballing CV to call upon, with Real Zaragoza, who'd beaten Arsenal in the final of the European Cup Winners' Cup just two years beforehand, being another of his former clubs.

Fleming and Grant had been signed to provide both experience and a little steel to a side that had been dependent for so much of the previous season on its young players and sometimes seemed as if it wasn't always able to cope with teams that adopted a seasoned and more physical approach to the game, one that had been typified in the 5-1 loss at West Brom when, to all intents and purposes, the Canaries had rolled over and given up on by half time. Fleming, in particular, looked an excellent acquisition at £600,000, still, at the time, one of the biggest fees the club had ever paid out but, given his experience, still something of a bargain. Fleming had already played for three seasons in the top flight for Oldham, earning, during that time, a much publicised sobriquet from Alex Ferguson, who'd labelled him the 'best man marker in the country'.

That need for on field steel had also been taken into consideration when Walker spent a further £850,000 on Wolves striker Iwan Roberts. Roberts was seen as the type of player that City had been woefully lacking in recent years, a powerful striker who could bully opposition defenders, was good in the air and as adept at making chances for others as he was taking them for himself; in other words, the perfect foil for Robert Fleck, who had so prospered at Norwich when playing alongside Robert Rosario, a player similar in style and build to Roberts. Iwan certainly came with a reputation as a goalscorer, having notched sixty-eight goals in 183 appearances for Huddersfield before going onto averaging a goal in about every three games in his subsequent spells at Leicester City and Wolves where he'd endeared himself to the club's support by scoring a hat-trick in a game against their biggest rivals, West Bromwich Albion.

Segura, Fleming and Roberts were all picked by Walker to start the game against Wolves at Carrow Road, one that Roberts would, no doubt, have been particularly keen to impress in as it was not only his first competitive game for his new club but would also, as fate often has it, be against his previous one. For those Norwich fans expecting him to play alongside Fleck, however, there was disappointment, with Fleck named as one of the substitutes, Walker opting to play Darren Eadie alongside Roberts in attack with Neil Adams and Keith O'Neill expected to keep the new Norwich front pairing supplied with plenty of chances.

With so much of the pre-match attention focused on Roberts, no one among the 17,230 fans at Carrow Road on a warm and bright afternoon would have had any reason to think that Wolves' replacement for Roberts in their starting line-up would go on to steal his thunder as well as win the Man of the Match award, especially as he was a raw seventeen year old making his first ever senior appearance. Yet that is exactly what Robbie Keane did, dominating proceedings throughout as well as all the post-match headlines with both goals in Wolves' 0-2 victory, his opener a first-time volley while his second, scored in the sixty-fourth minute, came as he cut through the Norwich defence, placing a fierce, low drive beyond the reach of Andy Marshall in the Norwich goal.

Neither the performance nor the result the Norwich fans had been expecting. Wolves had impressed throughout the previous campaign, ending it on a down note by losing to Crystal Palace in the play-off semi-finals. They'd managed to keep the core of their side together though, as well as managing to add a little extra quality with the likes of the fast-tracked Keane as well as former Tottenham midfielder Steve Sedgley and Polish international defender Dariuz Kubicki. So they were hardly a side to be underestimated as their performance showed on that afternoon. For the Canaries, it was a severe wake-up call to any fans (or players) and a reminder that, for all the optimism that had accompanied them into the campaign, it was still an optimism that was riding on the back of the two mediocre seasons that had preceded it and a run at the end of the previous one that had seen the Canaries win just three of their final fifteen league games, a sequence that had seen them drop from a play-off place to a final position of thirteenth.

A cluster of new signings and some early August sunshine had, it was clear, done little more than paper over the cracks and Mike Walker had a major task on his hands. Yet even if Walker hadn't suspected it at that point, he most certainly would have known it during and after the Canaries next match, a 4-1 defeat at Nottingham Forest that saw his teams inadequacies exposed for all to see on live television. Yet it had all started so well when Keith O'Neill opened the scoring after just seven minutes, a lead that lasted for just a quarter of an hour before Kevin Campbell struck a fierce shot past Marshall to make it 1-1. With the scores level at half time, there would have been hope that Walker's renowned motivational skills would have helped turn things around after the break, yet, as Forest continuously pushed forward, Norwich simply laid down and surrendered within four second half minutes with Pierre Van Hooijdonk and Geoff Thomas (two) doing the damage.

'The way we caved in was a disgrace' said a furious Mike Walker in his post-match interview and he was right, Norwich had been woeful. Changes were duly made for the Canaries' next match against Crewe at Carrow Road with, to nobody's surprise, the defence bearing the brunt of Walker's fury as Kevin Scott, Carl Bradshaw and Victor Segura all found themselves dropped, with Danny Mills, new signing Peter Grant and Mike Milligan replacing them with Robert Fleck also recalled, starting his first game of the season alongside Roberts in the two-pronged attack that the Norwich fans had been expecting from the off. Now, in a match against somewhat supposedly more 'humble' opposition than the sides the Canaries had come up against in their opening two fixtures, normal service was now expected to be resumed, although, it must be said, in front of an attendance that was nearly 6,000 down on the total that had been at Carrow Road for the Wolves game.

Those who chose to stay away didn't miss anything as Norwich cruised to their third consecutive defeat, Mark Rivers (who would later become a Norwich player) and Shaun Smith scoring in Crewe's unexpected but thoroughly deserved 0-2 win. It meant that, as the season's first 'official' league tables were printed, Norwich were firmly in bottom place, a region of the old Division Two that they hadn't visited since the 1960s. At such an early stage of any season, of course, league positions are irrelevant but what was a lot more worrying to Norwich fans was that, taken over a longer period of time, the form they found their club was in was a lot more relevant and worrying. That woeful early season form of played three, lost three with eight goals conceded to just one scored now came on top of their run in at the end of the previous season; league form and results over the longer term that now read as just three wins from eighteen games, which was relegation form.

Unthinkable of course and, at such an early stage of the season, fanciful as well. But just three wins from eighteen games? Not good enough. Mike Walker, who was now beginning to feel the sort of pressure that he'd have been used to at Everton rather than in his previous stint at Carrow Road, would have been very well aware that, regardless of everything that he'd accomplished before at the club, he'd have to turn things around, and quickly. Admittedly, and in his defence, City had been hit with a terrible run of injuries to key players. Summer signing Peter Grant had made his debut in the Crewe match only to fall victim to injury himself and have to come off, while another new signing, Craig Fleming, had also been ruled out of contention. Fleming's initial injury had been thought not too serious and he'd missed five matches after the Wolves defeat, returning to the side from the bench in the home game against Charlton and starting three of the Canaries next four matches before having to be taken off during Norwich's home game with Stockport County on 18 October and not returning to the team until the following January.

His absence from the team for such a long period of time meant Walker had to increasingly shuffle his limited options around as injuries continued to take their toll on the Canaries squad, recalling midfielder Karl Simpson to the side for a couple of games in October before bringing in Lee Marshall, who could play in defence or midfield, from non-league Enfield Town and giving him his debut against Bury at Carrow Road. Norwich ended up getting just a point from this match, despite taking an early 2-0 lead through goals from Craig Bellamy and Neil Adams before a stoppage time goal from Lenny Johnrose rescued a 2-2 draw for Bury. Marshall impressed enough to keep his place in the team for the trip up to West Bromwich Albion just three days later but, typical of the Canaries run of bad luck at the time, proceeded to brake his ankle, the injury severe enough to mean that his participation for the rest of that season was restricted to a couple of appearances off the bench the following March.

By the time Norwich travelled down to play Charlton Athletic at The Valley on Boxing Day 1997, they'd slipped to thirteenth in the table with only the club's most optimistic fans still feeling a place in the end of season play-offs was still within reach. It had been, again, a frustratingly inconsistent campaign so far for the Canaries with the occasional good result thrown in to a sea of general inadequacy. Take, for example, a 2-1 win at Birmingham on 8 November, a game that had seen a composed and disciplined performance not unlike the Norwich of the original Mike Walker, with Adrian Forbes, scorer of two goals, particularly outstanding. Yet, a week later, a team that should have been full of confidence after that win welcomed Middlesbrough to Carrow Road and even took the lead, courtesy of Iwan Roberts, whose first league goal for the club, one that was met with as much jubilation from the big striker himself as it was the Barclay Stand, who he gleefully shared his celebration with. Would the club's fortunes now take a turn for the better, just as they had now done so for Roberts?

In short, no. It took Middlesbrough just six minutes to equalise through Mikkel Beck, the Danish international striker's shot hitting both posts before crossing the line. Paul Merson proceeded to make it 2-1 early in the second half before Tony Ormerod added a third just three minutes later. Game, set and match to the Teesiders and back to the drawing board, for the proverbial umpteenth time, for Walker, who had, at least, been able to give a debut to Norwegian left back Erik Fugelstad. He'd recently signed for the club on a Bosman from Viking FK amid no little publicity at the time with the signing, which had been a long and drawn out affair, seen as something of a coup for the Canaries.

Four days after their defeat at Charlton, Norwich had a golden opportunity to make amends against struggling Portsmouth at Carrow Road and did just that, easing to a comfortable 2-0 win via goals from Matt Jackson and Craig Bellamy. Yet, once again, a good result only culminated in generating false hope as Norwich followed up that result with two heavy defeats, 3-0 to Grimsby in the FA Cup round before being comprehensively outplayed at Wolves with Robbie Keane once again their tormentor in chief, although the real damage was done, in this case, by Dougie Freedman, whose hat-trick made the day a particularly unhappy one for Bryan Gunn, playing his first game for the Canaries since the previous April. That, coincidentally, had also seen Norwich lose at Molineux with Iwan Roberts one of the Wolves scorers in their 3-2 win.

This latest capitulation in Wolverhampton had been Norwich's twenty-sixth league game of the season with Roberts, whose first season at Norwich was being hampered by ongoing injury and fitness concerns, starting seventeen of them. He would have felt the pain of that defeat more acutely than anyone, having arrived at the game determined to prove a thing or two to the home support who had never really taken to him during his short time at the club. Yet, with just one league goal to his name in those seventeen games, the big-money signing was now very much aware that a growing section of the Norwich support hadn't really taken to him either, with Roberts later admitting that the 1997/98 season was the worst season he'd ever had and that, despite Walker seeing him and signing him as the last 'piece of the jigsaw'*, he'd let his manager down.

In retrospect, Roberts was, maybe, being a little bit overcritical of himself by claiming he'd let Walker down. The season was, without question, turning out to be another extremely disappointing one, yet for much of it, Walker had struggled to name the same starting eleven for even two consecutive games, let alone a run of them with Norwich ending the season having used thirty different players, eleven of whom, nearly half, had been debutants. Four of them (Adrian Coote, Darren Kenton, Chris Llewellyn and Daryl Russell) were graduates from the youth side while a fifth, twenty-one-year-old striker Neale Fenn, was a loanee from Tottenham where he'd made just eleven league starts in his six years at the club. Injuries had also taken their toll on Walker's squad with Roberts joining Craig Fleming, Darren Eadie and Keith O'Neill in missing out on much of the campaign.

No club could afford to be without such pivotal squad members, especially when they didn't have the resources to adequately cover them with equally capable replacements. Walker had therefore had to put his trust into players who, for one reason or another, were not up to the pressures of playing and performing well for a club that had aimed on getting back into the Premier League and, while no one could have doubted the commitment and professionalism exhibited by the likes of Drewe Broughton, Shaun Carey, Adrian Coote, Victor Segura and others, they had all struggled to impose themselves on the team and, almost as importantly, the affections of the Norwich fans.

Victor Segura, in particular, came in for a lot of criticism. He'd arrived at the club during the previous summer with the sort of reputation that comes with having played his previous club football in the Spanish equivalent of today's Championship with CD Logroñés and UE Lleida, arriving on a free transfer from the latter, who'd released him after a disappointing season that had seen them flirting with relegation to the Spanish third tier. In today's digital age, the arrival of Segura might, given that any and all of his underwhelming career statistics would have been available to any Norwich fan with an internet connection, might have been questioned. Back in 1997, however, the fact that he'd been playing in Spain was enough to whet the appetite and his arrival was greeted with no little excited anticipation, with his presence in the side expected to provide the Canaries' defence with a

---

* *Roberts, Iwan (and) Buchanan, Karen 'All I Want For Christmas' (VSP, 2004)*

little continental flair and artistry, a player who would be an unquestionable upgrade on the archetypal English defender who, even on the sunniest of days, always looked as if he was battling through the rain and mud.

Unfortunately for Norwich and for Segura in particular, he never really looked like the aforementioned typical English defender, never mind a cultured Spanish one. It wasn't as if he didn't get an opportunity to shine. Mike Walker started him in twenty-two of Norwich's league matches during the 1997/98 season as well as for all three of the Canaries' cup ties including a League Cup tie against Barnet, which brutally illustrated his footballing deficiencies to a small but very critical Carrow Road crowd. Segura's woes were in stark contrast to the ongoing success story that was Craig Bellamy, who was fast establishing a reputation for himself as one of the standout players in the division. He would, at least, have had one thing in common with Segura in that both players had worked their way through the ranks of their first club, having initially signed for them as a youth team player.

But the similarity ends there. Segura was released by Real Zaragoza without having made a single senior appearance for them while Bellamy gatecrashed his way into the Canaries' first team, making his senior debut at just seventeen in a 2-0 defeat at Crystal Palace. The Cardiff-born forward never looked back from that moment onwards, attributing much of the success that he achieved in the game to the footballing 'education' he'd received at Norwich; among the regular duties he had was cleaning John Polston's boots and car, as well as making him numerous cups of tea, the usual tasks that apprentice professionals were expected to do for seniors, responsibilities and a part of the game that has pretty much disappeared today, much, you suspect, to Bellamy's disappointment.

Bellamy was, unquestionably, a live wire, full of himself and his ability, convinced that he was set to achieve great things in the game. He made thirty league starts for the Canaries during the 1997/98 season, ending it as the club's top scorer with thirteen goals, forming, in the process, a very formidable striking partnership with Iwan Roberts, who ended a personally disappointing season still as the club's second highest scorer with seven goals to his name, four of which had come during games when he had been playing alongside Bellamy. Admittedly, Bellamy's confidence, which some may have mistaken for arrogance, had a tendency to play on the nerves of his older colleagues, the famous story of him being locked in the toilet on the club coach en route to an away match testimony of that with his release being conditional, according to Roberts, that he 'kept quiet'.

Following a 2-1 win over Sunderland on 28 January, Norwich went on a winless run of fourteen league games, the absolute nadir of which was a 5-0 defeat to Ipswich Town at Portman Road on 21 February, a game that saw Alex Mathie grab a first half hat-trick in what must count as one of the most disappointing and hard to take results and performances in the club's recent history. The dreadful run of form that included that game eventually came to a spectacular and most unlikely halt on 13 April when a Norwich side that had scored only twelve goals in those fourteen games racked up a 5-0 win over Huddersfield Town at Carrow Road before going onto repeat that result twelve days later in seeing off Swindon Town by the same score. These two impressive home wins pretty much secured Division One safety for a Canaries side that had, after losing at home to Bradford City on 4 April, slumped to twentieth place in the table, just three points clear of the relegation places and with an inferior goal difference to three of the four clubs beneath them.

The aforementioned 5-0 wins had given the Norwich board and fans an opportunity to see what might have been that season, the conviction of the wins and the confident way the Canaries played in both games reflecting the fact that, for once, the manager had been able to pick a side that wasn't so far away from what might have been his preferred starting line-up all along as injury worries started to subside. Thus, the likes of Craig Fleming, Matt Jackson, Neil Adams, Darren Eadie, Iwan Roberts and Craig Bellamy were all able to feature in at least one of those games, with Roberts, aided and abetted by Bellamy in the Norwich attack, scoring three goals, one of which, against Swindon, came directly from a free-kick.

But it was all too little and much too late for the Canaries manager, whose second spell in charge of the club came to an end five days after the win over Swindon, his departure being announced as being by 'mutual consent'. It's a typically bland example of 'football talk', one that, to this day, you might want to treat with a little caution as it seems rather more likely that Walker, buoyed and revitalised by those two emphatic wins, would have been hoping they were enough to persuade the board that an injury-free Canary squad would have more than a realistic chance of returning to the Premier League at the end of the following season.

Walker's disappointment was made clear in an interview he gave to the *Norwich Evening News* given just after his departure: 'I am', he admitted, 'bitterly disappointed to say the least. They [the club board] have decided to make a decision which is their prerogative and, at the end of the day, that's the way it is. I think I have worked hard under trying circumstances this year, but the decision has been made.' Walker therefore left Carrow Road for the second and final time, albeit with a glowing reference from Canaries vice-chairman Roger Munby, who, also talking to the *Norwich Evening News*, said, 'Mike has been an unstinting worker on behalf of this club. His first spell was outstandingly successful and during his second spell we would pay tribute as he worked unstintingly in trying to achieve our number one objective of Premiership status.'

Walker's departure was not only sudden and relatively unexpected but also came just three days before the Canaries' final match of the 1997/98 season, which saw them travel to Reading for what would be the home side's last ever game at their Elm Park ground. It was an otherwise meaningless clash that at least saw some entertainment value with the fact that the recently departed Robert Fleck, who'd joined the Royals at the end of the previous month, would be lining up for the home side against his old teammates. Luckily for Norwich, Fleck had a quiet game and a Canaries side selected by John Faulkner won 1-0 with Craig Bellamy, inevitably, having the last word on a forgettable season with the only goal of the game, the three points won on the day meaning that Norwich ended the 1997/98 season in fifteenth place.

Walker's ill-fated second spell in charge at Carrow Road is a fine example of that old footballing adage that you should 'never go back'. How often are players and managers tempted to return to former haunts after a time spent away, time that has seen their status and part in a club's history rise to that of legend? Those among Walker's peers who had found the allure of returning to past glories had been Howard Kendall and Terry Venables. Kendall had enjoyed a trophy-laden spell at Goodison Park in his first stint as Toffees manager from 1981 to 1987 before experiencing a disappointing second spell on Merseyside from 1990 to 1993, when, ironically, his successor had been Walker. Yet, despite that, he'd still been tempted to return for a third spell in charge at Everton, one that had ended, as had Walker's second spell at Norwich, with his needing to find a new job at the end of the 1997/98 season*. Venables, meanwhile, oft tainted as the saviour of English football, had returned to Crystal Palace for a second time as manager in March 1998 only to leave less than a year later when the club went into administration. Both Kendall and Venables would now always be aware that no matter what glories they'd achieved in their first spells in charge at their respective clubs, there was always the chance that, as time passed, younger fans would only remember them for the periods laced with disappointment and failure, something that Mike Walker would have known was a future possibility for him the moment he returned to Carrow Road.

Canary history, however, has tended for forget and even forgive him for the footballing failings that endured for him second time around and he has mostly

---

* *Kendall and Walker's next managerial jobs after their third and second spells at the clubs, which they will forever be associated with, were in Greece (Kendall) and Cyprus.*

kept his reputation among Norwich fans positively intact. And rightly so. No one will ever know, had he been given the time he needed to turn things around following that hugely frustrating 1997/98 campaign, if he would have ultimately succeeded in taking the club back into the Premier League but my own view is that, given the quality of the players he had at his disposal throughout that season, he would have done exactly that, providing, of course, that squad had remained largely injury free throughout the following campaign. To do that, to hedge their bets in such a way, was not, as far as the Norwich board were concerned, something they were prepared to risk doing and the decision was made to not only replace Walker but, in doing so, bring in someone who had absolutely no previous experience or connection with the club, something that hadn't been done at Carrow Road with regard to a managerial appointment since John Bond's arrival a quarter of a century earlier.

One of the more intriguing names that ended up doing the rounds as a possible replacement for Mike Walker was Ruud Gullit, with more than one claim being made that the former Chelsea manager was looking for a 'long-term project' following his departure from Stamford Bridge and, as a consequence of that, he'd been intrigued enough by an initial enquiry from Norwich to want to find out more with claims he had been seen at Carrow Road subsequently appearing online. Gullit's candidature was, of course, an extremely unlikely one from the start, although the fact he'd been mentioned in dispatches was, as it is now, an interesting one as it has to be assumed that his was a name that wouldn't have been thought of by even the most dedicated rumour-monger unless there was a snippet of truth in the story.

Other more realistic names that might have been added to the mix that close season would have included Ian Atkins at Northampton, the up-and-coming Sam Allardyce at Notts County and Jim Jefferies, who'd just won the Scottish Cup at Hearts with a side of exceptionally good players including David Weir, Gary Naysmith and Neil McCann. There was also support and some renewed speculation surrounding the claims of former Canary Steve Bruce and, quite prominently for a while, the ex-Chelsea, Liverpool and Rangers midfielder Nigel Spackman, who was available having resigned from his position as Sheffield United manager a few months earlier.

All candidates were far more realistic possibilities than Gullit, who ended up at Newcastle, had ever been.

Yet, in the end, the Norwich City board still managed to spring something of a surprise on their supporters and the football world in general when, on 12 June, it was revealed that the club's new first-team manager would be former Middlesbrough, Bolton, Millwall and Arsenal boss Bruce Rioch. But not only that, as it was further announced that former Ipswich midfielder

Bryan Hamilton, whose last role had been in charge of the Northern Ireland national team, was coming in as the club's director of football, a newly created position at Carrow Road and the first instance of Norwich specifically recruiting someone in that position. With Rioch's remit being team selection, tactics and the buying of players, Hamilton would shoulder some of the other responsibilities normally undertaken by the manager, including coaching and other internal footballing matters.

The hackneyed phrase 'dream team' soon became a byword in the local media as Rioch and Hamilton settled into their new roles. They both were, unquestionably, extremely well-known and respected names in the football world and the appointment of Rioch had certainly been something of a coup for the Canaries. But would they be able to work together and, furthermore, would their very different roles dovetail as well as the Norwich board would have hoped? Alternately, with both of them being very strong willed characters, would there be any conflict between them with regard to some matters as both men had grown very much accustomed to being the man in charge of everything in previous positions rather than part of a managerial duo. It was quite a gamble. But what if it came off?

More to the point however – what if it didn't? A sobering thought. You couldn't help but think that, in appointing Rioch, the Canaries board had put everything they had and put it on black. A gigantic gamble. Why? Simple. Rioch was a big name in the game, a former Arsenal manager who, in his time at Highbury, had been persuasive enough to tempt no less a name than Dennis Bergkamp to play his club football in England, the man who had, upon departing Dutch giants Ajax in 1993, stated that the only other European country he was interested in playing in was Italy as Serie A was 'the biggest league at the time'.

So much for the hype of the Premier League. After signing for Inter Milan (for whom he played for against Norwich during the Canaries UEFA Cup campaign in the 1993/94 season), Bergkamp declared that Inter had met 'all of my demands. The most important thing for me was the stadium, the people at the club and their style of play'. English football, clearly, was never going to be an option for Dennis Bergkamp. He was twenty-four and had just spent seven years with Ajax.

He and Inter seemed a match in heaven, with a long stay at the San Siro looking a certainty before the Dutchman, weighed down with winners' medals and adulation, would return home to see out his career at his first club. Yet, somehow, Bruce Rioch, whose only previous managerial experience had been with Torquay United, Middlesbrough, Millwall and Bolton Wanderers, had persuaded him to join Arsenal. No mean feat.

Clearly, he was a man to be respected, a man who knew what he wanted and would take whatever steps he deemed necessary to go out and get it. No nonsense, confident in his own ability and with the sort of single-minded determination to succeed that doesn't suffer fools gladly, something he'd ably demonstrated at Middlesbrough where that tunnel vision had taken them, kicking and screaming, to second place and promotion from the old Division Three at the end of the 1986/87 season. This had all happened just months after the club looked to be permanently on the way out; locked out of its Ayresome Park ground by the official receiver and on the verge of bankruptcy. No one would have been surprised if, at that moment, the club hadn't just given up and curled up to die in a quiet corner somewhere. Rioch wouldn't allow that sort of thinking at his club and, following that promotion, he followed it up a year later by taking the club up into the First Division, an astonishing and, to this day, much understated achievement.

He was, clearly, someone who wouldn't let anyone stand in his way. And that, you assumed, would include club directors if he deemed it necessary. Or directors of football come to that. He didn't really seem a typical Norwich City appointment.

Yet that, of course, is exactly why the club had done everything in its power to convince Rioch to come to Norwich; because he was a fighter, because of the grit, the internal fire, the desire to drag his players and teams over the finish line in first place, no matter what the consequences. Norwich needed someone with that icy cold resolve. Yes, he would have been brought up to speed on the club's current financial worries but would still have some transfer funds as part of his wider remit, which was to rebuild the Canaries in his own image. That image was uncompromising, single minded and with a steadfast determination for progress and success.

Hamilton's responsibilities at the club would have been established in consultation with Rioch. For an old-fashioned footballing man such as Bruce Rioch, the presence of a director of football alongside him; a position that, even today, is considered with a lot of suspicion within the game, would previously have been a non-starter. But football was changing and he knew that he'd have to give a little in his demands if he was to get back into the game at the highest level and begin to rebuild his managerial reputation. So it is fair to assume that, while he would have made what he regarded as his sole responsibilities clear to the Norwich board, he would also have been happy to farm out those less desirable ones to his new number two. He wanted to be clear on what he would be doing and what the club would rely on him to do and with no interruptions or interference.

Because as far as Bruce Rioch would have been concerned, it was as much Norwich City applying to him to take on their managerial vacancy as it was he applying for the job himself. Fortunately for all parties, mutual common ground, interests and ambitions were all established fairly swiftly with the announcement that he was the new man in charge at Carrow Road being met with a mix of surprise and delight from the Norwich support, many of whom had been expecting their new manager to have a much lower profile in the game.

Rioch and Hamilton's arrival at the club coincided with some departures on the playing front, the most significant of those being that of John Polston, who joined Reading, and Rob Newman, who left for Southend United. The arrival of Hamilton also led to the departure of John Faulkner while, in the club boardroom, where a revolving door might have been fitted to cope with all the exits and entrances over the last few years, directors Gavin Paterson and Martin Armstrong bade Carrow Road a fond farewell while Bob Cooper, a former director of Sainsbury's, took up one of their vacated positions on the club board.

The Canaries' preseason took them, once again, over to Ireland where they played four matches in seven days, starting off with a 2-1 win over Bray Wanderers before games against St Patricks Athletic (1-2), Longford Town (4-0) and Home Farm Everton (2-2). A trip to non-league Enfield Town followed on 25 July, a game that Norwich won 4-0 before two consecutive home friendlies against Premier League opposition and two defeats, against Tottenham Hotspur (1-3) and Leicester City (0-1), the game against Martin O'Neill's side coming just five days before Norwich's opening Division One fixture at Crewe. The Railwaymen, humble in stature and a team of modest size and reputation, could still teach Rioch and his Norwich charges a thing or two about team spirit and fighting for the common cause. That never-say-die attitude had seen them finish four places and four points ahead of the Canaries at the end of the 1997/98 season, doing the league double over City in the process by winning 2-0 at Carrow Road and 1-0 at their Gresty Road ground.

With no additions being made to the Canaries squad over the close season, Rioch had to select his first Norwich team from the squad he'd inherited from Mike Walker. It was a decent enough side, however, one that saw Matt Jackson and Craig Fleming team up in the centre of City's defence, while Shaun Carey and Peter Grant provided some equivalent bite in midfield. With Iwan Roberts missing out due to injury, Craig Bellamy and Darren Eadie made up a dynamic front pairing with the wide support coming from Neil Adams and Keith O'Neill, the latter making a welcome return to the

Norwich starting line-up with his first appearance for the club since the previous January.

Norwich's impressive 2-1 opening day win was sealed by two first half goals from Craig Bellamy and Darren Kenton, both goals early candidates for the August Goal of the Month contest, particularly Bellamy's, which came as a result of a glorious 40-yard pass from Daryl Sutch right into Bellamy's path, the talented striker clipping it past Jason Kearton in the Crewe goal with all the aplomb of a player who everyone, especially Bellamy himself, knew was en route to bigger and better things in the game. That win was followed by two more in the league, 2-0 over Stockport at Edgeley Park and a 4-2 win over QPR at Carrow Road on 22 August. That had been quite a match, one that had seen its first four goals scored within the opening ten minutes, much to the delight of the home support who saw themselves go 3-1 up after Matt Jackson's eighth-minute strike found its way past Lee Harper. That win meant that Norwich had won their opening three league games for the first time in a decade, leaving them top of the table and, even at this early stage, looking as if they were going to be one of the teams to catch, with Bellamy, once again, outstanding, his two goals in that game bringing his total of goals scored in those three games to five. With Swansea having been seen off in a two-legged League Cup first-round match prior to the match against the West Londoners and Bellamy having also scored in one of those games, it was fast becoming clear that the Welshman was now the hottest young talent in the British game and questions began to be asked as to how much longer Norwich might reasonably have expected to hold onto him before a Premier League club made the inevitable offer.

A week after the win over QPR, Norwich met West Bromwich Albion at the Hawthorns, losing 2-0 in a game that showed up the lack of a physical presence in the Canaries side, something that Rioch swiftly addressed by signing Celtic defender Malky Mackay on loan in time for the game against Sheffield United at Bramall Lane on 19 September. Mackay didn't make the starting XI on this occasion but still made it onto the Norwich bench, replacing Victor Segura in a game that Norwich lost 2-1 despite another loan signing, Manchester City midfielder Ged Brannan, equalising after Marcelo had put the Blades a goal up in the first half.

Brannan and Mackay, who signed for the Canaries permanently shortly after that game, were one of three new additions at the club at that time, Rioch having also added a new goalkeeper to the Norwich ranks. The man in question was Aberdeen's out of contract Michael Watt, who won thirteen caps for the Scotland U21 team. Watt might, quite reasonably, have thought that his time at Norwich would have been spent providing cover for regular Canary number one Andy Marshall for the rest of that campaign but that proved to be anything but the case as, in the game at Barnsley on 8 September, which Norwich won 3-1, Marshall succumbed to a back injury, giving Watt an unexpected debut, one of nine appearances he would make for the club that season before returning to Scotland in order to play for Kilmarnock in time for the start of the 1999/2000 campaign.

Much to Rioch's frustration, Norwich, all too typically, blew hot and cold over the opening weeks of the season. Take, for example, the trip to Crystal Palace on 17 October, a game that saw the Canaries go a goal up late in the first half as Craig Bellamy set up Iwan Roberts for that opener. Maybe it would have been better had Norwich not scored as Palace, captained by former Italian international Attilio Lombardo, rallied superbly to score twice before the interval, adding another three in the second half to win 5-1. Yet, just three days later, Norwich took on high-flying East Anglian rivals Ipswich Town at Carrow Road, winning that game 1-0 thanks to an inevitable Bellamy goal before following that up with a stunning 4-1 win over Huddersfield at Carrow Road, Bellamy and Iwan Roberts again demonstrating the potential of their attacking partnership by scoring two goals each. Those two wins were followed by a run of a further five games without defeat meaning that, after another impressive away win, this time to the tune of 3-1 at Tranmere, Norwich welcomed struggling Oxford United to Carrow Road on 29 November knowing that another win would leave them only a few points short of a top-two place.

Bellamy, yet again, opened the scoring after just three minutes, running onto a Matt Jackson pass, and for a while it looked as if Norwich would rack up their fifth win in eight games with some ease. They hadn't counted on the sheer bloody mindedness of their opponents, however, who, led by former player Malcolm Shotton, had a reliable goalscorer of their own to call upon, one Dean Windass. He, remember, was the man who had been at the epicentre of Martin O'Neill's departure from the club a little under three years earlier. Long gone but never forgotten, Windass now proceeded to show the Norwich fans what they were missing by scoring one of the three Oxford goals scored within a fifteen-minute spell as Norwich found themselves outplayed and outwitted by a team that would be relegated at the end of that season.

Rioch's response was to drop Andy Marshall for the Canaries next match at Grimsby, which turned out to be the only change he made for that game. Was that harsh on Marshall? He'd performed exceedingly well since taking his chance to be the Canaries' number one goalkeeper, seeing off, in the process, Bryan Gunn, who'd been at the club since 1986. Gunn would have been thirty-four at the start of the 1998/99 season, hardly vintage for a goalkeeper, and he'd have felt he had a couple of seasons left in him at least. And, being the complete professional he was, Gunn would have wanted to play, not sit around and be paid for doing next to nothing. He therefore made the decision to return to Scotland in order to play for Hibernian where he made twelve appearances before suffering a hairline fracture to his leg during the 1998/99 close season, one that was bad enough for him to have to quit playing the following March.

Gunn may be a proud Scot but he will always be regarded as a man of Norwich and Norfolk, and he spoke of his sadness in leaving Carrow Road after twelve eventful years with the club by saying the decision he made to leave Norwich had been the hardest he'd ever had to make. Contrary to that, Rioch's decision to drop Marshall hadn't been a hard decision to make at all as far as Rioch was concerned. Marshall had been at fault for at least two of the Oxford United goals in the 2-1 defeat at Carrow Road, which included completely missing the corner that led to Brian Wilsterman's opening goal. Michael Watt came in to replace Marshall for the Grimsby game, which ended in a 3-1 win for the Canaries with Iwan Roberts and Craig Bellamy both scoring in the last ten minutes of that game. That win was followed by a 1-1 draw at Swindon Town three days later, a game that saw another young Canary make his senior debut, nineteen-year-old defender Che Wilson.

Christmas saw Norwich back up to fifth place in the league following a 2-1 win over Bristol City at Carrow Road, one highlight of the game being the return to his former club of striker Ade Akinbiyi to his former club. His twentieth-minute goal had briefly seen the Robins draw level before Iwan Roberts' second goal of the game retained Norwich's lead. Those two goals were the Welsh striker's eleventh and twelfth of the season, one which was seeing him and fellow Welshman Craig Bellamy beginning to establish a striking partnership that looked, potentially, as good as any the club had previously had and certainly up there, goals wise, with the likes of MacDougall and Boyer and Deehan and Bertschin. Roberts owed his yellow and green renaissance to the arrival of Rioch at Norwich, recalling that, when the Canaries' new manager had arrived at the club, he'd taken one look at Roberts and commented that Tom Walley, Roberts old youth team coach at Watford, would have been ashamed of him. It was a comment that inspired Roberts to get as fit as he could and, in the process, not only prove himself to Rioch but to any Norwich fans that might still be questioning the wisdom of his big-money purchase. It had worked to such an extent that Roberts was now having the season of his life, one that ended with him having scored a total of twenty-three league and cup goals and being voted as the winner of the club's Player of the Year award, a remarkable turnaround for a player who, the previous season, had been on the end of a lot of terrace criticism.

It should have been a platform for Norwich to build on into the new year, one that provided them with the impetus to push on for one of the automatic promotion places. Yet, once again, their chances of doing so ended up being considerably hamstrung by injuries to three of their most important players, the most high profile one coming about as a result of a shocking lunge at Craig Bellamy by Wolves Kevin Muscat in the game at Molineux on 12 December. That had led to Bellamy missing five games and, upon his return to the side, never quite recapturing the spark that he'd had at the start of the season. Another injury victim was Darren Eadie. He, like Bellamy and Roberts, had enjoyed a tremendous start to the season only to see it also interrupted by injury in November, one that saw him miss five of the ten games that followed that match before suffering a reoccurrence following the Canaries' 1-1 draw against West Bromwich on 16 January, one that was bad enough to see him miss the rest of the season.

And then there was Keith O'Neill, who'd started the club's first four games of the season before missing another eight due to injury. By the time he returned to the side, interest in him was at such a high level among other clubs that it soon became clear that, once he had fully regained his fitness, he would almost certainly be off to bigger and better things. That proved to be exactly what happened as, six days after the Canaries had endured a miserable 4-1 thumping at Bradford City, he signed for Middlesbrough for a fee quoted as being in the region of £1 million, the Canaries cashing in on one of their prized assets as it became clear that O'Neill, who was out of contract at the end of the season, would be able, and fully intent if it came to it, on leaving for nothing once his contract had expired at the end of June 1999.

A not altogether satisfactory state of affairs that, in the post-Christmas period, saw Norwich win just one of their sixteen games between their Boxing Day defeat at QPR and yet another defeat, this time at Crystal Palace on 3 April. Sixteen games, ten points from a possible forty-eight and just twelve goals scored in a run that saw the Canaries drop from that promising post-Christmas league position of fifth in the Division One table to fourteenth and fifteen points shy of the play-off places, another forgettable season of mediocrity already guaranteed.

Rioch had, in the face of injuries, tried his best to give his squad a boost. But the opportunity given to him to do so came far too little and much too late, even if, in hindsight, the players he did manage to bring in were all of undoubted quality. The first to arrive was midfielder Paul Hughes, signed on loan from Chelsea in time to make his debut as a replacement for Adrian Forbes during the 1-1 draw at Huddersfield Town on 24 March. This game sprang to life when Andy Marshall received a red card for hefty lunge at

Marcus Stewart, who'd end up as a future teammate at Ipswich Town. Let's hope they made up. Marshall's red mist moment meant that Daryl Sutch was now able to give full credence to his reputation as a 'utility player' by taking the gloves and going in goal in Marshall's place as Rioch had not named a substitute goalkeeper. Sutch revelled in the situation and was having the game of his life until a Ben Thornley corner ricocheted off Hughes and into the net, a goal that was typical of the bad luck Norwich were having at the time. Yet, for all that, Hughes impressed enough in his cameo appearance to start the next game, one that saw two more new signings make their Canary bow, Phil Mulryne, signed from Manchester United for £500,000, and Paul Dalglish, son of Kenny, who arrived on loan from Liverpool before signing for the Canaries on a permanent basis for around £300,000.

But perhaps the most interesting of the Canaries four new arrivals at that late stage of the season was that of midfielder Cedric Anselin, who became the club's first ever French player when he arrived from FC Girondins Bordeaux on 25 March. Anselin, who was just twenty-one when he arrived at Norwich, had been anticipating spending all of his career at Bordeaux so had been surprised, to say the least, when he was told that there had been interest in him from Norwich in England, later admitting that he had to look on a map of the UK to see exactly where Norwich was. Yet he settled at Carrow Road quickly, making his debut in the 1-0 win over Grimsby on 5 April, won via a spectacular free-kick winner from Phil Mulryne that sealed Norwich's first win since 20 February. It was a desperately needed three points that lifted the Canaries up to twelfth place in the league. With four of their remaining six matches due to be played at Carrow Road, it was now hoped that the new quartet could at least play a full part in Norwich enjoying a strong end to the 1998/99 season, a campaign that had, yet again, started with a lot of promise and expectation only to fall away to disappointing and occasionally completely unacceptable levels of performance.

The simple truth was that the Canaries had, again, endured another season that had seen a combination of long-term injuries and poor form contribute to an eventual finishing place of ninth, an improvement on recent seasons admittedly but still a considerable distance behind what everyone at the club had expected and been building towards the previous summer. And not least the new manager. There had been a few high points in among it all, most notably the goalscoring form of Iwan Roberts as well as the win against Ipswich at Portman Road that October and a steady rise in home attendances, which, at the end of the campaign, gave an average Carrow Road gate of 15,761 as opposed to 14,444 (1997/98) and 14,719 (1996/97).

Yet holding up any of these more redeeming features of the Canaries' 1998/99 campaign was just clutching at yellow and green straws, because Norwich had also gone for eleven games without a home win during the season, an appallingly poor statistic for a side that regarded itself as particularly strong at home. Only in this case, sixteen of Norwich's fellow Division One sides didn't particularly think so as they'd all come to Carrow Road during the course of the season and got at least a point for their troubles. Even relegated Bury had won more games at their own ground than Norwich had, while the number of league goals scored by the Canaries at Carrow Road that season (thirty-four) was bettered or equalled by fifteen other teams including Bristol City, who ended the 1998/99 campaign twenty-fourth and bottom of the league.

Norwich had, furthermore, lost three games that they had previously been leading against Crewe Alexandra, Oxford United and Crystal Palace; three defeats and a possible nine points that could have been won that would, had Norwich have held out in those matches, seen them end the season on seventy-one points-but still have been five points adrift of sixth-placed Bolton Wanderers.

Ninth place doesn't sound so bad if you say it quickly. But this was a very distant ninth place from a side that looked, more often than not, more ready for the division below them rather the land of Premier League flavoured milk and honey that was now fast receding into the distance. Hopefully the new signings, all quality players, would make a difference. Yet, for now, the Canaries couldn't even draw solace from the fact they'd fallen just short. They'd been cut well and truly adrift from the part of the table that mattered and, in truth, had been also-rans since early December. The club and its supporters had now endured four consecutive seasons back in English football's second tier and were very much looking, barring a miracle, as if they were destined to spend quite a bit longer at that level.

Among events that took place off the pitch during the season was the demise of the club's yellow shorts, voted out during a vote held at Carrow Road prior to a game, while, in the boardroom, Bob Cooper succeeded Barry Lockwood as Canaries' chairman that December as the restructuring of the club hierarchy continued to fall into place. Changes at the highest level saw a new man in charge who you couldn't help but think might, just might, start to get a little itchy in the trigger finger with regard to Rioch and Hamilton's tenure at the club if a real and sustained genuine promotion push didn't materialise in the 1999/2000 season

Yet the club's chances of doing just that would be dealt a series of serious blows before that campaign had even started.

CHAPTER SEVEN

Football's New Reality

You might have been tempted into thinking that it couldn't have got any worse for the Canaries at that time. Yet it could and it did.

Craig Bellamy, who wound up his teammates so much they locked him in the coach toilet. (*Photo courtesy of Norwich City Football Club*)

The close season prior to the 1999/2000 campaign was a fairly quiet one for the club, one that, in terms of incoming players, saw just two significant new arrivals in Jean-Yves de Blassis and Pape Diop, signed from Red Star de Paris and RC Lens in France, respectively. Of the two, Diop had made the biggest impression on Bruce Rioch, his athleticism and frightening pace having impressed him when Diop, who was signed on loan, turned out as a trialist for the Canaries in Daryl Sutch's testimonial match against Dutch side AZ Alkmaar. Diop then agreed to follow up that cameo appearance in another trial match, this time in a reserve team friendly against Ipswich Town. The fact that he'd been as committed in a low-key reserve match as he had the high-profile testimonial was enough for Rioch, who was normally a lot more fastidious in his player recruitment (although that probably wasn't needed for the likes of Dennis Bergkamp) to be convinced by Diop's performance in those two games to step in with the loan offer to Lens before one of Norwich's Division One rivals made a move themselves.

The Canaries had hoped for a quiet yet productive preseason tour of Sweden but it turned out to be anything but that. Norwich played two low-key domestic friendlies to start their preparations, these were against Colchester United (1-1) and Southend United (1-2 loss) before playing three matches in Sweden. These were against Helsingborg IF (1-0 win) and Nordost (2-1 win) before a disappointing 4-1 defeat at the hands of Orgryte. Yet those matches and results, dispiriting as some of them had been, were never going to be the main talking points of that tour, although you can be fully assured that Bruce Rioch would have given almost anything for that to have been the case.

Norwich had been struck down by the injury curse that had hung over the club over the last couple of seasons. The difference this time around was that the new campaign hadn't even began when Craig Bellamy damaged his cruciate ligaments in the friendly against Southend before Darren Eadie's knee injury flared up while the club were in Sweden. Significant blows, of course, for both players who would have been anticipating the new season with relish, not least Bellamy, who was fully aware of the interest in him that was now being shown by numerous Premier League clubs. He would have been more mindful than anyone that a good start to the season with Norwich would almost certainly seal his long-awaited (and expected) move onto bigger and better things. Yes, Norwich would miss him on the pitch, but the club's dwindling resources would be missing the anticipated seven-figure transfer fee his imminent departure would have brought in even more.

Make do and mend for Rioch again then, who now had to start the season with a game against West Bromwich Albion at the Hawthorns without two of his most important players. It was a livelier than usual opener that ended in a 1-1 draw; Paul Dalglish having put Norwich a goal up shortly after half time before the Baggies scored a fortuitous equaliser through substitute Paul Raven. A decent point then, especially for a team that was lacking two of its greatest talents. And Norwich had played well with Anselin excelling in midfield while debutant De Blassis had an equally good game alongside him. Things got even better for Norwich when, after the game, West Brom manager Brian Little had admitted that the Canaries had deserved to win and he was right, with only some wayward finishing coming between Norwich and a convincing win.

Norwich followed up that point with a routine 2-0 win over Cheltenham Town three days later in a League Cup first round, first leg match that saw Anselin, impressive again, see his early goal disallowed before Iwan Roberts, as tough as they come and blessedly injury free, scored twice before half time. Paul Dalglish and Phil Mulryne had also impressed in the routine win, one that meant the Canaries' home support was in fine voice as well as a good frame of mind prior to the side's first home league game of the season on 14 August against Birmingham City.

Bruce Rioch had also been impressed, so much so, it seemed, from team's performance in the draw at West Bromwich to name an unchanged starting XI for the Birmingham game. He may well, however, have been questioning his loyalty to those players when some woeful Norwich defending early on saw Jon McCarthy run onto a pass from Stan Lazaridis from the halfway line before hitting a fierce shot on the run that gave Andy Marshall no chance. It was a bitter early blow for Norwich to experience but worse was to follow when centre half Matt Jackson sustained a knee injury soon afterwards. Rioch was able to swap like for like with the appearance of Malky Mackay from the bench as Jackson's replacement but the damage had been done and the Norwich players, shocked at the departure to injury of another key player, struggled to make any sort of impact on the game; the nearest they came to scoring coming from a Mulryne free-kick, which was parried away by Blues keeper Kevin Poole. Iwan Roberts and Cedric Anselin also had chances saved by the visiting keeper and, although Rioch was able to bring on Diop for what turned out to be an impressively feisty cameo, Birmingham's defence was held out and the visitors left with all three points, a result and performance that would have delighted manager Trevor Francis.

Rioch, on the other hand, would not have been happy with the manner his side had lost the match. Yet, as dark as his mood might have been at around 4:50 p.m. on that Saturday afternoon, it would have been nothing compared to how he would have been feeling a fortnight later after the Canaries had suffered another league defeat at home, this time at the hands of Blackburn Rovers. Norwich had travelled to Charlton the preceding week and lost 1-0 with only an outstanding performance from Dean Kiely, the present-day Canaries goalkeeping coach, preventing them from getting anything from the match. So, as with the West Bromwich game, there was some post-match cause for optimism, even if, again, the team's performance had not got them the result they deserved. Yet all of that renewed hope came to nothing against Blackburn on 28 August in a game that saw Norwich comprehensively outplayed as two goals from Egil Ostenstad gave Brian Kidd's side a richly deserved victory, one that, in the process, dumped Norwich to the bottom of the Division One table.

From top of the Premier League to bottom of Division One in just under six and a half years. It wasn't exactly the greatest ever fall of grace that a club had suffered in English football, but it was still a dramatic and rapid one. And it hurt like hell.

You might at least have been tempted into thinking that it couldn't possibly get any worse for the Canaries at that time. Yet it could and it most certainly did. With Darren Eadie and Craig Bellamy already out of early season contention due to injury and Matt Jackson now having joined them on the sidelines, Norwich lost yet another key player to injury in the Birmingham match when, following a tackle from Christian Dailly, Phil Mulryne suffered a broken leg, which kept him out of the side until the following April.

By now, Rioch and Bryan Hamilton were beginning to feel the pressure that came with managing a club that, as far as its demanding supporters were concerned, was only meant to have spent one season at this level (remember the 'On loan to the Endsleigh' T-shirts from back in 1995) but were now, after losing three of their first four games of their fifth consecutive season in Division One, were now bottom of the table. To add to accompanying sense of ennui, the fact that there were barely any funds available to the manager to bring in new players meant that it didn't look as if Norwich would be vacating that lowly position with anything like the haste that put them there in the first place. The Canaries had even struggled to see off Cheltenham Town in the second leg of their League Cup first-round tie at Whaddon Road after goals from Neil Grayson and Jamie Victory had brought the aggregate scores level prior to the game going into extra time. Luckily for Norwich, a goal from Lee Marshall eventually earnt them a 3-2 aggregate victory but anyone who was at the game that evening will surely never forget Marshall's celebrations following his goal, a display of unbridled joy and excitement that would have appeared far more fitting had he scored in a World Cup final rather than a scrambled winner in a League Cup tie against a side that had been playing in the Conference twelve months previously.

Norwich had been winning at Bayern Munich a little over five years prior to this game. Yet, as magnificent as that achievement had undoubtedly been, those post-match celebrations seemed nothing on those that greeted Lee Marshall's toe-poke winner at Cheltenham Town. The Olympic Stadium and Gossy's wonder strike all seemed a long, long way away now.

So why had Norwich fallen so far from grace in such a relatively short time? The Canaries had finished the 1992/93 season in third place in the Premier League having led it, and, at one time, been eight points clear at the top for much of that campaign. They'd then gone onto prove that it hadn't been a fluke the following season by virtue of that UEFA Cup run as well as securing impressive Premier League victories at Blackburn, Leeds, Everton (and by five goals to one), Chelsea and Liverpool before spending nearly all of the opening six months of the 1994/95 campaign comfortably placed in the top ten of the Premier League before that dreadful run of results from February through to April had seen them relegated.

It was as if the club was still struggling to comprehend that unexpected fall from grace and the relegation that had accompanied it in May 1995, one that, for once, not even the most cynical of pundits might have suggested might have happened that season. Yet, following that run of twelve defeats from their last twenty games, the Canaries had continued to struggle with Division One finishes of sixteenth, thirteenth, fifteenth and ninth in the following four seasons, none of which had seen the club even remotely suggest it was capable of putting the sort of run together that would have been needed to return to the Premier League, a time that had seen clubs such as Barnsley, Charlton Athletic and Bradford City do exactly that – and in some style.

So what were they doing right that Norwich, who remained locked and bolted onto the bottom of the Division One table after a 2-2 draw at Walsall on 30 August, were most definitely not doing?

One possible answer is that the biggest and most inevitable price the Canaries had to pay for their unexpected but much lauded Premier League and UEFA Cup prominence from 1992 through to Christmas 1995 was that the club had not been prepared for the consequences of that unexpected success, the most telling of which was the interest it would generate in the Canaries' best players.

Norwich's remarkable run had been put together on a squad that included the likes of David Phillips, Ruel Fox, Chris Sutton, Mark Robins and Efan Ekoku, all of whom were now long gone to clubs with bigger wallets and salary budgets than the Canaries can ever have hoped to offer. Even Nottingham Forest, relegated at the end of the 1992/93 season, had been able to tempt Phillips away with a wage that far exceeded the one he'd been on or offered at Carrow Road. It was a sign of things to come. For Phillips, it was about the money and no one can blame him for that. For the likes of Fox and Sutton, however, it was about the opportunity to win domestic honours, the opportunity to do so clearly, as far as they were concerned, being much greater at Newcastle and Blackburn Rovers, respectively. This was, of course, the same Newcastle that had, while Norwich and Fox were barn storming their way through that inaugural Premier League season, been plying their trade in Division One – and only a year after narrowly avoiding relegation to Division Two.

Norwich and Newcastle were, effectively, in the process of trading places with Ruel Fox now seeing them as a far better long-term bet for him than Norwich City. He'd upped and left Carrow Road to head north for just £2.25 million in February 1993 (at which time Norwich were ninth in the Premier League table) after, like Phillips, having turned down the Canaries offer of a new contract. Chris Sutton had, on the other hand, agreed to sign a new contract with the club, the news of his having done so being announced by then chairman Robert Chase with the sort of hyperbole that was more likely to draw cynicism than joy from the Canary support. They were long used to seeing fan favourites depart the club and were under no illusions that Sutton wouldn't soon be joining their ranks, no matter what the chairman said. It was cynicism that would have been well judged. Sutton had, by the end of the 1993/94 season, spoken to nine different clubs, all of whom were interested in signing him and not, in the process, distracted one bit by either the fact he had recently signed a new deal with the club or Chase's now infamous claim that, if Sutton was sold before the start of the 1994/95 season, he would stand down as chairman.

Sutton eventually joined Blackburn for £5 million with John Deehan being granted only £800,000 out of that sum to sign a replacement for Sutton, the player in question being Mike Sheron, who arrived from Manchester City at the end of August 1994. A like for like replacement he most definitely was not.

And that was the problem. The Canaries were losing some of the best players they'd had in their history but were, time and time again, either unwilling or, given the ever-increasing transfer fees and player wages abounding in the game at that time, unable to commit to replacing them with players of equal ability. Even players who had been brought in and proved themselves to be high-class performers – for example, Jon Newsome – came and went with alarming haste; likewise Efan Ekoku and Ashley Ward. In addition to that and, while the club's schoolboy and youth set up had seen players of undoubted quality like Andy Johnson, Darren Eadie and Craig Bellamy work their way up to the Norwich first team, a lot of the other up-and-coming young Canaries, upon whose shoulders a lot of hope and investment had been made, were not able to make a similar impact upon the first team with many making only a handful of appearances before drifting away from the club and, in some cases, the senior game altogether, examples of which included Jason Minett, Johnny Wright, Karl Simpson and Che Wilson.

For all that the club had achieved during the latter part of the 1980s and early part of the 1990s, it now seemed as if the Canaries now found themselves up against the new glass ceiling that Sky's massive investment into the game had created. Prior to Rupert Murdoch's broadcasting behemoth bludgeoning itself onto the English game in 1992, there was always a chance, a possibility that one of the English football's so-called 'lesser' clubs could make an impact on the game and become, even briefly, one of its leading lights.

This had happened most prominently with Nottingham Forest from 1978 through to 1980, during which Brian Clough's side had not only won a League Championship with a team that was completely devoid of stars but, remarkably, gone onto win two consecutive European Cups, one of only eight clubs to have won the trophy (now the Champions League) in consecutive seasons since it was first contested in 1956. Their surge to the top of the English game beget other unlikely successes. West Bromwich Albion finished third in Division One in 1979 while Ipswich Town (second, 1980), Watford second, 1983), Southampton (seconf, 1984) and Crystal Palace (third, 1991) all, briefly, made welcome headlines themselves. Yet, until Leicester City's improbable Premier League triumph in 2016, Norwich's own unexpected rise to the top – third in 1993 – was the last time one of English football's lesser clubs made a serious enough impact on our domestic game to be thought of as potential Premier League champions.

Norwich City had indeed gatecrashed the elite. But they had done so at the last possible moment before, slowly and inexorably, England's Premier League became a closed shop for the exclusive use and gratification of the game's elite and their billionaire owners. The end of the 1990s had for Norwich, just as it also did for Nottingham Forest, West Bromwich Albion, Ipswich Town, Watford, Southampton and Crystal Palace, started to bring in the very grim reality that not only was the dream over, it was going to be virtually impossible to achieve again.

The grim cloud of truth that hung over the Canaries as they scraped to that 2-2 draw at Walsall on 30 August 1999 was that the result and their place at the bottom of the Division One table wasn't so much an aberration that needed to be corrected as soon as possible but a case of English football's new reality. Contrary, therefore, to all the expectation that had accompanied them when they'd been relegated from the Premier League in 1995, expectation that said we're a big club now and we'll be back (at the risk of labouring the point, remember those T-shirts?), the slowly dawning truth was that English football, as it hurtled towards the twenty-first century, was no longer a sport but a business and, as with all businesses, if you weren't one of the perceived long-standing elite, then you were going to struggle.

Which was exactly what the Canaries had been doing over the last four and a bit seasons. The only problem with that was that, despite all the logic that pointed to how this was probably what it was going to be like for Norwich over the coming years, the expectation that the club would, against now near insurmountable odds, still return to its so-called 'rightful' place in the Premier League.

Something that, by this time, Bruce Rioch, a footballing realist in an industry populated by dreamers, might have began to think wasn't going to be as straight forward as it might have initially seemed when he'd first been presented with the opportunity of taking the job.

Better news for Rioch and the Norwich support was to follow that hard won point at Walsall, however, when, after a period of eight months out through injury, Darren Eadie was restored to Bruce Rioch's matchday squad for the home match with Crewe Alexandra on 11 September. It started positively for the Canaries as well, when Erik Fugelstad's floated cross from the left was met by Iwan Roberts, whose glancing header was too good for visiting keeper Jason Kearton. Despite taking the lead, however, Norwich soon let Crewe back into the game and, shortly after Paul Dalglish had missed a good chance to put the Canaries 2-0 up, Colin Cramb appeared from nowhere at the other end to bring the scores level, much to the disquiet of an increasingly frustrated home crowd who were not slow in making their feelings known as the players departed the field of play at half time. It was the sort of communal discontent that might have been particularly telling for Rioch, who, up to this point, had enjoyed both a playing and managerial career free from the sort of pressure and criticism he and his players were now regularly on the receiving end of.

Rioch's conundrum at half time would have been whether or not he dared bring Eadie off the bench in order to try and spark his side into life and get their season moving. The fact that he had been declared fit enough to be part of the matchday squad was one thing; yet, despite his importance to the team, there was always the risk that Eadie might, again, break down once he became a regular starter again. It's a ridiculous premise of course. No club would ever want to keep any of its players out of the side for fear they suffered an injury once they started playing, which would then make them unavailable for a long period again, yet, as he began his warm-up towards the latter part of the game, the Norwich fans watching would, as one, have been overcome by a combination of delight at his potential return and dread that it might yet end in further injury to one of the teams' two talisman, so bad had Norwich's luck been over the previous year and a half or so.

In the end Rioch knew he had to give Eadie a chance and he duly made that first appearance since the previous January when he came on for Cedric Anselin, with Eadie himself putting the final touches to a script worthy of Hollywood when, with just two minutes to go, he capitalised on good work from Iwan Roberts and Adrian Coote to fire home the winner. It was, six league games in, Norwich's first win of the season and one that was good enough to haul them off the bottom of the league and into twenty-first place. Heady times at Carrow Road to be sure, and a much needed return to the side of a player who so much of the Canaries' future hopes were depending on. Providing, of course, that he was able to stay fit even if that much hoped for prolonged run of games that everyone now wanted to see him have in the side would mean, once again, admiring glances from elsewhere. And, much as Norwich would have wanted to keep him and, certainly for the time being, Eadie would quite likely have wanted to stay put, part of that new reality of football was that, if a bigger club wanted one of your better players, then they would come along and take them. And there was nothing Norwich could do about that.

Which is exactly what happened. Except to make it doubly galling for the Canaries, the club that eventually made the offer for Eadie that they couldn't refuse was not only one that Norwich might have considered their equal, but the delighted manager who sealed the deal was one who had previously been at Norwich and was now able to spend the sort of money that he could only have dreamt about having at his disposal during his time at Carrow Road. Cue then, Martin O'Neill, who happily spent £3 million of Leicester City's money in order to take him to Filbert Street. It hadn't, given Eadie's ongoing injury concerns, been the most straightforward of deals to complete; indeed, at one point the medical specialist who was giving Eadie the obligatory once over before the deal was confirmed had advised O'Neill that the state of Eadie's knee meant that he could either play for another ten years, or for barely another ten games before it gave out for the final time, further admitting that it could go either way and that he couldn't be certain either.

'I don't care' was Martin O'Neill's reply. 'I want him here'. And that was that, Darren Eadie had gone, another name on the increasingly long list of players that Norwich had to sell but this time in order to do nothing more than continue functioning as a business and football club with little to no chance of Bruce Rioch being given a fraction of the fee received for Eadie's considerable talents.

It was a watershed moment for me and, I dare say, many more Canary fans. The days of selling a player to a bigger, wealthier and more famous club and using the money received in order to add to your own squad had passed. Norwich were now selling players to clubs that they might, once, have considered as their equals and using the money received just to keep going, to try and maintain the near hand to mouth existence that they were now having to get used to. Football's new reality was biting hard.

The Canaries badly needed to respond after Eadie's departure. His last game for the club had been in a 2-1 win over West Bromwich Albion at Carrow Road, one that had seen him make the winning goal for the latest young Canary who was making his way through the playing ranks, nineteen-year-old midfielder Darel Russell. The Canaries followed up that victory with two more in the league, registering, in the process, three consecutive league victories, the first time they'd managed such a run in nearly eighteen months. That mini run had continued with a 2-1 win at Tranmere Rovers followed, on Boxing Day, by a win by the same margin against QPR at Carrow Road with the Canaries winning goal coming from Chris Llewellyn in the eighty-seventh minute. It had come late but better late than never, the precious three points won enough to push Norwich up to eighth place in the Division One table, four points behind Stockport County in that all important sixth place, and with a game in hand.

Maybe the new millennium would see a renewed push for promotion after all. Maybe.

To be continued...

Acknowledgements

Where to start? Whenever I begin a new book relating to the Canaries, I tell myself, solemnly and with no little conviction, that this will, definitely, without fail, be the last one.

There is, after all, a veritable phalanx of Norwich City writers out there now, all doing their thing, either in print or digitally, while the skills and creativity of those Canary fans who regularly feature on social media and YouTube repeatedly grab my attention, admiration and respect with their work.

Plus I've got other things to do, other books, projects and ambitions. As the modern-day footballer might say when he moves clubs, 'I felt it was time for a new challenge.'

It feels as if it is time I was put out to grass, at Carrow Road, and, preferably, on the first day of a new season, when its verdant green is a symbol of the bright and vibrant times we all hope lie ahead.

And yet, and yet ... there always seems, just as there is always one last Malteser in the box, one last Norwich City project to get started.

Which means that *Norwich City: The Noughties* will soon be following this one off the shelves and, hopefully, into your homes. Plus a couple of other things. All hush hush you understand. So watch this space.

As for *Norwich City: The Sixties* or *Norwich City: The Fifties*, well, if someone asks me, why not. While in around four or so years' time, maybe I'll be sat at my desk writing something along these lines for *Norwich City: The 2010s*.

But that will, definitely, absolutely, without fail and cross my heart etc. etc., be my last Norwich City book. Probably.

There are, as usual, a lot of people to thank as this book reaches its conclusion. First and foremost to Amberley Publishing for having so much faith in my work. Thank you from the bottom of my heart for everything.

Acknowledgements

To all at Norwich City FC, good people past and present, who have always been happy to help and support me in my work. So, thank you Dan Brigham, Daisy Simpson, Delia Smith, Tom Smith, Peter Rogers and Michael Wynn-Jones.

Thanks also to Jon Newsome for letting me interrupt him on an especially busy day at his business in Sheffield for what I promised would be a very quick interview only for Jon to happily chat for what seemed like half the afternoon about his time at the club and in football. An absolute gent who had nothing but good things to say about the club and Norfolk.

Likewise John Polston for writing the foreword for this book. Jon Newsome isn't the only ex-Norwich player to raise a quizzical eyebrow when they hear that John owns and runs a boot camp fitness business near Reading (www.wokinghambootcamps.co.uk) as, apparently, he wasn't always that keen on training. Poacher turned gamekeeper then.

I'm also indebted to Rob Butler, Dave 'Spud' Thornhill, Paul King and Kathy Blake for the memories of supporting Norwich which they have contributed to this book. I wouldn't like to hazard a guess at the number of Canary games that they've all been to, home and away, between them through the years but it must be in the thousands. Maybe one of them should write a book about it?

A nod of appreciation and respect is most certainly due to BBC Radio Norfolk – in particular Chris Goreham, Rob Butler and Paul Hayes – for making me feel so welcome during my visits to *The Scrimmage* as well as Michael Bailey, Darren Eadie and Jessica Howson for doing the same with Mustard TV.

Likewise Chris Rushby and Carole Slaughter at Jarrold and Ben Richardson at Waterstones in Norwich. Plus Mick Dennis, David McDermott, Jeremy Goss, Simon Moston, Linzi Rawson and everyone at the Maids Head Hotel in Norwich (www.maidsheadhotel.co.uk) and Russ Saunders.

This is beginning to read like a speech from the Oscars so I'll shut up now. If I have forgotten anyone then please let me know who you are and why I should have mentioned you so I can make the appropriate amendments for any subsequent reprints of this book. The same applies if you spot any errors within the text, factual or otherwise.

Thank you. OTBC!

Edward Couzens-Lake
August 2017
Twitter: @edcouzenslake

P.S. I wrote at the very beginning that this book was dedicated to all twenty-two Norwich City players who made at least one League appearance for the club during the 1992/93 season. In case you are trying to remember who they all were, look no further:

Darren Beckford, Mark Bowen, Ian Butterworth, Ian Crook, Ian Culverhouse, Efan Ekoku, Ruel Fox, Jeremy Goss, Bryan Gunn, Andy Johnson, Gary Megson, Jason Minett, Rob Newman, David Phillips, John Polston, Lee Power, Mark Robins, David Smith, Daryl Sutch, Chris Sutton, Mark Walton and Colin Woodthorpe.